WE ARE THE MUTANTS

T0062050

Repeater

WE ARE THE MUTANTS

THE BATTLE FOR HOLLYWOOD FROM *ROSEMARY'S BABY* TO *LETHAL WEAPON*

KELLY ROBERTS

MICHAEL GRASSO

RICHARD MCKENNA

Published by Repeater Books

An imprint of Watkins Media Ltd

Unit 11 Shepperton House

89-93 Shepperton Road

London

N1 3DF

United Kingdom

www.repeaterbooks.com

A Repeater Books paperback original 2022

1

Distributed in the United States by Random House, Inc., New York.

Copyright © Kelly Roberts, Michael Grasso and Richard McKenna 2022

Kelly Roberts, Michael Grasso and Richard McKenna assert the moral right to be identified as the authors of this work.

ISBN: 9781914420733

Ebook ISBN: 9781914420740

All rights reserved. No part of this publication may be reproduced, stored in a retrieval system, or transmitted, in any form or by any means, electronic, mechanical, photocopying, recording or otherwise, without the prior permission of the publishers.

This book is sold subject to the condition that it shall not, by way of trade or otherwise, be lent, re-sold, hired out or otherwise circulated without the publisher's prior consent in any form of binding or cover other than that in which it is published and without a similar condition including this condition being imposed on the subsequent purchaser.

Printed and bound in the UK by TJ Books

MIX
Paper from
responsible sources
FSC® C013056

CONTENTS

PREFACE

We Are the Mutants is a critical reassessment of what is arguably the most discussed and beloved stretch of movies in American history. Documenting the tumultuous and transformative years between the arrival of US combat troops in Vietnam and the end of President Ronald Reagan's second term, we've chosen mostly to avoid the restrictive (and, if we're being honest, overanalyzed) "auteur cinema" canon, focusing instead on an eclectic selection of films and filmmakers across multiple genres—horror, documentary, cinéma vérité, disaster, vigilante action, neo-noir, post-apocalyptic sci-fi— that together capture the push and pull of old and new Hollywood, New Deal and no deal America.

Each of our chapters pairs two films that at first glance may appear unrelated but ultimately intersect in meaningful and unexpected ways, both artistically and in the larger arenas of politics and culture. We've focused on feature films because those are the ones that, intentionally or not, fairly or unfairly, best capture the beliefs, hopes, and anxieties of the audiences that paid to see them, as well as the realities and preoccupations of the day. Even though (and because) the national psyche was reeling from what Andreas Killen called "the schizoid awareness that institutions were toppling and yet remained more firmly in place than ever,"[1] Americans always went to the movies, and in ever-increasing numbers. They went for new stories and old stories, for innovation and tradition, for engagement and escape. They went, and continue to go, because movies are how Americans choose to see the world.

We wrote this book during a global pandemic that, in the US at least, was made exponentially more catastrophic because of the ideological inheritance passed down by Richard Nixon and made permanent by Reagan: the idea that we must sacrifice our obligations to the community to enrich mercenary self-interest and "protect" individual liberty, even though liberty can only exist and be exercised *within* the context of community. The grueling and tragic events of the last two years (and how many more?) make any attempt to analyze the present moment just as urgent as it is futile. So we'll tell the story of how we got here instead.

INTRODUCTION

It was Theodore Roszak, a history professor at California State College at Hayward, who popularized the term "counterculture" and, in 1969, finally put into words the revolutionary impulse at its heart: "a culture so radically disaffiliated from the mainstream assumptions of our society that it scarcely looks to many as a culture at all, but takes on the alarming appearance of a barbaric intrusion."[1] Inspired by the civil rights movement and quickened by the piling mutilations of the Vietnam War, dissent became electric among the student body of the University of California at Berkeley (twenty miles north of Hayward) and jumped from campus to campus across the country. These barbarians at the gate, Roszak argued, who rejected not just the inhuman calculus of the industrial order, but also the belligerent god of Western scientific tradition itself, were in fact our liberators. What's more, they were the only hope of "[transforming] this disoriented civilization of ours into something a human being can identify as home."[2]

They were no such thing, of course, but they did radically shift those mainstream assumptions—about youth, community, commerce, sexuality, authority, duty, recreation, ecology, media, art—and they *were* an unprecedented generational phenomenon, especially through the eyes of their Depression-era parents. Born of postwar bounty and reared in the new suburbs, where the sorcerous glow of the first TV sets crossed the long shadow of the atomic bomb, literary critic Leslie

Fiedler compared them not to barbarian invaders but to an alien civilization. Specifically invoking the language of science fiction, the only genre equipped to imagine the kinds of visionary transformations the young were chasing, he called them "the new mutants": "drop-outs from history"[3] who were already living in a future state, one that admitted and required only unrelieved pleasure and freedom. They had been taught to expect nothing less.[4]

Spiro Agnew, poeticizing Richard Nixon's gruff disdain, called them "an effete corps of impudent snobs."[5] Ronald Reagan, who won the race for California governor in 1966 based largely on a promise to "clean up the mess at Berkeley," called them "sex deviants" and "filthy speech advocates."[6] In a 1967 speech, to the utter delight of a soon-to-be legion of "family values" conservatives, he described the prototypical hippie: "he had a haircut like Tarzan, he walked like Jane, and smelled like Cheetah."[7] The corporate media, sniffing the money, alternately lionized and scolded them—*Time* named the non-compliant "Twenty-five and Under" generation "Man of the Year" in 1966; by 1971, the same magazine lamented that there were "too many hippies. We can only afford so many people alienated from society."[8] But *they* were not all made of the same substance or kind, and their collective influence has been exaggerated on both sides of the political divide by countless insipid caricatures, and by the nostalgic narcissism of the participants themselves. The truth is that Roszak's young dissidents made up only a small minority of white middle-class and upper-middle-class young people,[9] and while thousands would embrace the activist ideals of the anti-war New Left as embodied by the Berkeley-born Students for a Democratic Society (SDS)—replacing "power rooted in possession, privilege, or circumstance by power and uniqueness rooted in love, reflectiveness, reason, and creativity,"[10] read a defining passage of 1962's Port Huron Statement—most were apolitical or even anti-political: they were lifestyle consumers who wanted to rebrand themselves, not rebuild society. Others believed that the only way to become truly free was to remake their own minds, by means of psychedelic drugs, spiritual experience, or both. Their attitudes and behaviors and interests, subsumed under the expansive aegis of youth culture, sometimes overlapped and sometimes didn't.

Either way, it was not all peace signs and tambourines. During 1967's Summer of Love, the bohemian hippies poured into San Francisco's low-rent Haight-Ashbury district by the tens of thousands, picking all the flowers in Golden Gate Park and scattering trash and excrement along the Panhandle (the rats soon arrived). They also swamped the health and housing resources (clinics and hospitals were overrun with cases of overdose, venereal disease, and malnutrition) that already fell well short of meeting the needs of the area's poor and working-class residents, who only wanted ready access to the material security and middle-class comforts that had underwritten the counterculture's great refusals in the first place.[11] In her apocalyptic 1967 essay "Slouching Towards Bethlehem," Joan Didion contemplates a society that could not be put back together again, and looks for answers in the Haight's "pathetically unequipped children,"[12] willfully uncoupled from the traditions and institutions of their forebears: addicts crumpled up on the floorboards, trust-funded runaways and burn-outs, black-caped paranoids, a tragically precocious five-year-old plied with LSD. Answers were not forthcoming.

As for the activist set, while hundreds of well-intentioned young whites temporarily abandoned their secure sinecures in Berkeley and Chicago and New York to volunteer for civil rights initiatives in the South, they had a habit of, in the words of Student Nonviolent Coordinating Committee (SNCC) Chairman and Black Power vanguardist Stokely Carmichael, "showing [Black people] how to do it."[13] Similarly, after the 1964-1965 Free Speech Movement at Berkeley led to a police presence and over eight hundred arrests, white students increasingly, and ludicrously, began to compare their struggles to those of Blacks, culminating in a widely shared and oft-reprinted 1967 *Los Angeles Free Press* article (expanded into book form in 1969) by civil rights activist and college professor Jerry Farber called "The Student as Nigger," which argued that students are "slaves" because they have "separate and unequal dining facilities" and are "required... to show up for tests at 6:30 in the morning."[14] At the time, less than 6% of college students were Black, and that number was as high as it was only because of equal opportunity mandates in the Civil Rights Act of 1964, as well as grants and loans supplied by the Higher Education Act of 1965.[15] And so young Black men, who could not claim student deferments or inconspicuously disappear into Canada, were disproportionately drafted into the Vietnam War and disproportionately sent to the front lines—where they disproportionately died.[16]

It was obvious that dissenting white youth, whether acid-heads or anarchists, in a sense wanted "to become more Black than White,"[17] as Fiedler had said, and as Jack Kerouac and the Beats had wished outright years before. Or they wanted to be Argentine rebel Che Guevara, or imitate a Native American culture they perceived to be more communal and natural and "authentic." It was the ultimate act of disaffiliating with their own privilege and the history of oppression that made such privilege possible. If they could somehow absorb the *claim* to that oppression without suffering its material *consequences*, then they might alleviate the suspicion that they were protesting against not having anything to protest against. ("The troubles of white people," wrote James Baldwin in 1961, reminded him of "children crying because the breast has been taken away."[18])

They were punished for their transgressions, though, this youthful opposition. They were beaten by the Hells Angels in 1965 on the Oakland-Berkeley border (the police, Hunter S. Thompson believed, moved aside to let the Angels do it).[19] They were beaten, wounded, permanently blinded, and shot dead at People's Park in May 1969 ("If there has to be a bloodbath," Governor Reagan had warned, "then let's get it over with").[20] They were beaten and gassed and driven through plate-glass windows at the 1968 Democratic National Convention by a maniacal Chicago Police Department unleashed by Democratic mayor Richard Daley—the same police department that murdered Black Panthers Mark Clark and Fred Hampton in their sleep in December 1969.[21] They were beaten in New York City by a coordinated legion of construction workers in steel-toe boots, May 1970 ("Thank God for the hard hats!" said Nixon).[22] They were executed and buried in shallow graves by Klansmen in Mississippi during 1964's Freedom Summer (Andrew Goodman and Michael Schwermer, white, were shot once through the heart; James Chaney, Black, was tortured, mutilated, and shot three times). They were shot and killed (four students, unarmed) and permanently paralyzed by National Guardsmen at Kent State on May 4, 1970, two years after Highway Patrol officers killed three unarmed Black students at South Carolina State and eleven days before National Guardsmen fired almost five hundred rounds into unarmed Black students at Jackson State, killing two. No officer or Guardsman was convicted. 58% of

7

Americans, said a Gallup poll taken a few days after Kent State, blamed the students for the bloodshed; 11% blamed the National Guard; 31% had "no opinion."[23]

It was as if the rod their parents had spared them in childhood (millions followed the nurturing, child-centric advice of pediatrician Dr. Benjamin Spock, who later became a vehement anti-war activist) was visited upon them a hundredfold for daring to talk back as young adults. What had they done to deserve such a punishment? They had mobilized against what history has proven to be an obscenely immoral war that three consecutive White Houses knew was unwinnable in every conventional sense. They rejected white supremacy, even if they did not always acknowledge white privilege. They denounced the genocidal stockpiling of nuclear weapons and demanded that the planet and all the life on it be nurtured. They made art in every medium that has always been revered and emulated. And yet, by the time Roszak put a name to their struggle, they had already lost: Richard Nixon was president, elected in 1968 by appealing, explicitly, to the "forgotten Americans," the "non-shouters" and "non-demonstrators."[24] By fall of 1969, when a majority of Americans had turned against the war, even more of them thought that the young people protesting it were "harmful to American life."[25] What future could there be in a nation that sanctioned the killing of its own children to sanctify the narcotic illusions of its elders?

"Jesus, I love to shoot film," says Chicago TV cameraman John Cassellis (Robert Forster) in Haskell Wexler's *Medium Cool* (1969). He's watching Martin Luther King Jr.'s "I've Been to the Mountaintop" speech on TV with Eileen (Verna

Bloom), the Appalachian widow he's falling in love with. The audience knows that King will be assassinated the next day; Eileen and Cassellis do not. She is moved to the point of "goosebumps" by the emotional appeal of the speech; he is in awe of the medium through which that emotion is transmitted, the revolutionary power of film. When the movie opens, we follow Cassellis and his soundman (Peter Bonerz) as they quickly and methodically take footage of a moments-old car wreck, including the unconscious female victim thrown from the passenger door, before they bother to call for an ambulance. Cassellis is brash, ambitious, mercenary (like television itself)—certainly not a countercultural figure. But when he learns that his network is selling footage (of draft card burners, among other things) to the police and the FBI, he is furious, and gets fired for demanding answers. He may be a square with a real job, but he's not a "fink," and he shares his generation's contempt for authority. He also shares his generation's love of the movies. On the wall of his apartment hangs a giant poster of French actor Jean-Paul Belmondo from Jean-Luc Godard's *Breathless* (1960), opposite a two-page spread of the instantly, gruesomely famous 1968 photo (taken by the AP's Eddie Adams) showing the moment South Vietnamese general Nguyễn Ngọc Loan casually shot a bullet into the head of Viet Cong officer Nguyễn Văn Lém on the streets of Saigon.

The baby boomers had grown up in front of the TV, but the movies were where they found themselves. Film was visceral, it was immediate and immersive, it was hallucinatory in essence, it fractured and remade and recuperated reality. But at the beginning of 1967, there was little in American cinema—a glut of singing nuns, copycat gunslingers, Biblical and historical epics, and B-grade sci-fi—for the emerging enthusiasts to identify with, so they turned instead to the small art theaters and nascent college film courses, where they discovered, like Cassellis, the unconventional, existential, and pointedly not-American work of Godard, François Truffaut, Michelangelo Antonioni, Ingmar Bergman, Sergio Leone, Akira Kurosawa. Inevitably, the revolution came to Hollywood, the great mythologizer of American life, evangelist of the American dream. There was no escaping the blitz of Arthur Penn's *Bonnie and Clyde*.

Nowhere would Roszak's generation of radical disaffiliation become more manifest than in the characters of Bonnie Parker (Faye Dunaway) and Clyde Barrow (Warren Beatty), so bored and broke and beautiful in nothing-town Texas during the Great Depression that they commit not only to each other but also to a life of violent crime within minutes of meeting. Premiering in August of the Summer of Love, which was also a "long, hot summer" of deadly riots in ghettoized Black communities, *Bonnie and Clyde* was, with few exceptions (notably Pauline Kael and Roger Ebert), excoriated by a critical elite that was just as baffled by the younger generation as the gerontocratic studio heads. (Warner Bros. president Jack Warner, who hated the film and thought it would flop, refused to give it a wide release until Beatty threatened to sue him.) It wasn't just the extravagant bloodshed, unprecedented in a studio picture—it was the French New Wave-style auteurism and irreverence, the violent repudiation of the same necrotic idealism that suckled Nixon's "silent majority." Bonnie, Clyde, and the motley gang they assemble flit from bank job to bank job across a desiccated Southwest, where the everyday victims of capitalism's crash lash their scant belongings (a shredded mattress, a rocking chair) to the tops of their trucks and say goodbye to the farms and homes they built from scratch—all of it now repossessed by the banks. "Why'd he try to kill me?" Clyde says of the butcher who attacked him for sticking up the general store. "I ain't got nothin' against him." Like his counterculture counterparts, he is stupefied as to why he or anyone else would willingly get a "straight" job or otherwise participate in the degenerate Establishment just "to get somethin' to eat around here."

Motion Picture Association of America (MPAA) president Jack Valenti, in a February 21, 1968 press conference, addressed the hostile reaction to *Bonnie and Clyde*: "When so many movie critics complain about violence on film, I don't think they realize the impact of thirty minutes on the Huntley-Brinkley newscast—and that's real violence."[26] He was undoubtedly leveraging his efforts, a year in the making, to kill the restrictive Motion Picture Production Code and institute a more flexible (and lucrative) ratings system, which would be formally introduced in November of the following year. But he was also right. His words came less than a month after NBC's footage of the Saigon execution was seen by twenty million viewers on that very same *Huntley-Brinkley Report*,[27] only a few hours after Adams' photo was splashed across the front page of almost every major newspaper in the country. The "film generation," as *The New Republic*'s Stanley Kauffman called them in his review of Antonioni's 1966 *Blowup*, a film about a fashion photographer who may have captured a murder while taking a surreptitious photo, was quite accustomed to violence on screen: the around-the-clock coverage of the JFK assassination, Jack Ruby gunning down Lee Harvey Oswald, Selma's "Bloody Sunday," and nightly footage of the carnage in Vietnam and the riots at home—in Watts, Detroit, New Jersey, Cleveland, Philadelphia, Washington, D.C.

The critics were irrelevant, as it turned out. *Bonnie and Clyde* cleared almost $23 million domestically on a $2.5 million budget. Mike Nichols' *The Graduate* (also 1967), another taboo-breaking youth draw, made almost twice that. Suddenly, the kids were alright. By 1969, when *Easy Rider* took in more than $19 million and became the first feature about hippies that was actually *made* by hippies— thirty-two-year-old Dennis Hopper and twenty-nine-year- old Peter Fonda—the majority of moviegoers, and almost all repeat viewers, were teenagers and young adults.[28] The "youth market" was aggressively courted by the studios, as were the young directors and writers from the nation's handful of film schools, especially the University of Southern California (USC) and the University of California at Los Angeles (UCLA). One independent production company had been doing those things for years: American International Pictures (AIP). Formed in 1954 by former projectionist and adman James Nicholson and entertainment lawyer Samuel Arkoff, AIP churned out low-budget exploitation fare for the drive-ins, and, thanks to ingenious producer-director Roger Corman, occasionally put out vibrant pictures that had something to say. Corman, always willing to take a chance on a young filmmaker with ideas—provided they would work for cheap, shoot quickly, and come in under budget—gave many of the central figures of "New Hollywood" their start: Francis Ford Coppola, Peter Bogdanovich, Martin Scorsese, Jack Nicholson, Robert De Niro, Robert Towne, László Kovács, Jonathan Demme, John Milius, Bruce Dern, and Peter Fonda. The idea for *Easy Rider*, in fact, came from Fonda's breakout role in AIP's wildly successful 1966 biker film *The Wild Angels*. (On Corman's advice, Fonda approached Arkoff to produce, but Arkoff wanted the right to pull unpredictable first-time director Hopper if he fell behind schedule. Fonda declined.) AIP's formula was simple enough, as Arkoff told it:

> We started looking for our audience by removing the element of authority in our films. We saw the rebellion coming, but we couldn't predict the extent of it, so we made a rule: no parents, no church or school authorities […] If they must appear, they will be bumbling, ineffectual people.[29]

In a fitting twist, it was the industry outsiders, scorned by the monolithic Hollywood establishment, who showed the way.

New Hollywood, however, like the counterculture itself, was an exaggeration—and for the very same reasons. Old Hollywood never died; it simply cannibalized the living, much like the ghouls in George A. Romero's 1968 *Night of the Living Dead*, a guerilla shocker about an undead uprising and a fractious resistance led by a Black man (Duane Jones) who, in the end, is shot in the head by the sheriff's Selma-reminiscent white posse. A new dawn had certainly arrived, anyway. Outworn genres were resurrected, revised, extended, and blended. Tried and trite narrative and cinematic techniques became idiosyncratic, and criminals and lowlifes became heroes and martyrs. This new breed of film was "not a means of escape," said *Cahiers du Cinéma*'s editor-in-chief Jean-Louis Comolli, "but a means of approaching a problem."[30] And yet the unfolding "cinema of sensation"—Stanley Kubrick's psychedelicized Star Gate, Sam Peckinpah's blood-orgiastic last stands, Scorsese's nihilistic and neon-washed mean streets—coexisted with James Bond super-thrillers and Sensurround disaster epics, and contained within itself the inflationary self-indulgence that would lead to its own implosion.

Despite the commercial success of these unrestrained new films, the motion picture industry faced a massive financial crisis from 1969 to 1971, losing an estimated $600 million on a series of big-budget flops aimed at repeating the windfall of 1965's *The Sound of Music*.[31] Auteurism, superior technique, and edgy social commentary had not inspired the studio execs to become patrons of the arts. "We want one big picture a year," Paramount president Frank Yablans told *Variety* in 1971. "The rest are budgeted to minimize risk."[32] Yablans had just overseen the cross-media marketing campaign for 1970's *Love Story*, a formulaic tear-jerker that became the highest-grossing film of the year and received seven Academy Award nominations. Paramount's next "one big picture" righted the industry and became, for a short time, the highest-grossing movie ever made: 1972's *The Godfather*, directed by the undisputed prince of the USC-UCLA New Hollywood enclave, Francis Ford Coppola. He had wanted nothing to do with the project initially, calling Mario Puzo's bestselling novel of the same name "pretty cheap stuff,"[33] and Paramount felt much the same way about him. But no one else wanted the job, and ultimately Coppola took it on so that he could pay off the debts of his production company, American Zoetrope, and fund the art movies he wanted to make.

Through Coppola's eyes (he co-wrote the screenplay with Puzo), *The Godfather* became a brooding and bloody period piece about contemporary America—an epic-sized *Bonnie and Clyde*, but without the ironic humor. Here the gangsters are a malignant but inevitable outgrowth of the inequities and iniquities embedded in postwar corporate capitalism and abetted by epidemic political corruption, and the sun-spangled America of white weddings and orange groves is underwritten by tawdry blood feuds and contract killings brokered by violent patriarchs behind closed doors. But the film is also a portrait of near-fanatical family loyalty and generational reconciliation amid chaos and war—a "reactionary" and "perverse expression of a desirable and lost cultural tradition,"[34] said Robert Towne, who worked on the script. Young, idealistic war hero Michael Corleone knows the family business is wicked and wants to go his own way, but he can't refuse his duty to his father, who he ultimately becomes.[35]

There were sleepers, too. Gordon Parks' 1971 *Shaft*, starring Richard Roundtree as a hardboiled Harlem detective battling the Mafia, lifted MGM through the recession. (Parks was the first Black director to helm a major studio picture, 1969's *The Learning Tree*, based on his autobiographical novel of the same name.) It was already in production when the first all-Black crewed film, Melvin Van Peebles' *Sweet Sweetback's Baadasssss Song*, made millions on a nothing budget, despite being "rated X by an all-white jury." 1971's little-publicized *Billie Jack*, about a half-Navajo Vietnam vet who defends a hippie school from the hostile townsfolk, made $10 million upon initial release and six times that amount in 1973, when director, producer, writer, and star Tom Laughlin re-released it using targeted TV ads and saturation booking techniques—the latter a gambit pioneered by exploitation houses like AIP and summarily adopted by the majors, who previously considered the practice unscrupulous. *Dirty Harry*, on the other hand, the sixth highest-grossing film of 1971, follows a vigilante cop (Clint Eastwood) who disdains effete liberalism and defends counterculture mecca San Francisco against a hippie assassin. A profoundly different animal, Tobe Hooper's 1974 *The Texas Chain Saw Massacre* is suffused with images of industrial collapse and moral decay; running out of gas, a group of innocent youngsters are entrapped and slaughtered by a family of monstrous cannibals.

These were all New Hollywood films, or none of them were. What mattered was that, for a moment in time, the studios had to a large extent surrendered control of the means of producing and manipulating the American image, and new technologies like the handheld Panaflex and Super 8 sound camera gave many more aspiring directors the chance to make films (distribution was another matter), be it for popular consumption or the flourishing underground circuit of the avant-garde. The result was a stunning succession of crisscrossing imagery steeped in violence and tragedy, self-destruction and desperation. The country had flipped over and, as in 1972's second highest-grossing film, *The Poseidon Adventure*, become "hell, upside down."

The identification of the counterculture with mutants crops up again in Theodore Roszak's third book, 1975's *Unfinished Animal*, in which his ongoing pursuit of the youth movement shifts to the "Aquarian frontier" and "a planet-wide mutation of mind which promises to liberate energies of will and resources of vision long maturing in the depths of our identity."[36] The book is introduced by an epigraph, graffiti seen by Roszak on a wall in Berkeley: "The bomb has already dropped, and we are the mutants." The author is unknown, but the essence of the idea may have been taken from a 1950 essay, "The Thing," by German philosopher Martin Heidegger:

Man stares at what the explosion of the atom bomb could bring with it. He does not see that the atom bomb and its explosion are the mere final emission of what has long since taken place, has already happened.[37]

Or maybe it's a nuclear age update of the opening of D.H. Lawrence's post-World War I novel, 1932's *Lady Chatterley's Lover*:

Ours is essentially a tragic age, so we refuse to take it tragically. The cataclysm has happened, we are among the ruins, we start to build up new little habitats, to have new little hopes. It is rather hard work: there is now no smooth road into the future: but we go round, or scramble over the obstacles. We've got to live, no matter how many skies have fallen.[38]

The concept and image of the radiation mutant had, by the early 1970s, become a sci-fi standard in both literature and film, grounded in 1950s American anxiety over the atomic bomb and what might happen if "they" dared use it against "us." For Roszak, the mutants are something quite different: the beneficiaries of an "*evolutionary* […] shift of consciousness fully as epoch-making as the appearance of speech" from whom "history demands more […] than mere survival" and "social revolution"[39]—a collective incarnation of the luminous "star child" glimpsed in the final shots of *2001: A Space Odyssey*. What he got instead was a mostly crass New Age of self-help and self-retreat and self-serving following the very public and very brash insurgencies of the previous decade, now all but laid to waste: Nixon's reelection in 1972 marked one of the biggest landslides in US presidential election history. In 1969, Roszak had warned about the insularity and "maniacal nihilism" of the counterculture,[40] and it had, in Malcolm X's phrase about the assassination of JFK, come home to roost.

And yet the mutants of the epigram are clearly not the elite, ethereal beings Roszak predicted. They are the "mere" survivors he rejected, everyone who had been changed, deeply and permanently, by the omnipresent menace of the bomb, yes, but also a scarcely endurable succession of mortal blows—Mỹ Lai and Manson, Kent State and Watergate, MLK and RFK, COINTELPRO and Operation CHAOS, Freedom Deal and Wounded Knee. Lawrence's words work just as well for post-Vietnam America, after all, where the cataclysm (or cataclysms) that happened became the ruins of the present: a festering and debilitating distrust of the government at every level, a procession of "sorry no gas" signs, predatory cults, copycat killers, hijacks, hostages, urban disinvestment and decimating inflation, the latter convincingly described by struggling Detroit autoworker Zeke (Richard Pryor) in 1978's *Blue Collar*: "Wages ain't the problem no more—it's the fuckin' prices. Everything's so goddamn high, the more you make, the less it's worth."

Maybe it wasn't a capsized ocean liner Americans found themselves in, but a shabby fishing boat soon to be dead in the water, a giant man-eating shark circling hungrily outside. With Steven Spielberg's 1975 *Jaws*, the blockbuster mentality became a syndrome that has never really been cured, but it was an unexpected hit from two years earlier, 1973's *American Graffiti*, that foreshadowed the greatest sea change, outside of the introduction of sound, in American film history. Although George Lucas's first feature, the dystopian sci-fi *THX 1138* (1971), had tanked commercially, it received some positive critical marks that focused mostly on the film's striking visuals. His friend and mentor Francis Ford Coppola suggested he make a more personal, more approachable film, and Lucas turned to his own teenage years in the small desert town of Modesto, California, a simpler time (through Lucas's eyes) of custom cars cruising on full tanks of cheap gas, harmless hijinks, and rock 'n' roll radio. Where *Bonnie and Clyde* and *The Godfather* were films set in the past that attacked the broken present, a prevailing New Hollywood trope, *American Graffiti* was a film set in the past that *idealized the past*. The nostalgia was explicit, and Lucas knew that audiences were hungry for it. "It had become depressing to go to the movies," he told the Modesto Rotary Club on the eve of the film's release. "I decided it was time to make a movie where people felt better coming out of the theater than when they went in."[41] The film's tagline—"Where were you in '62?"—both recalled and nullified the assassination of JFK, the turning point at which, in the words of Chief Justice Earl Warren, the "forces of hatred and malevolence" had begun "eating their way into the bloodstream of American life."[42] On a paltry budget of $750,000 (less than Lucas had raised for *THX 1138*), and all but forgotten by distributor Universal Pictures, *American Graffiti* won third place at the box office for the year, taking in more than $55 million. Lucas's next project, a science fiction fantasy based on the *Flash Gordon* serials of his youth, would unleash the full fury of the wistful forces he had cornered.

"I thought, 'we all know what a terrible mess we have made of the world,'" he told *Rolling Stone* about the genesis of *Star Wars*. "We also know, as every movie in the last ten years points out, how terrible we are, how we have ruined the world and [...] how rotten everything is." His new film would be something different, he pledged, a "positive" reinstatement of "dreams and fantasies, getting children to believe there is more to life than garbage and killing and all that real stuff…" The generation that had grown up "without fairy tales […] and adventures in far-off lands" would be put to rights.[43] In fact, every generation was swept away. *Star Wars* was a miracle salve for a wounded nation, a New Hollywood telling of an Old Hollywood epic using a revolutionary new grammar of hyper-elaborate special effects and four-track Dolby surround sound. Much like J.R.R. Tolkien's *The Lord of the Rings*, an early hippie obsession in the mid-Sixties, *Star Wars* projected moral clarity into moral fog, mythic pretense into mass malaise, a deep reverence for ancient magic and a deep resentment of modern technology—ironic for a sci-fi extravaganza, but what is the Death Star if not the perfection of the military-industrial technocracy? Lucas's unexpected global phenomenon reached "way past nostalgia," said Pauline Kael, "to the feeling that now is the time to return to childhood."[44] The same could be said of the second-best blockbuster of 1977, Spielberg's *Close Encounters of the Third Kind*, where a bored suburban electrician, Roy Neary (Richard Dreyfuss), abandons his family and the obligations of adulthood to take a ride into space with childlike aliens. Like one of Roszak's mutants, Roy is special, chosen.

Lucas gave the people what they wanted, and the result was the first "super-grosser"—by the end of 1982, after an initial run of eighteen months and three re-releases, *Star Wars* had returned a miraculous $530 million globally.[45] What was already a mercenary industry became a frantic, high-stakes gambling operation as studios vied for the next big score, each one manufactured from the ground up to become a "national obsession." The negative costs of making a film, including production, overhead, and financing, spiraled from $2 million in 1972 to $10 million in 1979, and the price of marketing alone often dwarfed those costs. The pre-sold film franchise was here to stay, and so were the multi-million-dollar merchandising deals (the original *Star Wars* trilogy brought in $2.6 billion in merchandising revenue[46]), multimedia cross-marketing, the careful grooming of (and subservience to) fandom. Many of New Hollywood's biggest names blamed Lucas, and to a lesser extent Spielberg, for "the death of film." "What happened with *Star Wars*," William Friedkin said, "was like when McDonald's got a foothold, the taste for good food just disappeared. Now we're in a period of devolution. Everything has gone backward toward a big sucking hole."[47]

But did Lucas's admittedly fluffy space opera really infantilize the moviegoing public and "prepare the ground for the growth of the right,"[48] as New Hollywood chronicler Peter Biskind suggested? Was Friedkin's exploitation art-horror *The Exorcist* (the runaway sensation of 1973), a movie that demonizes female adolescence, chastises single motherhood, and props up the medieval dogma of the Roman Catholic Church, "good food"? Like the phantom blonde Curt (Richard Dreyfuss) pursues throughout *American Graffiti*, the comforting but facile world of *Star Wars* doesn't exist, and the film-as-fairytale blithely glosses over the tragic waste of even the most "just" of wars: how many children and janitors and cooks and doctors did Luke Skywalker kill when he channeled the "good side" of the Force "that binds the galaxy together" to blow up the moon-sized Death Star? Not to mention Lucas's "far, far away" alternative future-past, teeming with colorful alien species but glaringly devoid of people of color, as actor and activist Raymond St. Jacques noted in a 1977 piece for the *Los Angeles Times*.[49] And yet Coppola's war epic *Apocalypse Now* (1979), which Lucas had been set to direct for almost a decade until he chose *Star Wars* instead, is equally fantastic. ("I mean the war is essentially a Los Angeles export, like acid rock,"

Coppola told Biskind. "The jungle will look psychedelic, fluorescent blues, yellows, and greens."[50]) While the surrealist parable wallows in the horrors that *Star Wars* could not face, it also reduces Vietnam and the Vietnamese to an ahistorical crucible that America must endure and transcend. The film is a sometimes cutting, sometimes juvenile exploration of the dualistic nature of humanity, the same theme running through *The Exorcist* and *Star Wars*.

Years before she pilloried *Star Wars* for sucking up to a "mass audience," Kael herself, in a 1973 piece called "After Innocence," took New Hollywood's insularity and "depressive uncertainty" to task:

> The movies have shown us the injustice of American actions throughout our history, and if we have always been rotten, the effect is not to make us feel we have the power to change but, rather, to rub our noses in it and make us accept it. Watergate seems the most natural thing that could happen [...] The acceptance of corruption and the sentimentalization of defeat—that's the prevailing atmosphere in American movies...[51]

Which is exactly what Lucas would later tell *Rolling Stone*. It wasn't *Star Wars* that put down the scrappy New Hollywood rebellion—in reality, not so much a rebellion as an unruly cash cow that was carefully massaged as it was carefully milked. It was New Hollywood that killed New Hollywood. What started with the bang of *Bonnie and Clyde* and *Easy Rider* ended with the thud of Scorsese's *New York, New York* (1977), Coppola's opulently inexplicable *One from the Heart* (1982), and the infamous $40 million fiasco of Michael Cimino's *Heaven's Gate* (1980)—a "scandalous cinematic waste," said

Roger Ebert[52]—that sunk United Artists. Most of the auteurs had lost their audience, so the studios dropped most of the auteurs. The country had changed. MPAA president Jack Valenti, a staunch defender of *Bonnie and Clyde* in 1968, had turned on outlaw cinema by 1980, shortly after former Hollywood B-lister Ronald Reagan was sworn in as the 40th president of the United States: "The political climate in this country is shifting to the right," he said, "and that means more conservative attitudes toward sex and violence. But a lot of creative people are still living in the world of revolution."[53]

Although few of the most popular films of the decade were as explicitly belligerent and reactionary as the 1985 Vietnam revenge fantasy *Rambo: First Blood Part II* and its progeny ("After seeing *Rambo* last night," Reagan quipped following the release of thirty-nine American hostages from Beirut, "I know what to do the next time this happens"[54]), almost all of the top draws followed the same formula: they were heavy on effects, they were action-oriented, and they were even less morally and emotionally complex than *Star Wars*. But because the cost of chasing blockbusters had become so prohibitive, the majors made fewer and fewer films. At the same time, the number of movie theater screens multiplied across the country, from almost 18,000 in 1980 to over 23,000 in 1989.[55] The studios, gobbled up by global multimedia conglomerates, in turn gobbled up the new theater chains, giving them a virtual monopoly on all three phases of the motion picture industry: production, distribution, and exhibition.

The new generation of moviegoers, 73% of them under the age of twenty-nine, was just as voracious as the old, and had arguably similar tastes. The murderous outlaws of *Bonnie and Clyde* and *Badlands* (1973) shifted into the psychotic puritanical slashers of *Halloween* (1978) and *Friday the 13th* (1980); Dirty

Harry and *The French Connection*'s (1971) "Popeye" Doyle, descendants of Leone and Peckinpah's wild-eyed Old West mercenaries, became the cowboy cops of *Lethal Weapon* (1987) and *Die Hard* (1988); irreverent generation gap comedies like *The Graduate* and *American Graffiti* got updates in *National Lampoon's Animal House* (1978) and *Fast Times at Ridgemont High* (1982); and of course, after *Star Wars*, science fiction feasted in every possible flavor. In fact, by 1980, sci-fi and horror films made up almost 40% of North American rentals.[56] And irrespective of genre, what bombed at the box office might hit big money "downstream" in the emerging home video and cable markets.

By 1986, independent releases outnumbered studio output by more than three to one[57]: all of those new theaters had to be fed. Most of them (with Cannon Films and Roger Corman's New World Pictures leading the way) were, predictably, bent on exploiting both the studio moneymakers and the many subcultures and short-lived fads of the vibrantly rapacious era, but others were as creatively subversive as anything released in the previous two decades. The difference this time around was that the films that went for the Establishment's throat rarely had the financial backing of the Establishment. But the sheer demand for film and the popularity of so many genres brought hungry backers, who gave a more diverse group of artists the chance to make their own movies. Of the 7,332 features released by major distributors between 1949 and 1979, only fourteen were directed by women.[58] In the 1980s, that number went up to approximately ninety, thanks largely to the efforts of the Directors Guild of America's (DGA) Women's Steering Committee, which in 1980 spotlighted a "30-year pattern of discrimination"[59] and called for studios and TV networks to introduce voluntary affirmative action programs and quotas. The studios refused, and the DGA filed a class action suit against two of them, Columbia and Warner Bros., in 1983. The case was thrown out in 1985—the DGA contract itself, the judge ruled, was discriminatory, and thus the DGA could not represent the women bringing the suit—but the tenacity of the Women's Committee and the resulting press coverage scared the studios into action, at least for a while.[60] The Guild's Ethnic Minority Committee had made the same argument with less luck, and it wasn't until the financial and critical success of Spike Lee's *Do the Right Thing* (1989) that Black and other non-white directors started to get more opportunities in Hollywood.[61]

The ghosts of Vietnam—not the inexcusable suffering or the inexcusable dead, but the infantile resentment of soiled American pride—continued to linger, as did the sense that a corrosive "crisis of confidence," in the words of President Jimmy Carter, "strikes at the very heart and soul and spirit of our national will."[62] And so nostalgia continued to thrive. In 1978, the three highest-grossers were *Superman*, a throwback to the gee-whiz superhero who was originally the "champion of the oppressed" but quickly became the patriotic "defender of law and order," *Grease* (set in the summer of 1958), and *National Lampoon's Animal House* (set in 1962, the same year as *American Graffiti*). A host of boomer reminiscences followed: *Porky's* (1981, set in 1954), *Diner* (1982, set in 1959), *Stand by Me* (1986, set in summer of 1959), *Dirty Dancing* (1987, set in summer of 1963), *Splash* (1988, begins in 1964), *Dead Poets Society* (1989, set in fall of 1959), to name a few. None were as impeccably entertaining or as consummately facile as 1985's highest grosser (beating *Rambo* by more than $40 million),

Robert Zemeckis's *Back to the Future*, an openly reverential and more or less literal adaptation of Reagan's 1980 campaign slogan: "Let's Make America Great Again." Upping the ante on *American Graffiti*, the protagonist actually travels back in time, thanks to good ole American know-how and uranium stolen from Libyan terrorists, to mend the decadent present by restoring the timelessly "ideal" values of the 1950s.

The following year's *Peggy Sue Got Married* takes the premise even further. This time, forty-something Peggy Sue (Kathleen Turner), recently separated from her cheating husband and former high school sweetheart Charlie (Nicolas Cage), passes out at her twenty-five-year high school reunion and wakes up as her teenage self in gloriously uncomplicated 1960. Given the chance to relive her senior year, she breaks up with Charlie, beds the class poet (Kevin J. O'Connor), gives the class science nerd (Barry Miller) inside info from the future that will make him a billionaire, and falls in love with her husband again. Returning to 1985 (she wakes up in a hospital bed: was it all a dream?), she takes back the groveling Charlie, and the patriarchal suburban order is restored. The film's director was not alleged cinema assassin George Lucas. It was former guerilla-auteur Francis Ford Coppola.

PART ONE

APOCALYPSE AMERICANA 1968–1973

RADIO NEWSCASTER: At this hour, we repeat, these are the facts as we know them. There is an epidemic of mass murder being committed by a virtual army of unidentified assassins. The murders are taking place in villages, cities, rural homes, and suburbs with no apparent pattern or reason for the slayings. It seems to be a sudden, general explosion of mass homicide. We have some descriptions of the assassins. Eyewitnesses say they are ordinary-looking people. Some say they appear to be in a kind of trance…

Night of the Living Dead, 1968

1. *"AREN'T* YOU HIS MOTHER?"': *ROSEMARY'S BABY* AND *BLOODY MAMA*

The first time we see Rosemary (Mia Farrow) and Guy Woodhouse (John Cassavetes), it's from on high: they are specks of shadow, barely, as they move down the sidewalk and turn to enter the massive, brooding Bramford, a storied and highly coveted apartment building facing Central Park West. The lofty perspective is not the protective gaze of God, as we'll find out, but the long distance of indifference. The young married couple meet Mr. Nicklas (Elisha Cook), the Bramford's leasing agent, who takes them up in a finicky cage elevator and down a dingy hallway of crumbling tile and plaster patches to apartment 7E, which has become available due to the elderly tenant's days-old death. By New York standards, the four-bedroom suite, shuttered in black drapes and still cluttered with Mrs. Gardenia's old-world belongings, is a miracle. Rosemary is giddy, and we know right away that she's an innocent—"Oh, it's a wonderful apartment—I *love* it," she enthuses in front of Mr. Nicklas, as Guy winces. But she is not stupid. A hefty chest of drawers blocks one of the closets, and while Mr. Nicklas is perplexed, Rosemary points out the streaks on the carpet: it was dragged there on purpose. A self-confessed "country girl" from Omaha who moved to the big city for bigger experiences, estranging her traditional Irish Catholic family in the process, she is not like the throngs of drifters and runaways and seekers of her generation. She knows exactly what she wants: Guy, three kids two years apart, and a cozy and stylish home for family and friends. Her only sin, and it can be called that only after more than fifty years of increasingly venomous national schism, is that she trusts her husband, her neighbors, her doctors, her political and religious leaders, and the integrity of the Establishment to which they belong. And *that* is why she is raped by Satan and gives birth to the Antichrist.

1968's *Rosemary's Baby*, Roman Polanski's sly, voyeuristic adaptation of Ira Levin's 1967 bestselling neo-gothic novel, seeded the American consciousness with infernal terror at precisely the moment the country was suffering its most desperate crisis of faith since the Civil War. More than that, the film, released only six days after the assassination of presidential hopeful Robert F. Kennedy, who had told a crowd at Vanderbilt University in March that his opponent Richard Nixon "represents the dark side of the American spirit,"[1] took on the air of prophecy. The supernatural thriller, which begins in August 1965 and ends in July 1966, is fleshed out and grounded by cultural cues and real events that marked a great transformation in American life—John F. Kennedy's assassination and its conspiratorial aftermath, the decline of religiosity and the ascendancy of all manner of freeform occult beliefs, the civil rights movement during what is arguably its most critical phase—and ultimately the severing of a liberal consensus that would forever split the country into hostile camps. Rosemary's pregnancy, and her growing awareness of the malevolent circumstances surrounding it, is the story of that gestating national apocalypse.

While Rosemary's older friend Hutch (Maurice Evans), something of a surrogate father, warns her and Guy about the Bramford's dark past, especially its harboring of a witch named Adrian Marcato, who claimed in the 1890s to have "conjured up the living Devil," Rosemary is unswayed—as we know she will be—and she sets to work making over the apartment: in a happy montage, workmen paint, roll carpet, deliver fashionable and expensive furniture (Guy, a theatrical actor who resents the delay of his big break, pays the bills with commercial work that he despises), and hang yellow and white and green floral print wallpaper (a visual motif throughout) in the room that Rosemary intends, sooner rather than later, to be a nursery. In the basement laundry room—because young Rosemary, though a reader of the *New Yorker* and the Kinsey Reports, is a dutiful stay-at-home wife—she meets Terry Gionoffrio, a former prostitute and drug addict taken in by Minnie (Ruth Gordon) and Roman Castevet (Sidney Blackmer), an elderly couple who live next door to Rosemary and Guy. (Rosemary mistakes Terry for actress Victoria Vetri, who is in fact the actress playing Terry, billed in the film as Angela Dorian: no one is who they seem to be.)

In the next scene, as Rosemary and Guy approach the Bramford after a night at the theater, they're met by a crowd outside the building and the flashing sirens of police cars. Terry has apparently jumped out of the Castevets' seven-story window. The "European" "good luck" charm that she showed off to Rosemary in the laundry room, a gift from Minnie and Roman, is still hanging around her neck, bathed in a pool of blood. The Castevets arrive on the scene, archaically and garishly dressed, identify the body, and confirm with the police (a little too emphatically) that the suicide note is in Terry's writing. Rosemary introduces herself and pays her respects, and the two couples, one of which presides over a coven of Satanic witches, become fatefully entwined. Rosemary has a dream that night while sliding in and out of sleep: the image of Terry's face—"watching the sky with one eye, half of her face gone to red pulp," as Levin described it and as Polanski shot it—is superimposed over the new bedroom wallpaper. Rosemary is transported to the Catholic school of her childhood, where she is chastised in front of her class by a furious Sister Veronica. The words are really Minnie's, though, heard faintly through the bedroom wall, and they describe Terry's fate—and Rosemary's:

> Sometimes I wonder how come you're the leader of anything... If you would've listened to me, we wouldn't've had to do *this*. We would've been all set to go instead of having to start all over from *scratch*. I told you not to tell her in advance. I told you she wouldn't be open-minded.

Guy—described in Levin's original character sketch as "totally self-centered, a mirror-looker, an actor"[2]—is turned quite easily. After dinner at the Castevets on the night following Terry's death, as Minnie washes dishes and casually grills Rosemary about the fertility of her sisters, Rosemary notices a conspicuous silence from the living room: Guy and Roman are unseen, their presence betrayed only by tendrils of cigarette smoke crossing the kitchen doorway. When the camera cuts to both men sitting on the sofa, Guy is leaning in, obviously shocked by one of Roman's "stories": he has already been offered the deal; he will quite literally sell his soul (and his wife's body, and her unborn son) to the Devil in exchange for the promise of stardom. From that point on, he is playing a part. The deception and ruination of his wife is the role of a lifetime.

For starters, he suddenly and enthusiastically agrees to have a baby, a project we suspect he had always planned to postpone indefinitely. He even knows (Rosemary does not question how) "the right time to start" trying, and on that night they get dressed up, start a fire ("I hope we have the coldest winter ever," Rosemary purrs), and eat dinner by candlelight. Dessert is a mousse, concocted by Minnie and pushed by Guy, that's filled—one of the helpings, anyway—with black-magic-brewed tranquilizers.[3] But Rosemary doesn't eat the full serving, and, as she is again caught between states of consciousness, she dreams that she is sitting on former President John F. Kennedy's yacht—first naked, then in a bikini—as Guy undresses her and preps her for the ceremonial sacrifice to Satan incarnate. Several other bikini-clad women are on deck with her as womanizer Kennedy himself (Paul Denton) looks on, stately and serene in his Navy officer's uniform, returned from the dead without a scratch.

Although this is the only explicit reference to JFK in the film, his assassination permeates the subtext of *Rosemary's Baby*. The tragedy in Dallas laid low a nation sky-high on postwar triumphalism, and it was especially painful to Irish Catholics, practicing or not, like Rosemary: Kennedy was, until the election of Joe Biden, the only Catholic US President, and at the time of his election Catholics were still widely scrutinized by what Kennedy called "the finger of suspicion."[4] JFK's very gruesome and very public death—recall Terry, "half of her face gone to red pulp"—was interpreted by the wider liberal majority "as a symptom of, and perhaps even a punishment for, some tragic moral flaw in American life,"[5] in the words of British journalist and historian Godfrey Hodgson. Americans simply could not believe that their preternaturally charismatic and telegenic young leader, after backing down the Russians the year before, had been felled by a disgruntled halfwit using a sniper rifle purchased through a mail order catalog—and they still can't, nearly sixty years later.[6] In Levin's novel, when the Castevets have Rosemary and Guy over for dinner, one of the topics of discussion is the Kennedy assassination, because "Mr. Castevet was reading a book critical of the Warren Report,"[7] which found in September 1964 that the assassination "was the work of one man, Lee Harvey Oswald. There was no conspiracy, foreign or domestic."[8] The irony, of course, is that Roman Castevet himself is the leader of the ultimate conspiracy: an international coven of witches that's working to revenge itself on the Biblical Prince of Peace and usher the Antichrist into power.

The day before JFK was shot, Columbia professor Richard Hofstadter delivered a lecture at Oxford University called "The Paranoid Style in American Politics," remarking on "the sense of heated exaggeration, suspiciousness, and conspiratorial fantasy" that was then rising on the "radical right"[9] but had been fossilized in the bedrock of the American project since the Salem witch trials and Indian captivity narratives, where "in every Nook" of the New World "the devil is encamped."[10] For the Puritans (who wanted to "purify" the Church of England from perceived Catholic elements) and their descendants, what else but subversives, working under cover of certain unalienable rights endowed by their creator, could deal privation and tragedy to the gleaming "city upon a hill"? In November 1964, right around the time Rosemary finds out she's pregnant, Hofstadter adapted his lecture into an essay that ran in *Esquire*. The archetypal "paranoid spokesman," he wrote,

sees the fate of conspiracy in apocalyptic terms—he traffics in the birth and death of whole worlds, whole political orders, whole systems of human values […] Like religious millennialists he expresses the anxiety of those who are living through the last days and he is sometimes disposed to set a date for the apocalypse.[11]

"There are plots against people, aren't there?" Rosemary asks Dr. Hill (Charles Grodin), who she has desperately called from a phone booth after discovering that her obstetrician, a friend of the Castevets who "delivers all the society babies," is part of the coven that plans (she thinks) to sacrifice her baby during a Black Mass. *Rosemary's Baby*, while very much the template for modern occult horror, is also a Cold War conspiracy narrative, and has a lot in common with that genre's quintessential film, and possibly the defining film of the Kennedy era: John Frankenheimer's *The Manchurian Candidate* (1962), about a Korean War veteran, Raymond Shaw (Laurence Harvey), who is brainwashed by Chinese communists and programmed by his ruthlessly autocratic mother (Angela Lansbury) to eliminate her husband's political rivals in a bid for world domination. The candidate of the title is US Senator John Iselin (James Gregory), entirely unaccomplished and unremarkable until he makes a startling allegation at a televised Department of Defense press conference that he has "a list of the names of 207 persons who are known by the Secretary of Defense as being members of the Communist Party… who are still nevertheless working in and shaping the policy of the Defense Department." This is nearly a verbatim quote from a real February 9, 1950 speech (just substitute State Department for Defense Department) by an unaccomplished and unremarkable junior Senator from Wisconsin, Joseph McCarthy, to a group of West Virginia Republicans. The tone was Biblical and apocalyptic, with McCarthy preaching "a final, all-out battle between communistic atheism and Christianity."[12] The line that would define McCarthy's loathsome and often brazenly unconstitutional campaign to weed out a conspiracy that he himself fabricated was attributed to an "outstanding historical figure" he never names: "'When a great democracy is destroyed, it will not be from enemies from without, but rather because of enemies from within.'"[13]

Rosemary's Baby manipulates this uniquely American-style fear of "enemies from within," except that here the threat is real and imminent—and cosmic in scope, more desperate even than McCarthy's craven and hysterical rhetoric. Black magic *works*. Satan *exists*, spiritually and physically. The conspiracy is real in *The Manchurian Candidate*, too, a liberal subversion of reactionary paranoia that recasts the McCarthy stand-in and his handlers as the conspirators. But where Frankenheimer's film enshrines the idealism, self-determination, and hawkish vigilance of JFK's New Frontier—an Army Intelligence officer (Frank Sinatra) unravels the plot, and sleeper agent Shaw redeems his unconsciously committed crimes by assassinating his mother and Iselin and killing himself—*Rosemary's Baby* ends in capitulation and fatal defeat, "the death of whole worlds... whole systems of human values."[14] By late 1968, there were no heroes left. Even the sacred myth of JFK's Camelot was breaking apart, exposing what J. Hoberman called "a shadowland of the vampire industrialists, Hollywood hustlers, militarist maniacs, and CIA-FBI-Mafia scuzzball hit men."[15] America, like the Bramford, had its own growing "high incidence of unpleasant happenings." And the list was becoming harder to ignore.

"Gas and Clubs Used to Halt Rights 'Walk'," read the front page of Rosemary's hometown newspaper, the *Omaha World-*

Herald, on March 8, 1965, the morning after Alabama state troopers and mounted deputies attacked over five hundred peaceful Black civil rights demonstrators with nightclubs and tear gas and, in the article's words, "drove them bleeding and screaming through the streets."[16] (A slightly smaller headline announced the arrival, for the first time, of US combat troops in Vietnam.) The Selma to Montgomery marchers encountered no resistance until they crossed the Edmund Pettus Bridge into Dallas County, where they met a wall of state troopers and a newly deputized white "posse" under orders from Alabama Governor George Wallace to stand firm and "enforce state laws." Newspaper and television coverage brought home the terror of "Bloody Sunday"—the victims included children and the elderly, and the marchers were "attacked... as they knelt to pray"[17]—and President Johnson sent the Voting Rights bill to Congress eight days later, signing it into law on August 6, 1965, three days after *Rosemary's Baby* begins.

To return to Rosemary's drugged dream (the sequence is a remarkable and masterful distillation of the entire film in symbolic terms): the President's yacht is hit by a typhoon. Naked again, consummately vulnerable, Rosemary approaches a lone sailor, an enlisted man, at the wheel of the yacht—we see them both from behind, heavy seas in the background. Rosemary taps the sailor's shoulder and he turns around: it's Diego (D'Urville Martin), the Bramford's elevator operator and the only recurring Black character in the film. "You better go down below, Miss," Diego says in close-up, "courteous but hating her," as Levin described it.[18] (Another reference in the book about Rosemary feeling "self-conscious, clumsy, and Negro-oppressing" around "a bevy of Negro laundresses" in the basement does not appear in the film.[19]) Rosemary walks past Diego and down the forward hatch. She is clearly in a residence now, and there is a stripped and frameless bed in the middle of an otherwise empty room ahead. As she walks down the passageway, a large structure to her right is visually and audibly engulfed in flames. It is actually a painting of a burning church or cathedral in the Castevets' hallway, the final act reveals—clearly an anti-Christian symbol, but the image also recalls the frequent burning and bombing of Black churches by white supremacists in the South during the civil rights era. As the "epicenter of the social and political struggles for African-American equality," targeting these churches "translated into an attack upon the core of civil rights activism, as well as upon the larger Black community."[20] That there are no Black members in the coven can be interpreted a few different ways: either the Satanists don't want them, or the Satanists understand that they could never turn them. Or both.

Of Selma, Martin Luther King Jr. had said that "again the brutality of a dying order shrieks across the land."[21] The sense of apocalypse is potent, but so is the hope of rebirth, the imminent "glory of the coming of the Lord." In a series of speeches, the last one a Sunday sermon delivered days before he was assassinated, he explained why the Lord was so late:

And I am sorry to say this morning that I am absolutely convinced that the forces of ill will in our nation, the extreme rightists of our nation—the people on the wrong side—have used time much more effectively than the forces of goodwill. And it may well be that we will have to repent in this generation. Not merely for the vitriolic words and the violent actions of the bad people, but for the appalling silence and indifference of the good people who sit around and say, 'Wait on time.' Somewhere we must come to see that human progress never rolls in on the wheels of inevitability. It comes through the tireless efforts and the persistent work of dedicated individuals.[22]

King is criticizing white liberals who peddle "the myth of time"—the idea that racial justice can be achieved, or *should* be achieved, only through "patience and prayer." (Even though Black votes were pivotal in the 1960 presidential campaign, JFK balked on civil rights legislation due to his narrow Southern support in Congress.) The juxtaposition of "the violent actions of the bad people" and "the appalling silence... of the good people" is probably an allusion to Irish poet William Butler Yeats' "The Second Coming," a 1920 poem—much-quoted during the late 1960s, including by Robert Kennedy in a February 1968 *New York Times* op-ed about the Vietnam War[23]—describing the deadly chaos of post-World War I Europe in apocalyptic Christian and esoteric language. "The blood-dimmed tide is loosed," Yeats wrote, "and everywhere / The ceremony of innocence is drowned; The best lack all conviction, while the worst / Are full of passionate intensity."

This grim verdict certainly holds true for the characters in *Rosemary's Baby*. When Terry Gionoffrio tells Rosemary how the Castevets' took her in, "starving and on dope," and treated her like "the daughter they never had," Rosemary says that "It's nice to know there are people like that, when you hear so much about apathy and people who are afraid of getting involved." The remark is telling, because, like so many "good" liberals, she is exactly one of those people afraid of getting involved. Terry's death obviously upsets her, but she is not bothered enough about it to heed Hutch's earlier warning about the laundry list of nasty happenings at the Bramford—child cannibals and newspaper-wrapped dead babies in the basement among them. And she does not mention Terry again. Seemingly indifferent to the struggles of her times and the emerging cultural revolution, cocooned in the bright suburban womb she has carved into the "black Bramford," Rosemary is committed only to the husband she admits is "vain and self-centered," keeping up with her upwardly mobile existence (she chides the Castevets for having "only three sets of dinner plates that matched" and a low-class joke book in the bathroom), and most of all having a baby. Compared to her sisters, she is already well behind, and the emptiness, in every sense, eats at her. Becoming a mother is her soul's desire, and ultimately the only conviction she carries that matches the unwavering resolve of the witches.

Rosemary is raped by a monster, but it isn't clear to her until the end who that monster is. She thinks it's Guy, who tells her the morning after that he "didn't want to miss baby night," and so went ahead and had his way with her after she passed out. Once again, Rosemary is naked (deep scratches from the Devil's talons cross her side and back), violated, mortified. She turns her back on Guy and tells him that "last night wasn't the only split second," but what can she do? (The "male sex right" exempted husbands from rape laws until the 1970s at the earliest; marital rape was not a crime in all fifty states until 1993.[24]) When Dr. Hill calls to tell her she's pregnant, all is forgotten: she cradles and rocks the phone as if it's her baby come to life. But pregnancy is not the bliss she expected: the pain is constant and excruciating, and it makes *her* a monster too, for a while. She develops a craving for raw meat, and once catches a reflection of herself in the toaster eating it—a cannibalistic ghoul like infamous former Bramford residents the Trench sisters, or a flesh-eating zombie from *Night of the Living Dead*, released a few months after *Rosemary's Baby*. She loses weight. She becomes deathly pale: "You look like a piece of chalk," a friend tells her.

After a housewarming party where she breaks down among her girlfriends, she confronts Guy about seeing Dr. Hill (who pretends to believe her witch story so that he can deliver her to the more prestigious Dr. Sapirstein) for a second opinion, because "pain like this is a warning something is wrong." It's the only time in the film when she speaks up for herself. Guy, his deal with the Devil on the line, is furious, and calls her friends "not-very-bright bitches" for putting the idea in her head. But suddenly, instantly, the pain stops. Guy is afraid the baby is dead, but Rosemary feels it kicking. And just like that, all is forgiven. Even though Rosemary is a reader and apartment 7E is full of books, Betty Friedan's 1963 *The Feminine Mystique* is probably not among them. (The only book she's seen reading in the film is Sammy Davis Jr.'s 1965 autobiography *Yes I Can*. Farrow was married to Davis's friend and fellow Rat Packer Frank Sinatra at the time, and when Sinatra demanded that she give up the role of Rosemary and her career to devote herself to him—to be more like Rosemary, in other words— she refused. Soon after, Sinatra's lawyer walked onto the set and served Farrow divorce papers.[25])

It's at the conclusion of the film's second and last happy montage—workmen wallpaper the nursery, carry in the bassinet—that Rosemary finds out Hutch, her confidant and only true ally since her arrival in New York, has died. She feels "awful" that she "didn't even think of him" since he had slipped mysteriously into a coma (a result, yet again, of the coven's black magic). Hutch is, in fact, the film's quintessential underachiever. An aging Englishman pegged right away by

Roman as a threat, it's Hutch who figures out the Castevets are witches. And though he is obviously learned and formerly distinguished—an inscribed photo of Winston Churchill sits on his desk—he makes his living churning out American boys' adventure books. All of which belies the coven's unrelenting and murderous devotion to Satan, the rebel angel who "came up from Hell" to "overthrow the mighty and lay waste their temples," to "redeem the despised and wreak vengeance in the name of the burned and the tortured." Those are Roman's words, and he is no less menacing because we have seen him as a doddering old man—spilling "vodka blush" on the carpet, absently dropping and smearing cigarette ash on his sweater. The danger is *magnified* because of his ordinary qualities, his human eccentricities. The same goes for Minnie's busy-body gossiping and her constant henpecking of Roman. The unmatched dishes, the joke book, the terrible meals, the eyeglasses on a chain, the caked-on make-up, the outlandish wardrobes—*those* things are not decoys. It's who the Castevets are: they just happen to also worship the Devil, even as Rosemary clings to the authority of her religion but not its spiritual core. "Well, he *is* the pope," she tells Roman at that first dinner, after he has accused all religions of being "showbiz," a sentiment shared by pre-Faustian Guy. "I was brought up a Catholic, now I don't know."

"It's the Pope at Yankee Stadium," Guy shouts at the TV as Rosemary scrapes the remainder of Minnie's mousse into the kitchen trash. "Christ, what a mob!" The footage he's watching is real. Pope Paul VI arrived in New York City, the first ever papal visit to the United States, on Monday morning, October 4, 1965. He would spend the next fourteen hours advertising the modernized and liberalized Catholicism of Vatican II—announced in 1962 exactly because so many people were brought up Catholic but now didn't know. He met with President Lyndon Johnson (they discussed poverty, civil rights, and the Vietnam War), addressed the United Nations ("Listen to the words of the great departed John Kennedy: 'Mankind must put an end to war, or war will put an end to mankind'"), and, a few minutes after Guy tunes in, delivered a "Mass of Peace" to 100,000 people in Yankee Stadium:

> We feel, too, that the entire American people is here present, with its noblest and most characteristic traits: a people basing its conception of life on spiritual values, on a religious sense, on the rule of law, on freedom, on loyalty, on work, on the respect of duty, on family affection, on generosity and courage...[26]

The Antichrist is conceived on that very night, the night that Guy chose, surely with a little help from his friends in the apartment next door. The last image Rosemary dreams before she finally blacks out is the pope (Michael Shillo), in full regalia, carrying an ordinary red suitcase. "Am I forgiven, Father?" she asks, as she is being raped. "Oh, absolutely," he says, thrusting his ring slowly, sexually into Rosemary's face until we see it is the Satanic charm first worn by Terry but bequeathed by the Castevets to her successor. Nearly nine months later, as Rosemary sits nervously in Dr. Sapirstein's (Ralph Bellamy) waiting room, she absently picks up a magazine on the table at her elbow. "Is God Dead?," the cover of *Time* asks, in red block letters against a black cover. The April 8, 1966 article, "Toward a Hidden God," discusses the apparent secularization of society at the hands of science and modernity and consumerism, and the proposals of some "radical" ministers "to carry on and write a theology... without

God."[27] There were hipper, cheekier idols to venerate, after all. Anton LaVey founded the Church of Satan, an all-too-secular consecration of the self-serving "carnal beast living in a cosmos that is indifferent to our existence,"[28] on April 30, 1966 (Sammy Davis Jr. was one of several Hollywood icons to become a card-carrying "Citizen of the Infernal Empire"). And John Lennon, in an interview with the *Evening Standard* a month before the *Time* issue hit the stands, declared that "Christianity will go," and that the Beatles were "more popular than Jesus now." In *Rosemary's Baby*, God isn't late, because God isn't coming. Only Yeats' "rough beast, its hour come round at last"—the "Year One," according to Roman's thundering pronouncement, of a vengeful new age. The end of the film is as the beginning: the camera pans up and away from the Bramford, backing into the empty sky.

Famously, we never see Rosemary's baby, the puritanical "punishment for […] some tragic moral flaw in American life." We see only her reaction to seeing the baby. She has a chance to kill it with the carving knife (the camera has caught the knife set hanging on the kitchen wall several times) she brought through the secret passage (the blocked closet from the first scene) leading to the Castevets' apartment, but the witches don't move. They know who she is by now; they know what she wants more than anything else. She backs away in horror, dropping the knife (Minnie, a fussy homemaker not unlike Rosemary, immediately plucks it out of the hardwood and tries to smooth the gash with her finger). The baby boy fusses as Laura Louise (Patsy Kelly) rocks him too hard, and for the second time Rosemary approaches the black bassinet, an inverted silver crucifix dangling from its hood. Arch-patriarch Roman, in the soothing tones of a proud grandfather, invites her to rock him, to join the family. "You're trying to get me to be his mother," she demurs. "*Aren't* you his mother?" Roman responds. And with that, he knows he's won.

"Gonna have me some boys," a teenaged Kate Clark (Lisa Linsky) says after her brothers hold her down and her father rapes her at the beginning of Roger Corman's *Bloody Mama* (1970). "And there wasn't any one of 'em who wouldn't kill for me, and didn't kill for me, or me for them. That's what you call family." Skipping forward thirty-something years later, we find out that Kate "Ma" Barker (Shelley Winters) has made good on her promise, as she bathes her four grown "boys"—much too grown to be bathed, and obviously arrested to the point of derangement—in a backwoods barn at the edge of the Ozarks. When the sheriff (Steve Mitchell) shows up accusing two of the boys of raping young Susie Turner, Ma calls it a lie and kicks him out, but she knows it's true and castigates the boys for raping the wrong kind of woman: "She's white trash and probably filthy with disease like all the other gals in this town." And then she leaves her husband (Alex Nicol), a "born loser" who "never did mount me proper," and gets the boys out of town in a stolen car before the sheriff comes back. Bigger trouble follows, as the Barker Gang heads southeast on a degeneracy spree that includes murder, robbery, drugs, prostitution, kidnapping, rape, and possibly incest.

Bloody Mama is partly a *Bonnie and Clyde* knock-off, for sure, but Corman's outlaws are deliberately uglier and unsympathetic, almost comically depraved: the film spontaneously captures how much worse things had become in the two years since *Rosemary's Baby* prophesied the end of the world. The Barkers' sadistic misdeeds during the "Public Enemy" era refract and distill the contemporary horrors of Mỹ Lai and Huế, the murderous insanity of Nixon decimating Cambodia so the North Vietnamese would think he was a "madman" and surrender. Meanwhile, monsters had multiplied on the home front as well: headlines across America on August 10, 1969 announced the "ritualistic slayings" of pregnant actress Sharon Tate (then wife of Roman Polanski) and four others at 10050 Cielo Drive on the Beverly Hills border. (Tate's friend Mia Farrow, who stayed with Tate and Polanski after Sinatra divorced her, was too terrified to attend the funeral: she believed she was "next."[29]) *Bloody Mama*'s tagline, brilliantly tasteless, left no doubt what the film was after: "The family that slays together stays together."

A moral panicky October 1969 issue of *Los Angeles* magazine called the Tate murders, and the following day's Leno and Rosemary LaBianca murders, assumed to be "copycat" killings, "a symptom of the sickness of our time": "somehow people identified with [the murders], in the way people seem to identify these days with strange movies like *Rosemary's Baby*." The "New Violence," said the piece, was fueled by "a half-million young Americans spontaneously creating a society based on drugs." [30] But the truth was much worse. What came out during the Manson "family" trial in the summer of 1970, shortly after *Bloody Mama* was released, was the apparent ease with which patriarch Charles was able to manipulate his many "girls"—most of them born and raised in all-American middle-class homes—into sexual servitude, abject fanaticism, and, for some, murder. Unlike Rosemary, Susan Atkins did not drop the knife: she plunged it into Sharon Tate over and over again, with passionate intensity, because she was "sick of listening to her… begging and pleading and pleading and begging."[31] Patricia Krenwinkel did not drop the knife: she stabbed Abigail Folger until Folger stopped screaming, because "I wanted to feel like someone was going to care for me, because I hadn't felt that from anywhere else in my life."[32] Shades of Rosemary, for sure, who gave her soul to an Establishment artist, cleaner and prettier on the outside, but equally small and vain and malignant on the inside (Guy is a struggling actor; Manson was a frustrated musician).

In *Bloody Mama*, the gender roles get reversed: for most of the story, it's matriarch Ma who calls the shots; her boys flop around their various safehouses like debauched sloths, until she commands them to become mad dogs. But Ma is no feminist. She's a misogynist, like Manson ("I can get along with girls," he told *Rolling Stone* in 1970, "they give up easier"[33]). Over 1920s newsreel footage of women in bathing suits, Ma laments how much the world has changed since she was a "little gal": "Women was showin' their bodies in public, smokin', doin' God knows what else. I'm sure glad I didn't raise me any *girls*." When a young woman, Rembrandt (Pamela Dunlap), refuses to let drug-addled Lloyd (Robert De Niro) "make it" with her, Lloyd rapes her and drags her back to Ma, who ties her to the bed and later drowns the "whore" in the bathtub. "We had to do it," she tells a dejected Lloyd the next day. "We weren't botherin' her none. She swam clear across that lake to come over here and mess us up…" The only other woman in the gang, Mona (Diane Varsi), is a world-weary prostitute pimped out and abused by oldest boy Herman (Don Stroud), who intends to marry her and make his conquest, his male sex right, exclusive—and so she is loathed and abused and alienated ("She ain't country folk") by Ma, who intends to keep Herman all to herself.

The posthumous historical portrait of Kate Barker as "the most vicious, dangerous and resourceful criminal brain of the last decade" is itself a misogynist myth, rooted in FBI director J. Edgar Hoover's febrile imagining of "gun molls" as "mainsprings" of American crime by virtue of their being women: "prodding" and "sneering" and "nagging" creatures addicted to sparkly jewels purchased with "blood money" and abetted by "American [male] chivalry."[34] Kate Barker had never been arrested, her fingerprints were never found at any crime scene, and those who knew her, including Barker Gang leader Alvin Karpis (who taught Charles Manson to play guitar when they were both incarcerated at McNeil Island Corrections Center in 1962), deny that she was anything but a "gullible, simple, cantankerous" old woman who gave "nearly foolproof cover" to her boys.[35]

Ma is also, like Manson, a white supremacist. "Some people even tried to put through an anti-lynchin' bill in Congress," she says, appalled, in the same newsreel sequence, "but a lot of folks went to Washington to help defeat it." The bill she's referring to is probably the Dyer Anti-Lynching Bill of 1922, killed multiple times in consecutive years by Southern Democrats in the Senate who said it would "encourage rape" of white women by Black men,[36] and the "folks" who marched on Washington, as we see on screen, were the Ku Klux Klan. For Manson, the apocalypse was not a baby with serpentine eyes in a black bassinet, but Black people rising up in ultraviolent revolution against "whitey," a "racial holocaust" that would eradicate all whites except for Manson and his disciples, the "master race" that would shelter in a "bottomless pit" in Death Valley, emerging at just the right time to wrest control from the Blacks, who "wouldn't be able to run the world without whitey showing him how."[37]

Sex, in *Bloody Mama*, is always weaponized, tainted with the "sickness of our time," a contagion made manifest in the "girls on the corner" who kept vacant vigil during the Manson trial, shaving their heads and mutilating their bodies in obeisance to "Charlie." And the sacrosanct "traditional" American family unit is mocked and perverted—just like in the Manson cult, just like in *Rosemary's Baby*. When Herman and effete Freddy (Robert Walden) get busted stealing the donations from a volunteer fire department fundraising event, Freddy ends up in a cell with sadistic Kevin (Bruce Dern), who, it is strongly implied, rapes him. Ma springs the boys—by robbing a bank and hiring "a smart, slick lawyer"—and Kevin tags along, now Freddy's "friend" and lover. Ma's own sexual appetites are aggressive and obsessive, and we are meant to identify them as deviant not because she's a criminal, but because she's a woman—an *older* woman, importantly—who takes what she wants. "We don't have to pay no mind to those respectable nice people rules," she tells the bound and blindfolded kidnap victim Sam Pendlebury (Pat Hingle) before forcing herself on him under the watchful eyes of Herman and Freddy. After Ma drowns Rembrandt, she tells Kevin, who is lounging in bed with Freddy, "I've been promising myself you for a long time, and I want you tonight." Kevin, with a lascivious smile, is happy to oblige: "Well honey, I'm ready." (In the original script for *Bonnie and Clyde*, Clyde is bisexual and has a ménage à trois with Bonnie and getaway driver C.W. Moss.[38] Director Arthur Penn and Warren Beatty thought the open depiction of homosexuality would lose the audience and kill the film. The character was changed to a heterosexual who is, for most of but not all of the film, impotent.)

Kate Barker was not only a primitive "animal mother" and a "veritable beast of prey," according to Hoover.[39] She was also "a monument to the evils of parental indulgence,"[40] a portrait on full and lurid display in Corman's satirical film, and one of several winking nods to the generation of youngsters that represented *Bloody Mama*'s target audience. In the late Sixties, the heir apparent agent of moral and social decay was "America's pediatrician" Benjamin Spock and his parenting bible, *The Common Sense Book of Baby and Child Care*, which conservative critics claimed "turned out a generation of infants," "small monsters" who "have grown up to be unkempt, irresponsible, destructive, anarchical, drug-oriented, hedonistic non-members of society."[41] A September 1968 *Newsweek* cover featured a drooling baby boy holding a yellow daisy and wearing anti-war pinbacks on his pajamas. "Is Dr. Spock to Blame?" the headline read. On the campaign trail, Spiro Agnew repeatedly blamed Spock for what President Nixon called "a fog of permissiveness" that was allegedly leading to the "erosion of respect and decency" among the nation's anti-authoritarian youth—"spoiled brats who never had a good spanking," Agnew chided.[42] Nixon's wife Pat, however, was quick to tell *McCall's* that "Dick… never said a harsh word to the girls… didn't try to dominate," and "always stressed that they should be themselves and not try to change their natural instincts in any way."[43] Ma, the "one mother only America could produce," the film's trailer boasted, would have voted for Nixon and his law-and-order ticket anyway—right after she robbed the closest bank.

After Rembrandt's body is dumped in the river, Ma tries to cheer up Lloyd and the gang by forcing them to sing "I Didn't Raise My Boy to Be a Soldier," a 1914 anti-war song and a strange choice for an uplifting ditty:

> I didn't raise my boy to be a soldier,
> I brought him up to be my pride and joy.
> Who dares to place a musket on his shoulder,
> To shoot some other mother's darling boy?

Let nations arbitrate their future troubles,
It's time to lay the sword and gun away.
There'd be no war today,
If mothers all would say,
"I didn't raise my boy to be a soldier."

It's an emotionally jarring scene that confronts and conflates both the exponential body count in Southeast Asia and the boys' terrified realization, as they reluctantly sing along, that there is no turning back now from the violence they have done; even Ma herself, as she rings the final chords on the piano, seems to feel some remorse for a moment or two—not for killing Rembrandt, obviously (some other mother's darling girl), but for raising her boys to be something worse than soldiers, and for consigning them to the same bloody fate.

This is not the only allusion to Vietnam in the film. Lloyd is a heroin addict who is "high" when he assaults Rembrandt—he shows her the tracks on his arm to prove it. By the time the gang arrives in Florida, he's "been stickin' himself with that needle," warns Arthur (Clint Kimbrough), "more and more and *more*..." Later that day, he's found dead in the reeds by the waterfront, the expended syringe resting on his corpse. By 1971, heroin addiction had become an "epidemic" among enlisted men in Vietnam[44]—"scag" was readily available on the black market, and it was harder to detect, smoked or snorted, than marijuana. Military command and the Nixon administration panicked to the point of obsession that "thousands of veterans, trained in violence and subject to the pressures of a protracted and unpopular war, may turn to crime when they return to civilian life to support the addiction they developed in Vietnam..."[45] Worst of all, those veterans and their "jungle" drugs "may soon invade towns in 'middle

America'." Nixon hardly cared that heroin had already invaded and fatally infected the inner cities that his betrayal of 1968's Fair Housing Act had rendered defenseless. The "'Nam junkie" turned out to be a bogeyman born of civilian fear and guilt, a conditioned response to what the media pathologized as "the most alienated generation of trained killers in American history."[46] Once the "ghetto conditions" of the war were removed, psychiatrists found, the vets largely kicked the heroin habit.[47] Meanwhile, Nixon's "war on drugs" further obliterated the sprawling ghettos of the home front, whose prisoners knew better than to expect an airlift evac.

So the Barker boys are stand-ins for "our boys over there," who came home not quite right; at the same time, they're a funhouse-mirror reflection of what Middle America—and a significant corps of American intellectuals—decided was the inevitable result of the counterculture's nihilistic hedonism. In the film's retroactive reality, the Barkers are outlaws driven to misbehave because the "proper" folks "always had everything, and we never had nothin'," but Ma's one-line attempts to parrot the revolutionary politics of *Bonnie and Clyde*—"You gotta fight the bastards always," "unless you're rich you ain't free"—are ultimately hollow. She and the boys are petty criminals, sociopaths, rotten to the core—and so, says *Bloody Mama*, were the celebrity-obsessed Bonnie and Clyde, who did what they did to get their pictures in the papers. The Barkers, on the other hand, prefer to lay low and keep their perversions in the family.

Even though the ransom is paid in full, Ma orders the boys to kill Pendlebury, because Herman insisted on removing his blindfold and blowing their cover. "I think I'm goin' right out of my mind," Herman says, shaken—"He's got Pa's eyes." ("What have you done to its eyes?" Rosemary screams when she sees her baby. "He has his father's eyes," Roman casually answers.) But the doting boys walk Pendlebury into a field and cut him loose, firing several shots into the ground. Herman makes his move the next day, as Ma forlornly and drunkenly sings at the piano. Defiant, arrogant, Herman tells her that Pendlebury is still alive. Ma slaps him, and Herman knocks her to the ground. "You're an old lady, mama," he seethes, "you can't just go beatin' up on four grown men like they was little babies. It just ain't ladylike." Herman takes over as gang leader, because the matriarchy is unnatural and dangerous. Because women are "prodding" and "sneering" and "nagging" creatures. If the boys had only stayed with their father, they might have grown up to be responsible members of civilized society—bankers, even. And if Rosemary had done the same, she might have had a boy without horns on his head.

In the final shootout, the boys drop one by one. Ma guns down Kevin herself as he surrenders to the Feds, telling them he "ain't a Barker." Ma agrees: "You bet your sweet ass you ain't!" At the end it is only broken, slobbering Mama moaning to Herman that she didn't think Lloyd was buried deep enough, that the animals might dig him up. Herman—Mona has left him, and he isn't going back to jail—shoots himself in the head, a negative image of Raymond Shaw's heroic suicide in *The Manchurian Candidate*. In the Frankenheimer film, the camera turns away before the shot is fired, but here, in post-*Bonnie and Clyde* Hollywood, in post-Manson America, the villain's face and head explode in red pulp—like Terry Gionoffrio, like JFK. As the battle rages, townspeople begin to pull up and watch, spreading out quilts and picnicking on the grass. It's a family affair: fathers stand sternly and mothers bounce their babies while the older kids drink Coca-Cola and eat bananas, everyone oohing and aahing as bodies fly and fall—just another day at the races. They are us, the audience; they are us, a nation strung out on and devoured by bloodshed.

Ma drags the Tommy Gun up to the attic window, where she makes her apocalyptic final stand. Rosemary drops the knife, opening hell's gate. They can't live without their boys, without being mothers. Rosemary gently rocks the bassinet, forgiving and forgetting, surrounded by her new family. Ma holds down the trigger for as long as she can, raining down fire upon the men who killed the boys she spawned to get revenge upon the middle-class fantasy that Rosemary must sell herself every day until the world ends.

2. "YOU THINK THEY DESERVE THAT FLAG?": *WILD IN THE STREETS* AND *PUNISHMENT PARK*

The movement to end the American war in Southeast Asia was at the center of the youth counterculture of the Johnson and Nixon years. The coddled children of the white middle class, all of them born into unprecedented prosperity and comfort, now faced the possibility of being sent to the front lines, just as the children of the working class and the poor had always been (and were again, overwhelmingly, in Vietnam). The war's manifest injustice and incompetent handling could be seen every day on the very same televisions these boomers had grown up in front of. This volatile combination of youth unrest, mass media, and the Vietnam War hovers over two very different satirical films bookending the most intense period of counterculture protest: Barry Shear's *Wild in the Streets* (1968) and Peter Watkins' *Punishment Park* (1971). Both the far-out teen-run dystopia of the former and the grim *vérité* desert landscape of the latter owe their visions of a radically changed near-future America to the contemporary tensions between Establishment and Youth. And in both films, the power of mass media itself proves capable of offering only the most harmless token resistance to the goliath, oppressive American military-industrial complex.

In *Wild in the Streets*, a youth revolution seems to completely transform the face of American society, and yet it becomes clear that this revolution, aided by the rebels' takeover of pop media, has only succeeded in replicating the most sinister and evil elements of the postwar American social control apparatus. Elected president and eventually proclaimed maximum leader of America's youth, pop star Max Frost imprisons his political opponents—the grown-ups—in detention camps reminiscent of America's darkest days of political and racial oppression, using hallucinogenic drugs to keep them quiescent, precisely as the CIA had been experimenting on American citizens in the postwar years. Even in Watkins' more chillingly realistic vision of a near-future where young rebels are placed in a "Punishment Park" for a four-day desert survival course—at the end of which they will be offered freedom from sentences in federal prison, only to be shot *en masse*—the fascist state cannot be dismantled (and is indeed only reinforced and recuperated) through the efforts of an American-British-West German documentary team. In the end, the oppression inherent in American society wins out: the dog-eat-dog generational warfare in *Wild in the Streets* will seemingly go on forever, generation after generation, while *Punishment Park*'s mechanized and bureaucratized slaughter simply brings the neo-colonialist forever-war home to destroy any hope of political change, whether incremental or revolutionary.

Wild in the Streets can trace its origins directly to the youth rebellion films that poured out of Hollywood in the 1950s. The schlock visionaries of American International Pictures, Samuel Z. Arkoff and James H. Nicholson, had by 1968 released dozens of teen exploitation B-movies since the company's founding in 1954. *Wild in the Streets*' screenwriter Robert Thom made his name in Hollywood with a trio of films about different kinds of Fifties rebels: the film adaptation of Broadway's *Compulsion*

(1959), inspired by the Leopold and Loeb case; Jack Kerouac adaptation *The Subterraneans* (1960); and Natalie Wood/Robert Wagner vehicle *All the Fine Young Cannibals* (also 1960). *Wild in the Streets* was adapted from Thom's own short story published in *Esquire* in December 1966, "The Day It All Happened, Baby!," and the film indeed uses the vocabulary of the older juvenile delinquent films: a gang with a charismatic leader rides into town (in this case, first Los Angeles, then Washington, DC) and wreaks havoc on the established order.

The mainstream press, when they did take notice of it, found *Wild in the Streets* a horrifying depiction of the revolution to come, despite its clear exploitation origins. *New York Times* film critic Renata Adler called it "the best American film of the year so far," taking Shear and Thom's depiction of a youth-ruled society very seriously and noting the cult of youth that had led to fascist and totalitarian movements throughout the twentieth century. Adler also makes a very canny observation that "any number of casts of mind are satirized" in the film, including "publicity as a value."[1] The underground press, however, found the film juvenile, reductive, and exploitative for the way it turned authentic youth revolution into a parodic carnival. *East Village Other*'s Lita Eliscu called it an "obscenity" and "offensive, repulsive,"[2] while the *Los Angeles Free Press*' Elliot Mintz memorably noted, "To say [*Wild in the Streets*] was one of the all-time bad movies would be too kind. To put it in the same class as [...] Ronald Reagan flicks would, at best, be an affront to our governor."[3] He goes on, presciently anticipating the New Hollywood around the corner:

Oh sure, [*Wild in the Streets*] will make bread. Certainly kids will go see it. But not after they have been offered an alternative. One day soon, some major studio will give a turned-on 21-year-old film-maker a chance behind a camera and that will change the direction of the entire industry. And they will never go back to AIP again.[4]

The opposition of the young to the postwar bounty and its attendant culture industries in mass media and advertising was a well-established fact by 1966, when Thom wrote his story for *Esquire*. Works such as Herbert Marcuse's *One-Dimensional Man* (1964) described a Western society in thrall to consumerism and increasing cybernetic management, a system that could only be defied by what Marcuse called the "Great Refusal—the protest against that which is."[5] The rhetoric of the students of the Berkeley Free Speech Movement, specifically Mario Savio, sought to resist the implacability of "the machine" of which the American university system was a crucial element.[6] Thomas Frank, in his 1997 study of how mid-century big business and advertising used youth disaffection to its economic advantage, *The Conquest of Cool: Business Culture, Counterculture, and the Rise of Hip Consumerism*, explains that without the mass media and marketing industry, there would be no counterculture, and vice versa:

It was and remains difficult to distinguish precisely between authentic counterculture and fake: by almost every account, the counterculture, as a mass movement distinct from the bohemias that preceded it, was triggered at least as much by developments in mass culture (particularly the arrival of The Beatles in 1964) as changes at the grass roots. Its heroes were rock stars and rebel celebrities, millionaire performers and employees of the culture industry; its greatest moments occurred on television, on the radio, at rock concerts, and in movies.[7]

Or, in the more succinct words of Marcuse, explaining how the technocratic society precludes his Great Refusal: "The works of alienation are themselves incorporated into this society and circulate as part and parcel of the equipment which adorns and psychoanalyzes the prevailing state of affairs. Thus, they become commercials—they sell, comfort, or excite."[8] After all, "The Day It All Happened, Baby!" appeared in the pages of *Esquire*, one of the preeminent sources of the new, hip, overwhelmingly white and male conspicuous consumption (along with *Playboy* and *Gentlemen's Quarterly/GQ*). In *Wild in the Streets*, Max Frost and his merry band of media pranksters—all of whom, in one way or another, wield impressive economic, political, and cultural power—*realize* that power and take it beyond the merely accumulative to the overtly revolutionary, subverting the subversion (all while being impotent fictional characters safely sequestered in a satirical piece of media). No wonder Renata Adler and her elite film critic colleagues found *Wild in the Streets* such a daring, provocative parable.

Why all the generational angst in the mainstream and underground press over the plot of a B-grade drive-in flick? Being released in the summer of 1968 didn't hurt. With actual young people in the streets from Paris to Prague to Chicago, *Wild in the Streets* hit screens—and deliberately so—at precisely the right time to leverage the uncertainty among both the adults in power and the youngsters looking to seize it. Over the course of the film, protagonist Max Frost (Christopher Jones) transforms from teen pop star to media provocateur to "owner of fourteen interlocking companies" to political king-maker to fascist leader of the United States. In a pair of vignettes expanded from Thom's short story, Max develops his skills in chemistry by making LSD in a home lab and blowing up the family's Fifties behemoth of a family car: two potent symbols of youth rebellion in an era where anti-Vietnam protestors were beginning to eschew dropping acid for dropping bombs (the militant Weather Underground would split off from the on-campus Students for a Democratic Society in the summer of 1969).

After the opening credits, we find that Frost (born Max Flatow; Robert Thom's birth name was Robert Flatow) has become the lead singer of a pop group, each of his band members holding not only a musical role but a strategic one as well, just like a corporate board: fey child prodigy Billy Cage (Kevin Coughlin) is Max's Yale-educated, computer-brained legal strategist; Richard Pryor's "Stanley X" is simultaneously a drummer, an anthropologist, social scientist, and a Black revolutionary; Sally LeRoy (Diane Varsi), "vegetarian, mystic [...] acid-head," is a former child actor with a heavily-implied traumatic past in Hollywood. And Shelley Winters plays Max's manipulative stage mother Daphne, who desperately craves her lost teen years in the midst of an era of youth-worship. It's in these scenes, as Max's following grows and his group plays some very suspect teen rebellion anthems like "The Shape of Things to Come" (written by Brill Building-adjacent stalwarts Barry Mann and Cynthia Weil and a real-world Top 40 hit), that *Wild in the Streets* is arguably the least fantastical and most gripping in its portrayal of the American generation gap in 1968.

Throughout *Wild in the Streets*, Max evokes mass movements of the American past, and not necessarily left-wing or youth movements either, but ones with popular patriotic appeal. He namechecks the Founding Fathers more than once, along with the suffragettes. He calls his fans "Troops." His campaign at first echoes the real-world campaign to lower the voting age in federal elections from twenty-one to eighteen, a reasonable request in an era when boys this young were being drafted to fight in Southeast Asia. This co-optation of American symbols and patriotism by the counterculture was nothing new: the American flag was freely accessorized by rebels as disparate as the Hells Angels,[9] *Easy Rider*'s Captain America (Peter Fonda), and the Merry Pranksters. And it is through this co-optation of mainstream political impulses that Max will eventually seize power. To wit, Max hitches his star to Congressman Johnny Fergus (Hal Holbrook), who seeks to advance his own career to the Senate. While Fergus represents every mainstream politician in 1968 seeking to ride a youth wave of discontent into office, he is obviously modeled on Robert Kennedy ("He's got a lot of teeth in that smile, don't he?" says Max), who would meet his own grisly end the same month as the film's release.

It's evident from the get-go that Max's rabble-rousing is tapping into forces Fergus cannot wholly control. When Max shocks Fergus by calling for mass sit-ins to secure the right of the young to vote at age fourteen (with a pop-chart ready anthem "Fourteen or Fight!," which again evokes a classic American political slogan, "Fifty-four Forty or Fight," a call for early nineteenth-century settlers to annex Britain's Pacific Northwest territories), Shear uses footage of actual protest, most notably from the November 1966 Sunset Strip riots[10] that became immortalized in Buffalo Springfield's classic youth anthem "For What It's Worth." These riots, which occurred in the epicenter of the American mass media machine only a year after the Watts Rebellion in the predominantly Black section of Los Angeles, arguably ignited mainstream America's awareness of the anger that the younger generation was feeling in the face of military escalation in Vietnam and perceived oppression culturally. (The riots were *actually* triggered by a curfew for high school-age kids in the rapidly multiplying nightclubs and after-hour gatherings happening on the Strip.[11]) In the end, the show of political force and the offer of a compromise voting age of fifteen satisfies Frost and his Troops, the politicians and industrialists backing Fergus go along, Fergus wins his Senate seat, and a new political order of youth rule takes hold.

Events turn from realistic to highly and implausibly satirical in the third act: Sally, older than the rest of the gang, wins a special Congressional election that brings to the fore a constitutional amendment lowering all *office-holding* ages to fourteen. Max deploys an LSD coup, mass-dosing Congress, and the amendment passes with Congress under the influence of youth drugs. The shady powers-that-be who negotiated with Max through Fergus now must accede to Max's run for President, which quickly leads to his being elected (as a Republican!) and implementing a final solution for the generational problem: all American adults over the age of thirty-five are relocated to "retirement" camps where they will be forced into cult-like, peace-symbol-emblazoned robes and fed a steady diet of LSD from water coolers, tripping all the livelong day.

The depiction of LSD as an instrument of social control is incredibly interesting considering the rumors and suspicions that were then flying across the counterculture's network of alternative media, and which, in the half-century since, have been proven true. The journey of LSD from Stanley Hofmann's bicycle ride in Switzerland in 1943, to a mainstream therapeutic drug in the Fifties and early Sixties, to one of the main instruments of the CIA's MK-Ultra mind control and political sabotage program would not even be partially revealed until the aftermath of Watergate and Richard Nixon's resignation.[12] The CIA had even planned to dose the Cuban leadership and media studios with acid[13] and stage the Second Coming in order to depose Fidel Castro[14], the baroqueness of which makes Max's plan to take over the government seem positively mundane. The fact is, Thom and Shear unconsciously tapped into prevalent currents in the counterculture at the time: paranoia around hallucinogen use and its uses in keeping youth sedated and inward-looking; the suspicion that the coming of a "groovy" victory in the cultural sphere would just lead to more oppression; and the realization that generational warfare is an impossible war to win, since the revolutionary young themselves will one day become the entrenched old guard. *Wild in the Streets*' pitch-perfect ending, where Max, traveling across America without any kind of secret police protection, comes across a group of little kids at an Edenic pond and stomps on their pet crawfish for kicks, puts this into sharp relief. One of the kids looks straight into the camera and says, "We're gonna put everybody over ten out of business." End credits, as we ponder the famous quote of the Berkeley Free Speech Movement's Jack Weinberg in 1965: "We have a saying in the movement that we don't trust anybody over 30."[15]

Punishment Park sprang from a very different strain of dystopian vision. Even though a mere three years had passed since *Wild in the Streets* was released, it was a radically different time: Nixon had been elected, the story of the Mỹ Lai massacre broke, the temporary elation of Woodstock and the Apollo Moon landings had faded under the assault of bad vibes from Cielo Drive and Altamont, and, most important to the mood of *Punishment Park*, the war came home to American soil at Kent State and Jackson State Universities. After armed troops opened fire on student protesters and killed six, the idea of draft boards turning into execution panels did not seem out of the question.

English-born expat Peter Watkins had been an international sensation with his 1965 release *The War Game*, another mockumentary, this one depicting the horrific aftermath of a nuclear war. His intervening features, 1967's *Privilege* (whose futuristic setting and pop star protagonist rallying the youth of Britain against the staid Establishment echoes "The Day It All Happened, Baby!") and 1969's *Gladiators* (about a futuristic televised game show that serves as a substitute for war) demonstrated Watkins' adeptness in painting nightmarish visions of times to come extrapolated from present-day trends, all presented in a nominally *vérité* fashion through the visual vocabulary of documentary film and on-the-spot news reporting, which itself had grown into its own during the Vietnam years on national network news. With *Punishment Park*, Watkins didn't even need to extrapolate all that much. The narrative action cuts back and forth between two groups of recently arrived inmates at the Park: Corrective Group 637 is preparing to take their chances in the desert survival course, while Corrective Group 638 is being processed for intake. Their crimes against the regime are read out before a tribunal of ordinary citizens, with a token defense bestowed in recognition of "constitutional" principles. As the group out in the desert quickly begins to flag and tire from the extreme heat and lack of water (the combined local sheriffs, state cops, and National Guard cruelly taunt the prisoners with a promise of water that turns out to be a lie), they also debate survival tactics: should they hide out from the cops and Guardsmen and try to escape the course later, take up arms against the cops and troops, or follow the rules and try to capture the American flag that denotes completion of the course? All of these approaches end up as metaphors for the larger internal arguments among revolutionaries and reformers in the late Sixties and early Seventies over tactics against the state. Meanwhile, in the tents that form the intake section of the camp, the new group is given the option between decades-long federal sentences as political prisoners... or three days in Punishment Park.

The prisoners, with one notable exception, aren't media sensations like Max Frost. They are ordinary young citizens of a near-future America where war has broken out on multiple fronts: radio news alerts playing over the proceedings at the Park hint at a much wider war in Southeast Asia, in addition to a hot conflict on the Korean peninsula and tensions in the Middle East and the Caribbean. They are draft-dodgers, pacifists, grad students, Black and Chicano activists, and rank-and-file youth resisters who are just another batch in a seemingly endless assembly line of political prisoners. The defense attorney (Frederick Franklyn), who must offer up a defense of the accused without benefit of being able to separate his defendants' cases from each other, or indeed without any customary constitutional protections at all, is an overworked law professor from a state university whose disheveled appearance simultaneously invokes the physical appearance of countercultural civil liberties legends such as William Kunstler and conveys the impossibility of his task. Interestingly, one of the members of the tribunal is a sociology professor from the very same fictional "University of Glendale" where the defense attorney is a faculty member. The implication is that, even though the counterculture grew out of the American university system, academia has always been part and parcel of the Establishment.

The panel of judges are made up of esteemed members of the (petite) bourgeoisie, respectable members of the community, and a single political commissar in the form of an agent of the FBI (Lee Marks), who reads out the more overtly revolutionary charges before the kangaroo court. The individual members of the tribunal are meant to evoke real-world persons and personality types that were standing in opposition to the student anti-war movement in real-life America. The Park tribunal's chairman, William C. Hoeger (Mark Keats), a "manufacturing executive and draft board chairman," was chosen because of his physical resemblance to the judge of the Chicago Seven trial, Julius Hoffman.[16] The others include a housewife-activist (Gladys Golden) for an organization called "Silent Majority for a Unified America," likely inspired by the then-new breed of anti-feminist conservative women activists such as Phyllis Schlafly, who tells the accused they make a "mockery out of everything we stand for: the home, true love..."; the aforementioned sociology professor, who describes the prisoners' complaints about American society as "self-gratification, mental masturbation"; and an industrial union leader (Paul Rosenstein), ostensibly in his twenties, like the detainees themselves, and coded through accent and mannerisms as a white ethnic, a real Hard Hat Riot type, who asks pointed questions about how these unwashed left-wing agitators would handle industrial production and economic management were they suddenly put in charge of the United States: "If it was up to you kind of people, we would just shut down these factories, we'd burn 'em down, we'd all go out and panhandle in the street, then what kind of society would we have then? How would you feed people then? So you want us to work to support you, that's what you want." The union leader echoes arguments seen in media from 1971's *Joe* to the 1971-debuting sitcom *All in the Family*: these lazy bums need to get a job, at gunpoint if necessary.

The members of the tribunal regularly offer the argument that American youth don't have it that bad in purely economic terms as compared with their counterparts in the Soviet Union, that they are ungrateful for all America has given them, and that they are basically crybabies. Any of the accused who fight back verbally or strike out physically are restrained and further hectored, and those who offer little to no defense during interrogation are called cowardly, "traitors": there is no way to win in Punishment Park, even before the prisoners hit the course. Watkins demonstrates how important the systematic humiliation and recitation of predominant Establishment values are to the tribunal. These show trials, like Red Scares throughout American history from the original 1910s-1920s wave to the Congressional hearings and blacklists of 1950s McCarthyism, aren't really designed to assess guilt or even to trigger a confession or reconciliation to America on the part of the radicals. The point is to reassure the ruling class that its ideology and actions in the face of youth rebellion are justified.

The presence of the cameras is openly acknowledged throughout the film, both in the courtroom tent and on the course: chairman Hoeger says that present are the "television-film cameras of a national network, also those of Britain and West Germany... as we know [these proceedings'] import to be of vital concern to people of the Free World everywhere. Their coverage will be impartial." Many of the accused of Corrective Group 638 look accusingly at the camera multiple times; the fugitive runners of Corrective Group 637 are captured in "talking head" interviews all throughout their three days of sunbaked torture. This performative aspect of the tribunal scenes becomes even more pointed when considering that *Punishment Park* follows Watkins' tradition of using amateur actors who belong to the groups they play-act as, in this case Los Angeles locals who include, according to Watkins, "a trade union officer, a dentist, a housewife..."[17] And his creation of a pressure cooker of generational anger, of young people pitted against the members of the bourgeoisie with mutual hate and distrust, recalls Cold War-era psychological experiments and methodologies as disparate as Yale University's Milgram Experiment and therapeutic group psychodrama. What is *Punishment Park*'s tribunal, after all, but an Esalen-style encounter group gone horribly wrong?

Probably the most memorable of all the exchanges in the tribunal tent is the one between the board and a "pop singer" named Nancy Smith (Catherine Quittner), whose "seditious" songs landed her in Punishment Park. Their lyrics, little more than revolutionary doggerel, are full-on exhortations to open rebellion in the manner of the Weather Underground (whose taped announcements and manifestos were very much in the news in 1970 and '71[18]), read by the FBI agent on the panel: "Santa Claus is coming with a bag of bombs and guns / Santa Claus is here, the revolution has come / Grab a handful, dip in quick / Grant a slug and make it stick / Right on, baby / Get yours and fight like crazy, we can win / Blow up buildings, watch 'em fall, for hours that we spent standing in the hall." The board offers their interpretation of these lyrics as evidence of a "neurotic and schizophrenic tendency," hinting at the real-world pathologization of political rebellion. The Schlafly analogue gets into a heated argument with Smith about the mere morality, not even the content, of her language; she is more concerned with what Smith is doing to "the children of this country." But Smith is no mere angry sloganeer. She and Max Frost are about as far apart as could be. Her appeal is from personal experience, and that experience crystallizes around Kent State:

> I had to quit school because I got so fucking paranoid [...] After Kent State I realized that I could put on a cheerleader sweater and an 'I Love America' pin and the people that were shooting weren't even aiming [at me] and it wouldn't do me any good. I could walk out of a classroom, be on my way to lunch, and get killed just as easily as I was in the front line of a barricade in a demonstration.

The judgments of draft boards during Vietnam were notoriously fickle and sui generis: Lawrence Baskir and William Strauss, in their 1978 study of the Vietnam draft *Chance and Circumstance: The Draft, the War and the Vietnam Generation*, write that "Consciously or not, a board's policy usually reflected its members' traditional values, treating deferments and exemptions as rewards for young men who shared these values."[19] Baskir and Strauss cite a case study published in 1969, where board members made judgments on draft fitness based on bourgeois and militaristic standards: one draft board member sees a scruffy long-haired potential inductee and says, "This is the sort of guy you would take down to the latrine and scrub down with a wire brush [...] Let's make this baby I-A ["Available for military service" draft classification]. We'll fix his trolley."[20] If anything, the language used by *Punishment Park*'s panel of upstanding citizens is muted and tame compared to the openly expressed prejudices of real draft boards.

The government act that endows the Punishment Parks with their authority cites first and foremost the need for "a necessary training for the law officers and National Guard of the country in the control of those elements who seek the violent overthrow of the United States government." Any "punitive deterrent" is seemingly an afterthought. Throughout the days Group 637 struggles to make it across the course, the police and Guardsmen spend their idle time comparing notes on weaponry and tactics against both detainees and the kids in the streets outside the walls. In another 1971 release, *THX 1138*, directed by USC wunderkind George Lucas, android cops are deployed to stop rebellion against the computerized, drug-aided system of control in the same white-helmeted Los Angeles Police Department/California Highway Patrol uniform seen in the streets of LA, Chicago, and the deserts of Punishment Park. The theatrical poster for *Punishment Park*, in fact, featuring a trooper pointing a shotgun at a kneeling park runner, echoes the scenes in *THX 1138* where the android troopers surround Robert Duvall's societal rebel and strike at him with electric cattle prods.

Running through each of these films is the specter of detainment camps. The American tradition of corralling, containing, and punishing potentially rebellious populations is as old as colonization itself. For centuries, both the chattel enslavement of Black Americans and Indian ethnic cleansing, extermination, and re-education had required the imprisonment and control of populations thought racially inferior. During World War II, this same logic was inflicted upon Japanese Americans who had been living in the United States for generations as loyal citizens. At the beginning of *Punishment Park*, the British narrator notes that the Internal Security Act of 1950 gave the President the power to create the Punishment Park system. And indeed, before the repeal of the McCarran Act's provision for detention camps in 1971[21], this Fifties Red Scare-era legislation did provide for internal forms of detention of political prisoners.

The tumult of the late Sixties led to all kinds of federal and state efforts to prepare for the control of large, politically rebellious groups. Ron Ridenhour, a GI who had served in Vietnam and was integral in exposing the Mỹ Lai massacre, contributed an article to the Winter 1976 issue of *CounterSpy* magazine that detailed US Army plans (Operation GARDEN PLOT) to handle widespread civil unrest in the aftermath of the riots/uprisings of the mid-Sixties.[22] Ridenhour's earlier 1975 article in *New Times* featured actual excerpts from GARDEN PLOT documents, including an account of a 1969 exercise (Operation CABLE SPLICER) simulating a domestic military action designed to quell civil unrest in the Western states of California, Oregon, and Washington.[23] Governor Reagan gave an opening speech to the personnel involved, which featured the ominous opening laugh lines, "You know, there are people in the state who, if they could see this gathering right now and my presence here, would decide their worst fears and convictions had been realized—I was planning a military takeover."[24] Reagan makes note of the combined forces participating, both from "the military and the national level" and "local law enforcement,"[25] again echoing the cross-service mix of authority figures gunning down the youth at Punishment Park. Future Reagan White House *éminence grise* and Attorney General Edwin Meese, then working for Governor Reagan as executive secretary, said of CABLE SPLICER: "This is an operation, this is an exercise, this is an objective which is going forward because in the long run… it is the only way that will be able to prevail."[26] The generational war is an existential war of attrition, pure Us vs. Them survival.

Punishment Park doesn't take place in the deserts of California for the scenery, or to represent the landscape of the new conservative Sun Belt pushed by Nixon, or the technocrats and scientists who, at thinktanks like the Stanford Research Institute, helped design and expand the secret defense and security regime that sought to forestall a second American revolution. It is because of that peculiarly American landscape that Jean Baudrillard called a "screen,"[27] represented by the cities and lost highways and vistas of the American desert: "Culture, politics—and sexuality too—are seen exclusively in terms of the desert, which here assumes the status of a primal scene. Everything disappears before that desert vision."[28] The primal performance of Oedipal rebellion finds purchase in Watkins' staging of the age-old generational revolt, and this blank canvas of the desert foregrounds the distance that Americans maintain from each other, socially and politically: "The inhumanity of our ulterior, asocial, superficial world immediately finds its aesthetic form here, its ecstatic form. For the desert is simply that: an ecstatic critique of culture, an ecstatic form of disappearance."[29] The young Corrective Groups of the park disappear as well, in a neo-Puritan erasure of the shining "city upon a hill." The lone American flag that is the runners' goal, simultaneously evoking the Marines at Iwo Jima in World War II, the recent Moon landings, and the patriotic symbol détourned by Abbie Hoffman and Jimi Hendrix and Max Frost, becomes the hollow symbol of the promise of America to its youth. And the media they trusted, the media they hoped would allow for revolution, is impotent to get the word out to the vast, TV-watching "silent majority" in any meaningful way. In fact, the narrator notes at the end of the film that one of the crew's American members was arrested in the aftermath of shooting the documentary. Is the next stop for such a "criminal"... Punishment Park Corrective Group 639?

At the end of *Punishment Park*, as Corrective Group 637 is murdered in the California dust, the British narrator and documentarian excoriates and threatens to expose the police and National Guardsmen, who simply smile in return and respond:

> You think we'd let them reach that flag? You think they deserve that flag? You're trying to make out like a big goddamn humanitarian, the only thing that you want is so you can sell this to your goddamn network and put money in your pocket.

The pigs know what kind of power rules America: corporations, capital, and self-interest. It's a system that eats up and transforms rebellion, makes it into a spectacle for an audience to safely consume. Any appeals on behalf of the kids' inherent patriotism, on behalf of their desire to see America become a better place, is as doomed to moral failure as Max Frost's youth-run "Shape of Things to Come".

3. "HOW DO YOU KNOW YOU'RE YOU?": *SECONDS* AND *WATERMELON MAN*

Arthur Hamilton (John Randolph) is a middle-aged white man, successful and well-respected. A Harvard graduate and former tennis champ, he lives in a palatial suburban home in New York and takes the train to the city during the week, where he works as the vice president of a bank. His homemaker wife Emily (Frances Reid) takes him to and from the station in the family wagon that is no longer necessary—their grown daughter has moved "out West" and married a doctor. They don't see her anymore, but she "writes now and then." On the car ride home, sounds of children playing in the neighborhood underscore the loneliness of the couple's empty nest. They rarely speak, they sleep in separate beds, and Arthur no longer returns his wife's affections. He doesn't realize just how bored and joyless he is—until a friend he thought was dead calls him and tells him he can be reborn into a better life.

In a separate but parallel universe, Jeff Gerber (Godfrey Cambridge) is a middle-aged white man, a successful insurance salesman who is loved (reluctantly, at times) by his homemaker wife Althea (Estelle Parsons) and their two small children and hated by everyone else. He is obnoxious, racist, and sexist, a self-centered health nut who works out in the attic ("Come on, Harvard!" he cheers while on the rowing machine) and tans himself under a sunlamp every morning. He lives in the Los Angeles suburbs and takes the bus to the city during the week—but only after racing it to a late stop, his favorite thing in the world; he wants to gloat about being "undefeated" to all the passengers who root against him, but he also wants to avoid paying the full fare. Althea, a good liberal who wants him to "show greater interest" in "the civil rights issue," complains that they lead a "boring life." There's "no passion," and Jeff no longer returns her affections. But Jeff is perfectly happy and content—until he wakes up one morning as a Black man.

Arthur reluctantly goes to the scribbled address that had been surreptitiously slipped into his coat at the train station. It's a laundry, and the old presser (Edgar Stehli) sends him to a new address—a meat-packing plant—where he's driven, in the back of a meat truck, to a nondescript office building. Here he meets Mr. Ruby (Jeff Corey), who describes in detail the "circumstances" of his prospective new client's "death": the high cost of "extensive cosmetic renovation" and the identification (by CPS, Cadaver Procurement Section) of a "fresh corpse" that exactly meets Arthur's build and "medical specifications," as well as "the question of death selection" (a hotel fire, Mr. Ruby suggests), which "may be the most important decision in your life." A revised will is trotted out that provides for his family and assigns all remaining sums to the "Company," but Arthur is having second thoughts about his second chance. When he doesn't sign, Mr. Ruby gestures to his associate, who pulls down a projection screen from the ceiling. Lights off, camera rolling, we watch Arthur, drugged when he first arrived, apparently "ravage" a young woman (Françoise Ruggieri) in her bedroom. An old Southern gentleman (Will Geer) wearing a bowtie and pushed back Panama hat—the "head of it all"—appears over Arthur's shoulder. He doesn't like to think of it as blackmail, "just kind of insurance": "Isn't it easier to go forward when you know you can't go back?"

Jeff can't go back either, despite hysterically trying to scrub, scald, and pray the Blackness off his body in the shower. Althea screams when she sees him, slams the bathroom door behind her, and screams again: *"Jeff, Jeff, Jeff, there's a Negro in your shower... Call the police, he'll kill us!"* His kids, though, recognize him immediately, even though he's got a "heck of a tan." Jeff, attempting to remain "logical and rational," blames the sun lamp. He races off to "one of *their* drug stores" and rakes all the hair straightening products, Afro Sheen, "Beautiful Bleach," and "Miracle Wash" into a box. He tries everything—no luck. "These creams don't work," he says, "no wonder Negroes riot!" He puts a mold on his face and bathes in milk to "cleanse" himself. He tries voodoo. But there's no putting it off; he has to go back to work, and the next morning, cheering up a little, he takes off after the bus. The journey is not quite the same this time around. The white woman watering her yard screams bloody murder, loses control of the hose, and calls for the police. Jeff is chased and corralled by a white mob who call him a thief. The cops nab him and make him open his briefcase. Onlookers press in, complaining that "the neighborhood isn't safe anymore."

Arthur goes under the knife and wakes up with a new face and a new name: Antiochus "Tony" Wilson (Rock Hudson). His "guidance advisor" (Khigh Dhiegh) informs him that he is to be a painter, based on his preferences given while under the influence of Sodium Pentathol (his first choice was tennis pro). He's supplied with "certificates of study" and "diplomas from reputable universities," ready-made canvases that show off his distinct style, and a "luxurious" studio in Malibu, California, where he can, at his leisure, develop his own style. "You see," says the advisor, "you don't have to *prove* anything anymore… You've got what almost every middle-aged man in America would like to have: freedom. *Real freedom.*"

Jeff, his sales dwindling, arranges to meet a client at the local yacht club, but the white glove of the doorman (Erik L. Nelson) turns him away—"This club has got rules." A Black man sweeps the sidewalk behind them, and a statue of a Black minstrel stands on the column at the foot of the stairs. A crowd gathers when Jeff refuses to leave. "Is this America?" he cries out, trying to force his way inside. A police officer hauls him back to his office, disheveled and humiliated, and asks his boss (Howard Caine) if he really works there. "He stole something," says the cop. "We don't know what it is yet." His boss doesn't care. He wants Jeff to exploit the "virtually untapped… Negro insurance market." Jeff sneaks off to the doctor (Kay E. Kuter) instead, who tells him that there must be a "Negro strain" in his family history. After three hours of tests, he goes home, where Althea is waiting up, clearly anxious. The phone rings. Althea tells him not to answer; it's the wrong number. He picks it up: "Jeff Gerber?" the voice says. "Yes." "Move out, nigger." Jeff hangs up, but the phone keeps ringing.

Tony's butler John (Wesley Addy) wants him to throw a party and meet new people, but Tony is just as unhappy and pent-up as he ever was—and now he's out of his depth, out of his skin, a ghost out of time. He meets free spirit Nora (Salome Jens) while wandering on the beach, and she tries to draw him out: "Somewhere in the man there is still a key unturned." She takes him to a bohemian grape-stomping festival in Santa

Barbara, where revelers guzzle wine from chalices, play flutes and tambourines, strip, and climb naked into the giant vat. Tony is mortified when Nora, who "came here to feel, to *be*," follows. Tony talks to her sternly, like a father—Arthur was old enough to be just that—and tries to extract her from her joy. Instead, the crowd rips Tony's shirt off and throws him into the teeming vat. He's terrified, choking on grape juice, lost in bodies and sensations and freedoms that repel him. Nora finds him and they embrace, kiss. He lets go. The key has finally turned.

Coming home after work, Jeff is confronted by several of his white neighbors. They're "concerned" that his "presence in the neighborhood can undermine the value of our homes." With some generous help from the local banks, they want to buy him out and sell the house to a "good family"—it's "nothing personal." They make him an offer and he prods them until they double it. Althea is upset that he's "taken advantage" of them. "Why do you insist on being Negro?" she yells. "What happened to the flaming liberal I married?" Jeff wants to know. "I'm still liberal," she assures him—"but to a point." Althea casually mentions that she's sent the kids to live with her sister in Indianapolis to protect them "when the newspapers find out." Later that night, Althea moves out too.

Tony finally throws a party for the neighbors, but he's confronted by several of them, menacing middle-aged men, when he gets drunk and starts telling the crowd he went to Harvard. They carry him to the bedroom and pin him down on the bed. He asks them who they are. "They're like you," John tells him—"reborns." Weeping, he calls for Nora, but Nora, a Company employee like John, tells him to "shut up." It's the last time he sees her. Charlie Evans (Murray Hamilton), the "dead" friend who convinced Arthur to visit the Company, calls Tony the next morning. The two of them are "tied together," he explains; he should wait right there until someone arrives to help him through his "adjustment period." Tony bolts, catching a plane to New York. He goes to his (Arthur's) old house to see his (Arthur's) wife, who thinks he (Arthur) died in a hotel fire. Tony tells Emily that he was a friend of Arthur's. He's come to pay his respects, perhaps take back a memento (he asks for one of Arthur's watercolors, but she has "cleaned out the garage"), and presses her to tell him more about Arthur. He was a "good man" full of "silences," she says. "The truth is, Arthur had been dead a long, long time before they found him in that hotel room." John is waiting with a car and driver outside. Tony gets in quietly; he wants another chance. "Begin again," he mutters, as the sounds of children playing echo through the neighborhood.

The first film is John Frankenheimer's *Seconds* (1966), and the second is Melvin Van Peebles' *Watermelon Man* (1970). Frankenheimer, one of live television's premiere innovators in the 1950s, was by this time one of the most sought-out directors in Hollywood, and his two previous films, conspiracy thrillers *The Manchurian Candidate* and 1964's *Seven Days in May*, had been greenlit only through the personal intervention of President John F. Kennedy—the studio feared the former would be "highly embarrassing" to JFK (it was horribly prophetic instead), and the Pentagon wanted nothing to do with the latter, which portrays an attempt by the Joint Chiefs of Staff to overthrow a liberal president and his cabinet.[1] In 1968, when Robert F. Kennedy announced his bid for president, Frankenheimer volunteered as his media advisor and filmed him on the campaign trail. The two became fast friends. RFK was staying at the director's Malibu house—used as Tony's home and studio in *Seconds*—the night he was assassinated. Frankenheimer drove him to the Ambassador Hotel in Downtown Los Angeles and waited outside to drive him back to the beach. Devastated, he and his wife Evans moved to Paris, where he took cooking classes and tried to forget that Richard Nixon was president.[2]

Van Peebles had been in Paris since the early 1960s, writing novels and plays and columns. Before that, he studied astronomy at the University of Amsterdam on the GI Bill (like Frankenheimer, he served in the Air Force). He was in San Francisco before that, where he made some short films and brought them to Hollywood. But Hollywood wasn't hiring Black filmmakers. Hollywood was only hiring Black elevator operators and parking attendants. Hence Paris, where Van Peebles had been invited by the founders of the prestigious Cinémathèque Française, and where he got a director's card and a government grant to make his first feature, *La Permission* (*The Story of a Three-Day Pass*).[3] A New Wave-styled love story between a Black American soldier and a white French woman that slashes at racism, the film won the Critics' Choice Award at the San Francisco International Film Festival in 1967 and premiered in the US just as Frankenheimer was en route to France.

Seconds is the third entry in what has been called Frankenheimer's "paranoia trilogy," although the paranoia in each case is justified, not just in the cautionary fictions but in the villainous political realities they anticipate and condemn. In *Seconds*, adapted from the novel of the same name by David Ely, the personal is the political: it's an existential parable about conformity and identity and vanity, about the limits and follies of American idealism, the insidious violence of the emotional detachment enshrined in the American man. The nameless Company is a satire of technocratic corporate capitalism, but the Company is also Hollywood sacrificing its own to appease the infernal tribunal of the House Un-American Activities Committee: Frankenheimer made it a point to hire blacklisted actors John Randolph, Jeff Corey, and Will Geer. Shot in phantasmagoric black and white by celebrated cinematographer James Wong Howe (a Chinese American who added "Howe" to his name because of persistent racism), the vertiginous close-ups and oblique and distorted angles capture the inhuman machinations of the smiling suits who claim to be "waging a battle against human misery." Because rebirth, although couched in liberatory religious language, is nothing but a pyramid scheme. Arthur is a mark and, as he finds out too late, he has sold his soul to a boss devil in a Panama hat.

The Story of a Three-Day Pass landed Van Peebles a three-picture deal with Columbia. He only made one of them. *Watermelon Man*, changed from waffling original title *The Night the Sun Came Out on Happy Hollow Lane*, was supposed to be a "feel good" comedy marketed to white audiences. "It won't happen to you," the poster remarks above Jeff Gerber's half-white, half-Black face, "so you can laugh." Columbia touted the "authentically black viewpoint" of their director, but reinforced that "Any message and/or social commentary" would be made "by indirection."[4] And no one had even considered hiring a Black actor for the lead, despite the protagonist being Black for all but the first twenty minutes of the movie. So, instead of Alan Arkin or Jack Lemmon, the studio's first choices[5], Van Peebles hired comedian Godfrey Cambridge, who plays the beginning in deliberately garish whiteface.[6]

Rock Hudson was not Frankenheimer's first choice. He wanted Laurence Olivier to play both Arthur and Tony, but Paramount wanted a "movie star" and pushed Hudson. Frankenheimer tried to talk him out of it, told him it would be too hard, but Hudson, himself leading a double life that did not become public until he died of AIDS-related complications in 1985, persisted.[7] In retrospect, Frankenheimer praised his "very gutsy, honest, marvellous performance,"[8] but still believed that casting him was a terrible mistake that destroyed *Seconds* commercially. He vowed not to repeat that mistake. "If I want to stay as a viable, mainline movie director," he recollected in 1989, "I've gotta do something that's not a collector's item."[9] His next film was the ensemble blockbuster *Grand Prix* (1966), a technical marvel and by-the-numbers drama about the "glamour and greatness" of Formula One racing.

Van Peebles had set out to violate mainline Hollywood from the beginning. His revised title itself refers to Black self-sufficiency: post-emancipation, many Blacks made a living by growing and selling watermelon (the "watermelon man" made his rounds through the neighborhood in a horse-drawn cart), and whites resented them for "flaunting their newfound freedom," subsequently stigmatizing the fruit and those who enjoyed it, depicting them as juvenile and lazy and messy and animalistic.[10] Jeff refuses to fleece his Black clients to fill the coffers of his white boss's company, just as Van Pccblcs refused to make a movie that made white people feel good. The original ending by screenwriter Herman Raucher had Jeff waking up white again, no doubt learning an important lesson about how to be a better liberal who shows "greater interest" in "the civil rights issue."[11] In Van Peebles' rewrite, Jeff wakes up on a different level, ditching incurable white

America and accepting his Blackness and everything that comes with it. He doesn't chase the bus anymore. He's "working out in the evenings now"—Black Power style. Van Peebles himself would follow Jeff's example, ditching Columbia and Hollywood to make 1971's incendiary *Sweet Sweetback's Baadasssss Song*, "Starring the Black Community" and "dedicated to all the Brothers and Sisters who had enough of the Man." At the time, it was the most successful independent film ever made.

Seconds is about being born again but never waking up. It's a condemnation of the privilege and quiet desperation of the white middle class, the plastic gestures of trimmed hedges and summer boats, and yet who else but the white middle class would find Arthur or Tony the least bit sympathetic? Who else would believe they're "owed" a second chance? Who else would demand a third? "There's nothing anymore, is there? Anything at all?" the old man asks Arthur in the Company office. The question is rhetorical. He knows Arthur's ego will expand until he feels sorry for himself, until he resents others for not making him happy, until he believes he deserves a resurrection without a crucifixion. But of course, Arthur already has everything. All he has to do is pick up the phone and call his daughter, tell her he loves her, get on a plane and go visit her; all he has to do is talk to his wife, touch her hand—she loves him dearly and wants only to please him; all he has to do is quit his job at the bank and paint watercolors on the beach. But plastic surgery is easier: he doesn't have to apologize or admit that he's not perfect; he gets to keep (he thinks) his pride. Arthur is fleeced by the Company, and he's not the only one. Reborns are everywhere. Because the men (and they are all men) who come to the Company are incurable when they arrive.

Jeff quits his job and moves to a Black neighborhood, where he starts his own insurance company. His walk changes. His style changes. He's part of the community. He's happy in a way that white Jeff could never have been happy. He has suffered for his new skin, and he's not going to give it up.

Back at the Company, Tony is "not the least bit sorry, because there were certain mistakes made in my case." Mr. Ruby will consider that, but first he wants to know if Tony can "recommend and sponsor a new client"—"a business associate, perhaps? Someone down the street?" Tony himself has been sponsored, Mr. Ruby explains. Tony wants to think about it, and in the meantime he's photographed from every possible angle, measured from top to bottom, and sent to an aseptic white room full of other middle-aged white men, all of them sitting silently at desks trying to pass the time: reading, doing crossword puzzles, playing solitaire and chess. (He's been here before, during his first visit to the Company, when Arthur got lost looking for an exit.) An orderly hands out pills in white cups and nods to a man sitting in front of Tony. It's Charlie Evans, but Tony doesn't recognize him—he's got a new face—until he talks. He's been waiting in that room a long time. He was there when he called Tony the first time, pitching rebirth as "something tremendous." He's Tony's sponsor, and thought Tony would have a "better chance." A man in a black suit enters, a buzzer goes off, and he calls for a Mr. Carlson. Charlie/Mr. Carlson stands up, a tear running down his cheek. His third life is about to begin.

Althea calls Jeff at his new apartment—it's poky, the miniature fridge is in the living room, the windows are barred. They exchange pleasantries and she says, laughingly, that it's almost like "it never happened." Jeff is curt: "Not on this end, baby." Althea wishes him well and wants to know if he's still getting his exercise. Yes, Jeff assures her, he is still getting his exercise. He hangs up.

Tony can't think of any names to give to Mr. Ruby, and Mr. Ruby accuses Tony of "not cooperating." Tony believes he deserves another "opportunity" at a "meaningful existence." Mr. Ruby wants a name. Tony can't, or won't, "think of a single soul." Mr. Ruby dismisses him to the "day room" and picks up the phone on his desk. He tells "processing" that it's time for Mr. Wilson to be moved to the "next stage." He hangs up.

Jeff, shirtless, is doing jumping jacks. He drops to the ground and disappears for a few heartbeats. The scene shifts: now he's in a dingy basement full of other shirtless Black men of all ages. They're pushing mops and brooms over their heads, shouting kiais as the makeshift weapons reach the high point. The men turn the mops and brooms around and jab them forward like spears—more kiais, louder. They're exercising. They're training for the revolution.

The old man wakes Tony up in the middle of the night, tells him he really hoped he'd make it, that he'd find his "dream come true." Tony admits that he "never had a dream," but this time around, he says, it'll be different. The old man explains, almost apologetically, that when he started the Company as a "young man with an idea," he only wanted to help others "find a little happiness," but the business grew and became a "financial responsibility"—profit-sharing, a board of directors—and there were a "high percentage of failures." Still, "We can't let the mistakes jeopardize the dream." Orderlies arrive with a stretcher to take Tony to surgery. "You're lucky we got a match so quick," the old man says, touting the Company's "efficiency." Tony is wheeled down a series of elongated hallways, where a priest explains that during the "next stage" he will in fact "face the creator." Tony screams and struggles to break free. The orderlies brutally bind and gag him while the priest reads the last rites. "Released for cadaver use last night," Tony, or CPS number 722, is sedated in the operating room. He'll be the corpse for a client who has selected "death by automobile accident"—a cerebral hemorrhage, to be specific. The doctor (William Richard Wintersole) tells Tony, still awake, that he was his "best work," and identifies the left occipital lobe as point of entry. As he pushes the drill through, we see Tony's last memory, or his last dream: he walks and runs on the beach with his young daughter swinging on his shoulders, holding her hands. The grinding whine of the drill fades. The image wavers, distorts, and disappears.

4. "EVERY GIRL SHOULD HAVE A DADDY":*THE EXORCIST* AND *MANSON*

The year 1973 was bookended by two films that would go on to be nominated for (and in one case win) Oscars, each of them detailing the rebellion of Middle America's adolescent girls under malign, demonic influence. The "documentary" film *Manson* (directed by Robert Hendrickson and Laurence Merrick, first released in January 1973) and the end-of-year box-office smash and pop culture hallmark *The Exorcist* (adapted by William Peter Blatty from his 1971 bestseller and directed by William Friedkin) spring from a similar source: a marked, profound anxiety throughout American culture concerning the seeming dissolution of the postwar nuclear family, and the consequent dissipation of the daughters within those families. *Manson*, a drive-in hit that was soon forgotten, was touted in its promotional material as a real-life peek inside the Manson Family, but, as one might expect from a film distributed by American International Pictures, exploitation elements abound. *The Exorcist*, excoriated in mainstream media at the time as an offense against Christianity and Catholicism specifically, had all the trappings of a supernatural horror thriller: ancient demons, foul blasphemies, elaborate (puke-and blood-filled) special effects, crises of faith. But the film's unsparing final act was as profoundly shocking as it was only because of the intimate, *vérité*-style realism of the first two acts, which so convincingly described an American (broken) family in turmoil—a mother and daughter living on their own. In truth, it is Friedkin's film that works more like a documentary, and it's *Manson*, with its sun-dappled hippie idylls punctuated with true-crime *Grand Guignol* details of the Family's crimes, that is the schlock horror exploitation flick.

Charles Manson and the Family's legacy of influence on the Sixties counterculture, the mainstream's perceptions of the counterculture, and mass media is, of course, massive. It has only been relatively recently that the conspiratorial elements in Manson's story—the prosecutorial and personal ethical misconduct of Vincent Bugliosi, the strange US intelligence assets that surrounded the Family and its associates, and the hands-off policy that local law enforcement had on the Family both before and after the murders—have been catalogued and explored.[1] In the aftermath of the sensationalistic trial in the latter half of 1970 and the penalty phase in 1971, the Family members imprisoned on Death Row (until the abolition of the death penalty in California in 1972)—including Manson himself, Susan Atkins, Patricia Krenwinkel, Leslie Van Houten, and later Tex Watson in a separate prosecution—had left a leaderless cult. Into this void plunged Hollywood acting school owner-director Hendrickson and exploitation director Merrick, who had met Manson at Spahn Ranch in 1969 while filming 1970 biker flick *Black Angels* (Manson reportedly ordered him off the property because he was employing Black actors.[2]) The two spent nearly three years shooting film and interviews with the Family during and after the trial. On the surface, despite the outré subject matter, *Manson* is a pretty bog-standard documentary for its time and place in both style and structure. Time is given to the witnesses, members of the Family, and Bugliosi, who would soon release his narrative-defining account of the Family and their trial, *Helter Skelter*, published in 1974. Bugliosi acts as a mouthpiece for the "straight" world while the various folks caught up in the maelstrom of the Family's activities, from witnesses to members, have their say about the emotional, psychosexual crucible to which "Charlie" had subjected them.

The film opens with Lynette "Squeaky" Fromme monologuing from within a survivalist's mindset in what looks like a cabin hideout: "You pick up a child, and you move him to the desert." She's cradling a rifle in her lap, opining about how it is necessary to kill: "Whatever is necessary to do, you do it. If somebody needs to be killed, there's no wrong: you do it," she says, unconsciously (and darkly, considering the Family's dreams of race war) echoing Malcolm X's famous maxim, "by any means necessary." The opening credits sum up the Family's legal problems circa late 1972 with images detailing each member's legal status, concluding with a posed shot of the cultists still free on the outside and "At-Large," as the caption says. All of this is overlaid with a treacly acoustic-strummed song by Family defector and *Manson* interview subject (referred to in the film as "Witness for the Prosecution") Paul Watkins: "When murder became [the Family's] lifestyle," the narrator tells us, "[Watkins] fled the pack." Watkins becomes a witness not just for the prosecution but for an entire hippie ethos (*Manson*'s narrator Jesse Pearson, a former TV western bit-part player and *Bye Bye Birdie*'s Conrad Birdie, rather cloyingly calls Watkins "a true flower child") that seemed to have died that night on Cielo Drive.

As Watkins' (and eventually Manson's own) gentle acoustic music weaves in and out of the talking head interviews, the primary thematic juxtaposition of the film becomes rapidly clear: violence is what happens when the freaks meet the squares. In fact, it's as soon as the credits and introductions are completed that Vincent Bugliosi greets us, the audience, outside the chambers of Charles H. Older's courtroom. Dressed in a three-piece suit, clean cut, and with movements and a vocal cadence like a politician on the campaign trail, he introduces the film in a rather overheated way as the tale of

> perhaps the most savage bizarre nightmarish murders in the recorded annals of crime. Sharon Tate's husband, movie director Roman Polanski, could not himself have conceived of a more monstrous, macabre scene of human terror and massacre than that which took place at his own residence on the early morning hours of August the 9th, 1969.

The evocation of Polanski's *Rosemary's Baby* is no accident. Like the spawn of Satan in that film, the Manson girls are a harbinger of deeper and wider societal disruption, which Bugliosi details in his "Helter Skelter" theory of the crimes: that Manson was trying to launch an apocalyptic race war with the Tate/LaBianca murders, that Manson was receiving "prophetic" messages from the works of the Beatles.[3] But a different reality keeps peeking through his supremely ordered theories, thanks to the editing decisions of Hendrickson and Merrick. For instance, after Bugliosi asserts the binding reality of Helter Skelter, Watkins, the dutiful witness, confirms that it was indeed Manson's "Helter Skelter trip" that changed everything. But before that trip took hold, Watkins offers a view of what the Family was all about:

And everything that everything was for was always for fucking. That's what everything was for. If we weren't doing that, we was leading up to it, and if we weren't leading up to it, we was doing that, and that's what it was all for, that's what everything we ever did was for...

Throughout *Manson*, the filmmakers give over a lot of rhetorical space to the Family to talk about the injustices in the world and in America during the period of the cult's formation and fame, including references to Nixon pointing his "bloody finger" at Charlie during the trial (the famous *Los Angeles Times* headline "Manson Guilty, Nixon Declares" was shown to the jury by Manson himself in an attempt to bring about a mistrial[4]) and the war in Southeast Asia. But it's the Family's hippie love-in antics that the film keeps returning to; with so much footage in evidence of the post-trial Family frolicking, singing, caring for ranch animals, and skinny-dipping, the filmmakers combine their prurient sensationalist exposé of the bloody details of the Family's crimes with the seeming innocence and freshness that resulted from the counterculture's rejection of the strictures of the repressed suburban nuclear family. These juxtapositions are deliberate and deployed by the filmmakers with irony. After a trippy psychedelic montage of "candid" footage of the Family having a group hug with some ranch horses (tracked with audio of their collectively chanting a mantra), the jailhouse cellmates of convicted murderer Susan "Sadie" Atkins tell in great detail how Atkins eagerly confessed every detail of the murders to them, with multiple-aliased cellmate Ronnie Howard offering the memorably macabre account of how Atkins compared the Tate murder to sexual intercourse: "And she told me that to stab someone is better than having a climax. To stab somebody is a sexual release in itself anyway, because the whole world is one big intercourse."

It's this sense of sexual satisfaction in violence and murder that connects *Manson* with its antecedents in the pulps and in AIP-style exploitation films (especially the biker films) of the previous decade. Lurid tabloid jailhouse "confessions," such as the Family's positively Ballardian plans to murder and skin Hollywood celebrities like Elizabeth Taylor and Frank Sinatra, are trotted out by the film for the viewers' enjoyment and horror. And it is in this detailing of the psychosexual brainwashing of the Manson "girls" that we arrive at the center of *Manson* as a document of the "traditional" family's disintegration in the face of the revolutionary Sixties. Both professional academics and armchair pop culture psychologists have long observed that Manson's power to isolate and control his cult grew out of the patriarchal, sexual power he exerted over its female members.[5] The interweaving of sex, fear, and death, as Atkins told her cellmate, was central to this control, and to his ability to build and grow the Family. The documentary pointedly evokes this during a montage of every single female member, with Paul Watkins talking about how he'd seen the girls around the Southern California scene, how they were "some of the prettiest girls I'd ever seen," and how he was essentially seduced (just like many other male members of the Family and other men in close association, such as Beach Boy Dennis Wilson) by the girls' sexual liberation. But *Manson*'s authorial narrator finds a clear parallel between the lives that the Manson girls left in the suburbs and the lives of sex, drugs, and ritual murder they inherited at Spahn Ranch:

> These little all-American girls Manson collected came equipped with a multitude of social and sexual taboos,

which Manson eradicated. Grateful, the girls worked slavishly for him doing the same menial chores they hated at home. They sewed fanatically and embroidered Charlie's ceremonial vest, which became as infamous as the Family.

Cooking, doing the "shopping" (actually dumpster-diving at LA's supermarkets, a popular practice among counterculture communes and organizations across late-Sixties America[6]), sewing, taking care of the Family's babies, and being readily available for sexual service: the same tasks that a square suburban American husband would demand of his own mate, and the same expectations feminists had been calling out for decades. It seems to be Charlie's successful subversion of these American patriarchal rituals imprinted upon the daughters of the baby boom, a grotesque mirror image of 1950s domesticity, that allows him to rule over his Family—using tricks he'd learned, and himself endured, in the American prison system where he spent so much of his life[7]—and fosters the film's own exploitation appeal. *Manson* leans into this argument quite nakedly, consistently painting the Manson girls as "good girls gone bad": "Wealthy debutante Sandy Good had earned her B.A. and was halfway through her Master's when she met Manson..."; as for Lynnette Fromme, she was

a typical suburbia USA child raised on kites, roller skates, and dancing lessons. She majored in psychology and aspired to be a social worker [earlier in the film the narrator makes special note of Cielo Drive victim and coffee heiress Abigail Folger's job as a social worker in Watts]. She was the second girl Charlie collected... and his favorite. Squeaky says every girl should have a daddy... just like Charlie.

Pearson dramatically pauses prior to whispering these final three words, punctuating the all-American horror story with kitsch amateur dramatics like a TV horror host. Delivery aside, this is the moment in *Manson* that is pregnant with the most macabre and society-shattering implications. The specter of toxic masculinity and poisonous patriarchy hovers over every interview with the Manson girls. When Bugliosi and some of the Family members compare Charlie to Hitler, it harks back to the central conceit of Wilhelm Reich's epochal 1933 *The Mass Psychology of Fascism*: that "we have to look upon [the family] as *political reaction's germ cell*, the most important center for the production of reactionary men and women[8] [...] In the figure of the father the authoritarian state has its representative in every family, so that the family becomes its most important instrument of power."[9] The cyclical, chicken-and-egg nature of the authoritarian state and patriarchal family is replicated in the Manson girls' devotion to Charlie and Charlie's own feints at becoming the next Hitler (leading a white tribe to victory in an American race war). As the narrator, Bugliosi, and various Family members openly opine about Manson's Jesus trip, Fromme exclaims, "Yeah! Yeah, he is God! And that's why they're hanging him, that's why they're killing him, that's what they want to kill, is God. That's what the preacher wants to kill when he wears his black robes and stuff. That's what the judge sits up there in his black robe and orders to death." Charlie is thus competing with every patriarchal symbol in mainstream American society: political leaders, judges, preachers, suburban fathers, even God or Christ himself.

In possibly the most memorable sequence of *Manson*, and one that has cast a long shadow over Manson Family lore, the narrator talks about the effects of violence in the mass media and the girls explain how their childhoods in front of the TV and movies had indelibly shaped them. "And the Establishment smugly dismisses the Mansons as an oddball phenomenon," Pearson informs us. "These kids came from our own schools, our own neighborhoods, our own homes. By the time the Sadies, the Katies, and the Leslies had reached the age of 14, they'd witnessed over 14,000 killings on television." "We are what you have made us," says Nancy Pitman, a.k.a. Brenda.

> We were brought up on your TV. We were brought up watching *Gunsmoke*, *Have Gun Will Travel*, [*The*] *FBI*, *Combat!* *Combat!* was my favorite show! I never missed *Combat!* I always watched *Combat!* because the guy that was the lead [...] was my hero. You know, he was a big strong dude and he shot 40 or 50 people in each show but he was still the hero. He was still the beautiful dude that was doing it for some kind of cause which they never, never told us.

Brenda goes on to cite gangster films and cartoons, and says that all of these violent protagonists, "characters that would catch the kids' attention," were held up as role models to admire. "We are what you made us," Pitman repeats.

This is the same rap, stentorian narrator and all, at the heart of the juvenile delinquent films of the 1950s and the biker films of the 1960s: these children, simultaneously coddled and exposed to pop culture's rebellious, violent undercurrents, are cuckoos in the nest, potential agitators whose demands need to be acknowledged by the "smug Establishment." In his 2019 paean to lost pre-Seventies Hollywood, *Once Upon a Time in Hollywood*, Quentin Tarantino punctuates the Family's decision to assault the home of the film's protagonist, washed-up cowboy actor Rick Dalton (Leonardo DiCaprio), with a version of Pitman's monologue, in the film attributed to Sadie (Mikey Madison). And earlier in the film, Rick and his stunt guy Cliff Booth (Brad Pitt) watch an episode of *The F.B.I.*, another reference to Pitman's favorite childhood shows; in another scene, a bus advertising *Combat!* re-runs pulls away to reveal fictionalized Family member Pussycat (Margaret Qualley) hitching. The Family created its own internal myth: that society was changing and that the world for which their generation's childhoods had prepared them simply no longer existed. Only with Charlie's messianic guidance could his girls survive in the post-Helter Skelter wasteland.

One of the biggest movies of the 1970s, *The Exorcist* is probably best known for the public response to its shock and blasphemy. Aping the sensationalist marketing of B-movies from the 1950s (like William Castle's famous gimmick films, such as 1959's *The Tingler*—electric shocks dealt from every cinema seat), ubiquitous TV and newspaper stories about the film during its holiday season release detailed the audience's visceral physical reactions of disgust and abjection: moviegoers were passing out, vomiting, screaming in terror.[10] Lapsed Catholics spoke of the film's evocation of their pre-Vatican II haunted childhoods,[11] while church officials were scandalized by the gross-out horror and sexual blasphemy of Linda Blair's child possessee Regan MacNeil.[12] In the film-academic world, contemporary critical response to *The Exorcist* was negative, and sometimes even vitriolic. *Film Quarterly*'s Michael Dempsey called it a "trash bombshell" that expertly appeals to both "reactionaries" as well as liberal "sophisticates" and "ruthlessly manipulates the most primitive fears and prejudices of the audience."[13] Dempsey and others look at the mania surrounding *The Exorcist* as evidence of a rapidly diminishing capacity for the contemporary American (and by extension Western) film audience to discern fantasy from reality, a condition expressed in both the personality cults and religious movements, new and revivalist, sweeping the country in 1973.[14]

Ruth McCormick, in *Cinéaste*, offered a more measured and detailed review, and unsurprisingly it is her feminist critique that gets at the misogyny at the center of the film:

> *The Exorcist* can be seen as an extended rape fantasy. It is a sadist's delight, and the repellent torture of an innocent young girl by an unseen, powerful male entity cannot but be a real turn-on to brigades of woman-haters unable to find happiness even in the sado-masochistic porno flicks in which the women seem to enjoy their degradation [...] I have also heard and read more than one male opinion that Regan's 'possession' is due to her awakened sexuality, with the definite implication that, at the age of 12, she needs a man and not just a daddy.[15]

So much of the criticism and analysis of *The Exorcist* over the past half-century has focused on the possession of Regan as an expression of her transition from childhood into adolescence that it's easy to miss what McCormick was able to see right away, living as she was in a milieu where the hard-won struggles of women's lib were encountering what Susan Faludi would later call a "backlash." Are Regan and her mother, film actress Chris MacNeil (Ellen Burstyn), being punished by Blatty and Friedkin for being independent women who not only are without a "daddy" figure in the aftermath of the Sixties, but perhaps don't even *need* or *want* a daddy?

In our first look at the MacNeil family, we watch matriarch Chris go into Regan's bedroom to shut a window. It's Regan's room that looks more like a home's traditional master bedroom, with its fusty, old-fashioned decor (including, apparently, a full china cabinet), while Chris's bedroom is tiny with a childlike bed, decorated with little-girl touches like lace pillows and patterned wallpaper. Chris has a whole staff of household helpers: a cook, a handyman, a personal assistant, and Regan's upper-class childhood is idyllic at the outset, full of horse rides and picnics by the Potomac. Mother and daughter seem very close despite all of Chris's professional engagements; they giggle about their appearance on a *Photoplay* magazine cover, taking Chris's wealth and fame in stride. It's during a bedtime conversation that we see glimpses of the family dynamic that has put mother and daughter together: "You're gonna marry him, aren't you?" Regan asks teasingly, referring to film director Burke Dennings (Jack MacGowran, who will later be flung by the possessed Regan down the film's infamous Georgetown stairs). Chris and Regan's father, we find out, are divorced. The sensationalistic and uncanny horror in *The Exorcist* has its roots in the quotidian and homely, as does Regan's compulsive cursing and acting out, the symptoms that lead her into a battery of invasive medical tests, and eventually priestly treatment for demonic possession. On the phone with the operator on Regan's birthday trying to reach Regan's father, Chris rages at his overseas absence as Regan peeks from her bedroom: "He doesn't even call his daughter on her birthday, for Christ's sake! He doesn't give a shit!"

The folkways and practice of divorce in America were going through a sea change in the early 1970s. Fittingly enough, considering Chris's Hollywood career, California set the new nationwide standard, passing the Family Law Act of 1969, which enshrined no-fault divorce.[16] Other states soon followed. Prior to this, American married couples who wished to separate had to use esoteric loopholes to prove harm (or go to states or abroad to other countries that offered quickie divorces).[17] The push to establish divorce laws that would allow for unilateral separation was part and parcel of the feminist movement. However, laws and customs that overwhelmingly protected male material interests in both marriage and divorce were already long on the books, and it soon became clear that husbands would benefit far more from these new laws than wives. Men were established as breadwinners; divorced women who had been housewives often found themselves with the short end of the stick as alimony and child support laws lagged behind. As the Seventies moved on and divorce rates skyrocketed across America, a new awareness of a structure half-built began to sink in among feminist scholars and legal minds: systemic disadvantages in the workplace and in American society's financial and social infrastructure left divorced women incredibly vulnerable.[18]

In the world of Hollywood, of course, divorce was and had been a regular fact of life for decades, fueling the gossip rags and movie magazines. Ronald Reagan himself, who signed the Family Law Act as California governor, was notably divorced from first wife Jane Wyman and would go on to become America's first divorced and remarried president ten years later. The wealthy movie stars in Hollywood's studio system were provided with all kinds of "fixer" infrastructure to prevent difficulty in their various personal and sexual relationships: secret abortions,[19] "beards" for gay and lesbian actors,[20] and the smoothing of actors' divorce and remarriage prospects.

Chris MacNeil clearly possesses all the material benefits of a Hollywood actress—a beautiful Georgetown rental property and servants to help bear the burden of single motherhood while shooting on location. The rot in the MacNeils' home is therefore a spiritual rather than a material one, and Chris and Regan, despite their economic class, are exemplars of any single parent and child we might see in a Seventies film, from Ellen Burstyn's own follow-up role as a widow in Martin Scorsese's *Alice Doesn't Live Here Anymore* (1974) to the decade-ending *Kramer vs. Kramer* (1979), which examined American divorce from the husband's point of view.

American audiences were riveted a few months before *The Exorcist*'s release by a documentary series that aired on the then-new Public Broadcasting System. Titled *An American Family*, it told the story of a comfortable middle-class California family, the Louds: patriarch Bill, wife Pat, and five children ranging in age from their early to late teens. Cameras and filmmakers documented the Louds' movements over the course of a few months in 1971 and ended up being present for the nominal disintegration of the formerly model suburban household: Pat demanded a divorce from Bill, and eldest son Lance came out as gay. Intimate, real portrayals of these formerly taboo topics—divorce, homosexuality, familial disintegration—were aired to an audience of millions, who were already reeling from the societal changes wrought by the younger generation over the previous five years. Tensions that had simmered under the surface of the inviolable American nuclear family unit throughout the Fifties and Sixties—housewives trapped in their homes, children chafing at "father knows best," feelings of meaninglessness among those fathers in their grey flannel suits—could no longer remain hidden. This breakdown is explicit in *The Exorcist*.

It makes perfect sense to consider Regan's foreboding introduction of a Ouija board and her imaginary friend "Captain Howdy" as the gateway to her eventual possession: in her review, McCormick notes that her macho male chauvinist moviegoer "will see perfectly that Regan turns to Captain Howdy in the first place because she needs her Daddy."[21] And however one classifies Regan's preternatural empowerment, it's that inherent *need* for a father that ultimately leads to her torment. This point comes to the fore when the medical and psychiatric establishment—science itself—can do nothing to cure Regan, and Chris must turn to Catholicism and the patriarchal power of both Church and priests for a "cure." In Friedkin's and Blatty's schemas, it's the power of God the Father who saves Regan, and the priests, celibate and unmarried, serve as surrogate father figures, although they can never take the place of the man who doesn't call on Regan's birthday. Both stern Father Merrin (Max von Sydow) and the young, tortured priest Damien Karras (Jason Miller) see their own personal psychodramas finally resolved through their intercession with Regan and battle with the Devil, but at the cost of their own lives. In a conversation between Karras and Merrin at the height of the exorcism process, Karras asks, "Why this girl?" And Merrin responds, "I think the point is to make us despair. To see ourselves as animal and ugly. To reject the possibility that God could love us." So, instead of a daughter to be loved and cherished and made whole as part of a family, Regan is merely an instrument of the priests' own inadequacies and doubts in the beneficence of patriarchy: a means to an end for their own self-actualization and crises of faith. She's a thing to be protected, much like the "innocent" suburban girls that the *Manson* narrator opines over.

Manson and *The Exorcist* expose, unconsciously or otherwise, the *rage* of America's daughters and wives, a rage leveled at the authoritarian fathers and husbands who relegated them to the role of helpmeets and dependents. Once that rage found expression, it blew apart the tranquilized and obedient homes of those self-same patriarchs. The fascination and disgust that both of these films focused on and dredged up in their audiences were symptoms of a new freedom, vertiginous and wild, blasphemous and sexual and violent. Even if Friedkin, Blatty, Hendrickson, and Merrick were merely allowing their own fears to creep onto the screen, their documentary efforts couldn't help but place young women—wild, inhuman, and seemingly demonic—at the fore of the momentous societal changes then possessing the country. "We are what you made us," says Nancy Pitman into the documentary camera; "I am no one," says Regan-as-Devil into Karras' tape recorder, backwards and backmasked, heard only because Karras is really *listening* to what Regan is trying to say. Both statements bear witness to the shattered postwar American family and the lost daughters of a system of oppression that left them unable to conceive of life without Daddy.

PART TWO

A HANDFUL OF RUST
1974–1980

ELIZABETH: Oh, Matthew, I can't go *on*! I wanna go to sleep. I can't stay awake anymore.

MATTHEW: You have to. You *have* to stay awake.

Invasion of the Body Snatchers, 1978

5. "THE COST OF ELECTRICITY":

THE TEXAS CHAIN SAW MASSACRE AND *HARLAN COUNTY, USA*

"They worked you like you'd work a mule or a brute," retired coal miner, union activist, and folksinger Nimrod Workman tells the camera at the beginning of Barbara Kopple's 1976 documentary *Harlan County, USA*. "I heard the bossman say one time... he said, 'you be sure [you] don't get that mule no place where the rock'll fall in on 'im. Don't take that mule to no bad place.'" Nimrod, green at the time, asks the bossman, "Well, what about me?" What happened if the rocks fell on *him*? The bossman replies, "We can always hire another man, but you gotta buy that mule." The casual, calculated cruelty at the heart of that answer, at the heart of the Eastover Mining Company's vicious and eventually murderous attempts to break a strike of Brookside, Kentucky coal miners forty years later, is hardly believable. That's why the closest kin to Kopple's Academy Award-winning feature is not any of the labor union-themed dramas that followed—*Blue Collar* (1978), *F.I.S.T.* (1978), *Norma Rae* (1979), *Silkwood* (1983)—but Tobe Hooper's unforgiving "true story" of class struggle taken to eviscerative extremes, 1974's *The Texas Chain Saw Massacre*.

Both films went into production as questions about American energy—how we get it, who controls it, how we use it and waste it and hoard it, who profits from it, and who we sacrifice to keep it flowing—pointed to a looming national emergency. The cost of the Vietnam War had plunged the country's spectacular post-World War II bounty into deficit, and even though domestic oil production peaked in 1970, drained by unsustainable expansion, the "energy orgy" rumbled on[1]—Americans made up only 6% of the global population, but consumed one-third of the globe's available power.[2] The joyride stalled in October 1973: the OPEC oil embargo, fronted by Saudi Arabia in retaliation for US aid ($2.2 billion worth of weapons and military supplies) to Israel during the Yom Kippur War,[3] led to an "energy crisis," as President Nixon described it in a November White House address,[4] that engulfed the economy. Oil prices shot up by 400%,[5] and drivers lined up for hours to get a turn at the costly pump. Severe inflation combined with high unemployment diagnosed a new capitalist malady: stagflation.[6] Truckers blocked the highways in protest, sometimes violently.[7] The supply lines were cut off; shortages and panic-buying ensued. Nixon's Secretary of State Henry Kissinger warned of "the moral and political disintegration of the West."[8]

This new world of scarcity and precarity—the result of great affluence, according to Nixon, because "what were once considered luxuries are now considered necessities"[9]—is the backdrop of *The Texas Chain Saw Massacre*, which begins with an apocalyptic radio report that tells of "a special grand jury investigation" (the Watergate scandal came to a head during the energy crisis), grave-robbing and corpse desecration (the "top story," obviously), oil fires, a cholera epidemic, a deadly building collapse, suicide, and serial murder. It's summer in Texas, but the heat is no ordinary heat: the sun sheds smoke against a black sky, like some surreal and foreboding eclipse. When our "five youths" on their "idyllic afternoon drive" (the voiceover is presumably satiric) roll up to the Gulf station in their gas-guzzling van, the owner (Jim Siedow), one of the Sawyer family cannibals known only as the Old Man, turns them away: the tanks are dry, and the supply may not get there until the next day.

The "kids," as the Old Man calls them, decide to visit Sally (Marilyn Burns) and Franklin's (Paul A. Partain) grandfather's house (they just stopped at the graveyard to make sure his corpse wasn't missing or mutilated) while they wait—they don't have enough gas to get them to the next closest station. When they get there, Kirk (William Vail) and Pam (Teri McMinn) head down to the creek, where Kirk hears the chugging of a nearby generator: the sound is a more or less constant presence throughout the film, displaced and drowned out only by its phallic counterpart, the gas-powered chainsaw. They head to the decrepit farmhouse to make a deal for some gas. Rusted pots and a pocket watch with a giant nail through the center hang and swing on a spindly tree: time has stopped for the savage Sawyers, but they have learned the value of modern tools when practicing their ancient trade. Camouflage netting disguises several cars in very good shape, including two very out of place Volkswagen Bugs. The generator is there too, hooked up to an oil drum, and there's a much bigger fuel tank squatting in the brush as the couple circles around to the front of the house, where Kirk finds a human tooth on the porch and unwisely forces his way inside.

The miners in Harlan County have almost none of Nixon's "luxuries" that have become "necessities" through "prosperity." The Brooksiders live in a coal camp owned by Eastover, the decrepit row houses rented back to the miners. Only a handful of them have baths and running water, and electricity costs extra. (50% of the nation's supply was generated by coal,[10] and coal profits in Appalachia increased by 150% between 1969 and 1976[11]; in 1973, Duke Power cleared $90 million, up 14% from the year before.[12]) There's no indoor plumbing, and the toilets built out over the river have "highly contaminated" the water supply, says the Harlan County Health Department.[13] Bad and missing teeth are the norm—no dental insurance. A mother in hair curlers washes her baby from a bucket on the porch railing. One of the older kids explores the carcass of a decomposing car. There is no mention of gas prices or rationing or recession; those are problems they'll be able to afford only with a better contract. Few of the miners have cars that work—the strikebreakers and "gun thugs," like the Sawyer family, have plenty—and they can't afford to leave the camp anyway: they're on strike wages paid by the United Mine Workers of America (UMW). And when the strike ends, even if all the safety concessions are met (they won't be), going back down into the mine, forty-eight inches high at its highest, will still be one of the most dangerous jobs on the planet.[14]

Coal miners have been at the center of the American labor movement and American radicalism since the late nineteenth century. They lived in company towns owned by the coal operators, rented company equipment, and got paid in company scrip that was good only in the company store, where price-gouging was the norm. The water supplies were routinely contaminated by the heavy metals that came out of the mine, and the unventilated coal dust gave the miners "black lung" (the older miners at Brookside and elsewhere are often gasping for breath during interviews, or hooked up to oxygen tanks). Private security hired by the company, often ex-cons, would intimidate, assault, evict, and blacklist union members, organizers, and sympathizers. In Mingo

County, West Virginia, this led to the 1920 shootout at Matewan (dramatized in John Sayles' 1987 film of the same name, inspired by *Harlan County, USA*) and the Battle of Blair Mountain, where thousands of armed miners faced off against local law, the West Virginia National Guard, company-hired biplanes loaded with explosives, and Federal troops. The strikers in Kopple's film talk a lot about "Bloody Harlan," a series of deadly skirmishes between miners and company men in the early 1930s. "I've been all around the bloodshed," says a retired miner who was there, "blood all around me. For a contract." It's not so much that time had stopped in Harlan County—it's that it didn't really exist. Time, like everything else, was owned by the company and measured out by the boss with his pocket watch.

"Hey, that's the ole slaughterhouse," Franklin remarks as the kids, leaving the defiled cemetery behind them, are overwhelmed by a noxious stench. "That's where grandpa used to sell his cattle." (Cattle barons: the greedy capitalist villains of many a Western.) Franklin animatedly and graphically describes how the slaughterhouse workers would do the deed— "they'd bash 'em in the head with a big sledgehammer"—and then tries to reassure the horrified Pam that they use a more efficient mechanized "airgun" now, as if it was the inefficiency that bothered her. The group stops to pick up a bloody-faced Hitchhiker (Edwin Neal), another Sawyer, who tells them that his brother and grandfather worked in the ole slaughterhouse, and that "my family's always been in meat." (The sign above the gas station advertises Coca-Cola, with "We Slaughter Barbecue" spelled out underneath.) Prompted by Franklin, the Hitchhiker says the airgun is "no good" and prefers, almost lasciviously, "the old way, with a sledge." The "new way," he says, "people put out of work." (The captive bolt gun, or stun gun, was invented in 1905 and became standard in slaughterhouses over the next two decades: time has not only stopped but regressed.) "*The Texas Chain Saw Massacre* is, at its heart, the story of unemployed abattoir workers applying the skills of their trade to the butchery of humans," writes Mark Steven in 2017's *Splatter Capital*.[15] The Sawyers have been "disenfranchised" and "made unemployable by the modernization of their industry and by the crisis in value caused by that very modernization."[16] The bloodshed on the near horizon, in other words, is labor's revenge—an indefinite strike, if you will, by rural workers against their big-city bourgeois oppressors.

In storied and isolated Harlan County, coal mining is all there is. It's not so much an occupation as a defiant family tradition. "There is no neutral there," sings seventy-three-year-old Florence Reece at a UMW event supporting the Brookside Strike, "You'll either be a union man/Or a thug for [sheriff and coal company strongarm] J.H. Blair." It's from "Which Side Are You On?," a song she wrote in 1931 during Bloody Harlan, and everyone in the audience, young and old, smiles and sings along. This generational struggle embedded in radical labor is parodied in the fictional town of Newt, Texas. The Sawyer family patriarch is the grotesque and vampiric Grandfather (John Dugan), who animates, barely, only at the taste of blood. He is revered and doted on by his son, the Old Man, and the Hitchhiker and Leatherface, his grandsons: three generations under one cursed roof, united under one bloody cause. Grandpa "is the best killer that ever was," the Old Man beams, telling hysterical captive Sally that "It won't hurt a bit." A slaughterhouse legend, he "did sixty in five minutes once." He's like John Henry, another mythic sledgehammer holder who challenged the machine, except Grandpa lived (kind of).

The Sawyers are all men, naturally. Grandmother, no Florence Reece, is a decomposed corpse propped up in a rocking chair in the attic (in 1960's Oedipal *Psycho*, the decomposed corpse of Norman Bates' mother is propped up in a chair in the cellar). Unlike the redneck brothers in *Bloody Mama*, who are led astray and deranged by the "prodding" and "nagging" misogynist matriarch, here it's the lack of a maternal figure—normally the "civilizing, humanizing influence," notes Robin Wood[17]—that contributes to depravity and dysfunction. And the sense of dysfunction, the moral universe they inhabit, is deeply absurd and ironic: the Old Man beats and berates his boys (older Hitchhiker is rebellious, younger Leatherface is submissive) not for killing people in cold blood, but for committing transgressions that challenge his authority as father and head of the household —endangering the family "business" by desecrating the graveyard, chainsawing and ruining the front door in pursuit of Sally. This line of patriarchal paternalism is passed down by the very land they inhabit: the Sawyers live adjacent to Franklin's grandfather's manor: they are serfs bound to their lord. "It's a feudal system, I think," says UMW organizer Houston Elmore about Harlan County. "There is a very rich class of people, and then there are the coal miners." The difference between the Sawyers and the Brooksiders, of course, even though both are "representatives of an exploited and degraded proletariat,"[18] as Wood describes the former, is that the miners and their families, just when bloody revenge seems inevitable, choose solidarity and a contract—not mercenary, incestuous brutality.

The Texas kids are hippie-types. We don't know if they

have jobs. We don't know if they're students. They seem to be drifting. Franklin constantly whines when he doesn't get his way. Pam pontificates about astrology. Kirk, approaching the farmhouse, cluelessly plans to "leave 'em my guitar, you know, give 'em a couple bucks" for some gas. And three of them barge into a house that doesn't belong to them, uninvited. "You don't want to go foolin' around other folks' property," the Old Man at the gas station warns the kids when they ask about grandpa's place. "Some folks don't like it, and they don't mind showin' you." Franklin tells him his father owns it, and the Old Man is noticeably disgusted. In short, the youngsters are entitled. The film, among other things, is about the undoing of the counterculture.

In the van, the Hitchhiker cuts himself deeply on the palm with Franklin's pocket knife, then takes a Polaroid of Franklin and burns it on top of a piece of foil in some kind of dark magical ritual, *Rosemary's Baby*-style. He folds the foil up and puts it into what looks like a Native American medicine bag. This is country magic, folk magic, not the commercial occult sham of Pam's big book of horoscopes. The Hitchhiker slashes Franklin's forearm with a straight razor, dashes outside, and mixes his and Franklin's blood on the side of the van: a sigil of some sort. "I'm about half ready to call a cop," Kirk says, disgusted at himself for thinking it. The dissenting adventures of his class, color, and generation, subsidized by the labor of the Sawyers ("I like meat," Sally complains, when she's finding out how it's made) and Appalachia's miners and Detroit's auto workers, are also something of a sham: when the struggle got real, the "revolution" wilted in the face of resistance, in the face of real violence. Meditation and vitamins were safer. The suburbs and stock options weren't so bad after all. "That's the last goddamn hitchhiker I ever pick up," says van driver Jerry (Allen Danziger).

"When you believe in somethin' strong enough that you're ready to die for it," says Lois Scott, who emerges over the course of *Harlan County, USA* as possibly the most important leader of the thirteen-month Brookside Strike, "that's when you get it." Nobody wilted here, not even the "hippie New York filmmaker" the miners suspected Kopple of being when she arrived. But they had nothing to worry about. "There was no contest," she said. "It wasn't about objectivity." She knew which side she was on, and she and her crew (mostly associate director Anne Lewis and principal cinematographer Hart Perry) immediately became part of the strike, sleeping on the floor of the miners' houses and showing up at the picket line at 5 o'clock in the morning "with film or without film" to protect the strikers: "Nobody," Kopple said, "wants to commit murder in living color." In one extraordinary scene, Eastover foreman and leader of the gun thugs Basil Collins calls Kopple over to his truck and asks: "Who're you workin' with, honey?" She tells him the United Press (it's not true, but she does have a press card). He asks for her ID. She tells Anne to go get it from the car. He's "twirling his gun" on the seat, the gun he's already pulled on the miners and will keep pulling on them. She asks him how he feels about the "people picketing"; it catches him off guard and he pauses, his head swivels away from the camera and back; he has "no comment on that." He asks for her press card again, getting impatient. She asks for *his* ID. He's "lost it," he says. "I think I might have misplaced mine too," Kopple shoots back. Collins winks at her—he knows he's beaten this time—and drives off.

In one extraordinary scene in *The Texas Chain Saw Massacre*, Pam wanders into the house after Kirk and gets captured by massive Leatherface (Gunnar Hansen), who picks her up, takes her into the slaughter room, and plunges her onto a hanging meat hook, where she writhes and screams and has no choice but to watch as Leatherface decapitates dead Kirk (killed "the old way, with a sledge") with a chainsaw (the "new way"). Things turn out better for Sally, who escapes in the end, but she spends the last third of the movie running for her life, jumping out of a window, getting beaten with a broom, gagged, stuffed in a sack, tied to a chair, her finger slashed and given to zombie Grandpa to suck on, her head held over a bucket so zombie Grandpa can sledge her, until she finally breaks free and jumps out of another window, screaming, forever screaming.

Had the men of the Sawyer family faced off against any one of the members of the Brookside Women's Club, the screams might have come from the other side. It's the women who show up on the line when the men don't. It's the women who lay down on the road to stop the scabs from getting to the mine. It's Sudie Crusenberry who breaks up a squabble about someone "running around" with someone else's husband: "I don't care who takes whose man [...] They can take mine. I'm not after a man, I'm after a contract." It's Lois who pulls a .38 out of her bra ("You'd be crazy *not* to carry a gun now") after she sees the strikebreakers toting machine guns. It's Kopple who gets a warrant for Collins' arrest when shots are fired on the predawn picket and she gets footage of him pointing his gun at her, after which she's knocked down and beaten by a scab. It's the women who force the sheriff to make Collins and the scabs turn around and go back down the hill: Anne Lewis gives the warrant to the sheriff on camera. And it's the women who pay the price: the miners get their contract only when a Brooksider, twenty-two-year-old Lawrence Jones, is shot in the face and killed by a scab, leaving behind his sixteen-year-old wife and five-month-old daughter. A miner points out a piece of his brain, like the viscera spilled from one of Leatherface's victims, that's splattered on the asphalt.

Eight months into the strike, the Brookside miners go to New York to picket Duke Power outside the Stock Exchange. Jerry Johnson, wearing a sign that says "Duke Power Is No Match for Coal Miner Power," tells a beat cop: "A lot of people don't understand that that 'lectricity burnin' over there... there's somebody dyin' every day for it. There's one man dies every day." A member of the Citizens Public Inquiry into the Brookside Strike agreed, concluding that "we're burning up people to make electricity." Even the union, we find out, eats its own. On New Year's Eve in 1969, UMW presidential candidate and rank-and-file champion Joseph "Jock" Yablonski was murdered in his house. So were his wife and daughter—shot to death in their bedrooms. The investigation pointed back to then-UMW president W.A. "Tony" Boyle, long suspected of being "in bed with the coal operators," who ordered the assassinations and used union money and the "blood and sweat of miners" to pay for it. At least the Sawyers eat what they butcher. Sally, with Leatherface in chainsaw-revving pursuit, bursts into the gas station and falls into the arms of the Old Man. She doesn't know he's Leatherface's daddy until it's too late. He knocks her out, binds and bags her, drags her to the truck, starts the engine. He looks back at the store, turns off the truck, runs back to the store, turns the lights off, and runs back to the truck: "Cost of electricity's enough to drive a man outta business," he says, chuckling. The meat has got to stay frozen until it's ready to be cooked.

Meat is meat. Cannibalism is cannibalism. The coal operators rip open the earth; the Hitchhiker digs up and desecrates the graves. The teeth and shears of the continuous drill rend and tear the walls of the mine; the chainsaw rips through bone and muscle; the Sawyers rend and tear the flesh. The miners extract the coal; Leatherface extracts the organs; the coal owners extract the profit. The Sawyers have to be careful to cover their tracks—they don't want the meat at the market anymore, and they can't afford it anyway. The owners have to be careful not to make the mines too safe, because safety costs money and $90 million is not enough. Miners suffer, miners die, miners strike, but the contract is signed only when the risk assessment algorithm determines that not signing will cost the owners more money in the end than signing. The owners of the cars hidden in the Sawyer's backyard were not careful enough: they were butchered, cured, consumed, sold to the next victims ("We Slaughter Barbecue") who rolled up to the empty Gulf gas tanks. Kirk, Pam, Jerry, Franklin: butchered, cured, consumed, fed to Sally. It's never enough. They have a taste for it now, the blood and the money, and the hunger is endless. Energy flows, blood flows, sometimes in geysers, but the country needs more. Poison the atmosphere, start a war, start another, sacrifice the young, civilian casualties galore, sell out the generations to come—whatever it takes. The coal is spent. The meat locker is empty. A new mine. A new van. The bodies pile up again. "They're treatin' us like animals, dogs," Lois says. Less, even. You gotta *buy* that mule. Life is cheap, and the Sawyers didn't learn how to eat people from the slaughterhouse. They learned it from Duke Power.

6. "WE'VE COME THIS FAR, WE MUST GO ON!": *ALIEN* AND *SORCERER*

As the 1970s came to a close, the United States shuddered under the impacts of economic instability, political scandal, and the consolidation of international capital under the aegis of a new petro-corporate order. Americans saw their buying power, consumer confidence, and postwar material gains shaken by coups and kingdoms far from home, while in satirical films like 1975's *Rollerball* and 1976's *Network*, mega-corporations did battle (literally, in the case of *Rollerball*) with each other as the stultified masses were hypnotized by the spectacle the mass media dished out. In each film, one man stands up to this new world order—James Caan's rebellious rollerballer Jonathan E. in the former, Peter Finch's mad prophet of the airwaves Howard Beale in the latter—but each character's ending, violent and ambiguous, revealed the power of the forces arrayed against him. Very shortly, this trope would solidify into something even more menacing. William Friedkin's 1977 *Sorcerer*, a loving yet brutal re-imagining of Henri-Georges Clouzot's existentialist adventure *The Wages of Fear* (1953), and Ridley Scott's 1979 *Alien* used two different genres—adventure thriller and sci-fi horror—to depict a disparate team on a desperate mission on behalf of a distant, uncaring corporation in an unsparing world.

In both *Sorcerer* and *Alien*, there is no corner of the Earth (or the galaxy!) that can escape capitalism's grasp. It doesn't matter if you're a former master of finance, a corporate collaborator, a science officer, a middle manager, a criminal on the run, or especially a working-class schlub looking for a lucrative bonus payout. All are disposable, and not even the bravery, intelligence, and determination of the heroes of the films— Roy Scheider's Scanlon and Sigourney Weaver's Ripley—can save them from the system: both "last 'men' standing" end up broken physically and psychically by the extremes of their experiences in the "jungle," reluctant pawns of an eternally victorious corporation. And in both cases, the penetration of the Company into the edges of what's deemed "civilization" ends up creating fantastical, hallucinatory liminal zones populated with singular hidden treasures, which provide the bosses with ever-widening vistas of plunder and profit.

This clash of a technically advanced, economically developed, rapacious outside world with the primitive wilderness on the edges of the imperial core evokes the concept of the "cargo cult," where the sudden appearance of the apparatus of modernity (and the instruments of war-making attached to it) among isolated native cultures leads to a belief in foreign gods and their intermediaries, who are able to conjure valuable "cargo" from nowhere. During and after World War II, Pacific Islanders erected facsimiles of antennae, air strips, and other forms of modern infrastructure to once again summon the valuable supplies that had disappeared from their islands after the war. Throughout the postwar period, the Western public was fascinated by the phenomenon, but the concept is ultimately less a sociological reality than a lens through which a "triumphant" Western world can view the "primitive" cultures it clashed with and exploited.[1] In *Sorcerer* and *Alien*, that cargo (serving as a MacGuffin that drives the plot) is an extremely dangerous prize, and the "workers" are sent on impossible missions to obtain it to satisfy, if only for a moment, the Company's endless greed for profit and power.

Sorcerer was released to middling reviews and not much box office success, despite Friedkin's winning ways throughout the first half of the Seventies: *The French Connection* and *The Exorcist* won a combined seven Academy Awards and collectively grossed nearly half a billion dollars. Critics and audiences found Friedkin's follow-up bleak and difficult to understand, at best a pulpy remake of a far more atmospheric late-noir classic. At exactly the same time, some of cinema's most promising "outlaw" filmmakers were choosing to make crowd-pleasing films full of wonder and spectacle: 1977 saw the release of both *Star Wars* and *Close Encounters of the Third Kind*, films that hearkened back to both Lucas's and Spielberg's love of classic film genres. Friedkin's impulse to remake *The Wages of Fear* fits right into this pattern, except that *Sorcerer* was doggedly pessimistic and pointed to the crushing realities faced by audiences of the 1970s, who apparently no longer wanted their noses rubbed in it. Friedkin himself defiantly cited these realities as factors in the film's rejection by viewers and critics: "My films became more obsessive, less audience-friendly, and would turn even darker in the future. They would continue to portray the American character as fearful, psychotic, and dangerous."[2]

Like the original *The Wages of Fear*, *Sorcerer* features four outsiders, stuck in a distant outpost of "civilization," who are called upon by an oil company to do a dangerous job for little pay (just enough for a ticket and travel papers out of the grim company town). The changes Friedkin and co-writer Walon Green made to the narrative are noteworthy: in a series of introductory vignettes, we get to see exactly how all four men have ended up in the purgatory of South America's Porvenir. The film opens with a brief and stylish scene where presumed professional assassin Nilo (Spanish actor Francisco "Paco" Rabal) takes out a target in the midst of a festival in Veracruz, Mexico. We then cut to Jerusalem, where a team of Palestinians (disguised as Israeli Jews), including Kassem (played by Moroccan-French actor Amidou), has just bombed an Israeli bank; he alone escapes death or capture by the Israeli Defense Forces in a sequence clearly inspired by Gillo Pontecorvo's 1966 anti-colonial urtext *The Battle of Algiers*. Victor Manzon (French actor Bruno Cremer) is a financier and banker who's married into old money and finds himself in need of a bailout after committing fraud that will implicate both him and his complicit brother-in-law Pascal (Jean-Luc Bideau). And finally, in the USA, small-time Irish-American hood Jackie Scanlon and his crew rob a local church's bingo hall and shoot a priest who happens to be the brother of a local Mafia chieftain. The latter three protagonists must flee their situations as the authorities—military, police, or criminal— close in on them.

Unsurprisingly, most of their crimes revolve around money and global finance. In a key scene in Victor's prologue, cited by Friedkin himself as the "theme" of the film,[3] he and his wife (Anne-Marie Deschodt) discuss a memoir she's editing about a French colonial officer in Algeria who must decide whether to fire upon an innocent female civilian. Victor snidely reads off the title page of the manuscript, "Adventure and the glory of colonial France," and then asks if the officer ended up doing it. Blanche says yes, and Victor, awash in cynicism and self-reproach, declares that the man Blanche calls "more philosopher than soldier" is simply "just another soldier." Blanche replies coolly: "No one is *just* anything." As Victor trades his wife, his wealth, and his beautiful life in Paris for the dingy hell of Porvenir, we see the conflict between bowing to the implacable system and standing up to it.

These preludes call attention to larger connections between the protagonists' personal actions of crime and fraud and the larger international system of finance and neo-colonialism in which they all participate. At a lunch right before Victor's brother-in-law shoots himself and Victor flees the country, Blanche's dining companion mentions that "they say Veracruz has the best lobster," linking her gourmet tastes as a wealthy Parisian to Nilo's assassination prologue in Mexico. The lobster comment hits harder given Blanche's revelation that Victor comes from humble working-class stock: his father was a fisherman. In the getaway car from the bingo robbery, right before the crew dissolves into recriminations and treachery and ends up in a crash of which Scanlon is sole survivor, an Irish member of Scanlon's crew joyously sings a song made popular by the Irish Rovers, "Goodbye Mrs. Durkin," about a potato-digging peasant finding succor and riches in the New World: "As sure as me name is Barney / I'll be off to Californy / Instead of diggin' praties / I'll be diggin' lumps of gold." It's an ironic foreshadowing of Scanlon's fate in Porvenir, digging not gold but oil.

All end up down on their luck, broke, and working in one way or another for the American oil company in Porvenir. ("Wherever there's oil, there are Americans," says one of the tramps in *The Wages of Fear*.) On Friedkin's set, the real world and the cinematic world would merge in uncanny ways: he filmed in the Dominican Republic because "[Gulf and Western chairman Charles Bluhdorn] had everything I needed in the Dominican Republic, which was then virtually a 'wholly-owned subsidiary of Gulf and Western'."[4] Gulf and Western in turn owned Paramount and a number of other business interests: everything from media (television production company Desilu and Black record label Stax[5]) and heavy manufacturing (interests in zinc, aluminum, and copper processing) to old-school colonial extraction in the Caribbean (tobacco and sugar).[6] Friedkin, well aware of this irony, famously framed a picture of the Gulf and Western board of directors, including Bluhdorn, to represent the oil company's board in their offices in Porvenir.[7] Ultimately, everyone in Porvenir—foreigner, criminal, native—ends up working for the company. As we take a leisurely tour through the various poverty-stricken corners of the town, we see how our protagonists live: stuck in seedy rooming-houses, drinking in filthy cantinas, working jobs full of drudgery, bearing false identities with Spanish aliases. This kind of company town has been a standard fact of life in the colonized world in the industrial era, from pre-Castro Cuba to pre-Ayatollah Iran to pre-independence Philippines to any of the Central and South American puppet republics that provided commodities and raw resources for the American capitalist machine over the course of the twentieth century. And company towns were not merely a colonialist exercise; there were plenty in America's own oppressive backyard, the coal-rich communities of Harlan County, Kentucky, among them.

When a fire that can only be extinguished by a concentrated explosion breaks out at the drilling site, this team of outlaws, men with literally nothing left to lose, is assembled to drive two trucks deep into the heart of the jungle and bring back a cache of highly unstable dynamite. Rabal's assassin joins the team late by killing one of the original recruits for the job, a German whose pseudonym "Marquez" (Karl John) hides the fact that he is a Nazi war criminal; presumably Nilo ended up in Porvenir expressly to assassinate him. The oil company nominally rules the town but also has the careful acquiescence of the nation's military leader, who appears on posters plastered everywhere. His ruling party slogan, "Unidos Hacia El Futuro"—"United Toward the Future"—recalls the neoliberal modernizing project of American puppet leaders throughout the world during the Cold War, including Chilean dictator Augusto Pinochet, who adopted free-market policies that, among other things, privatized or eliminated social welfare programs and made labor unions illegal. These nations became the laboratories for American corporations and laissez-faire economists, who brought the same kinds of policies back to the US in the Reagan Eighties and beyond.[8]

The oil company's workers and managers realize that the deadly terrorist bombing of the oil well in Porvenir is in some way merely the price of doing business: "In this country, terrorists who blow up American oil wells are heroes," says company official Lartigue (Peter Capell). *"El Presidente* cannot risk his liberal image by sending us troops to chase patriots." The game must be played and a sop given to the largely impotent revolutionaries, despite the fact that the company owns the president, the nation, and essentially all of its resources. Lartigue reads from a jargon-filled Telex from the company that demands answers on production numbers despite the attack: "Limitations on production... emphasize attention immediate supply obligations, with minimum concern R&D." "What the hell is R&D?" oil well supervisor Corlette (Ramon Bieri) demands to know. "Research and development," Lartigue responds, both informing us that good money is not going to be thrown after bad in the backwater of Porvenir and signaling the Rand Corporation (whose name originated from "R&D"[9]), handmaiden to Cold War American dominion. The executive who sent the Telex is named "Weber," a possible allusion to sociologist and historian Max Weber, who documented the march of Protestant capitalism across the colonized globe.

Throughout *Sorcerer*, and especially during its chilling latter half, as the four men handle and retrieve the boxes of nitroglycerine-sweating dynamite left behind by the company to cap the oil well, we see the representatives of "civilization" deal with the ultimate test: the indifference of nature to their giant modern machines, to their desires, to their lives. All the features of the frontier landscape—catastrophic weather, crumbling narrow roads and rope bridges, encounters with the natives—become deadly threats in the face of the company's need for the explosives. Why is the dynamite this deep in the forest, hundreds of miles from the damaged oil well? We never find out. It's hinted that it's a military cache, but in the end, as with all aspects of the political and military power structure here (the military are seen brutally cracking down on an uprising triggered by the post-bombing deaths of natives working the well), the dynamite belongs to the company. An engineer (Chico Martínez) angrily demands of the soldier who accompanies him and Corlette to the shack containing the explosive: "When was this stuff last turned?" Without maintenance, without constant attention, civilization's tools become a dangerous alien cargo. Two hundred miles away, the oil fire burns off the company's profit, while these four men—scattered to the winds by their own crimes and their entanglement within a global system of exploitation and corruption—battle nature itself and encounter the pre-modern inhabitants in a crucible of mutual mistrust and misunderstanding, a common theme in Seventies cinema from Werner Herzog's *Aguirre: The Wrath of God* (1972) to Coppola's *Apocalypse Now* (1979).

Vincent Canby, in his original *New York Times* review, cites a brief sequence where a single native cavorts and mocks the four drivers as they slowly usher their trucks, the names "Sorcerer" and "Lazaro" ("Lazarus," in English) painted on their sides, through what looks like a clear-cut area of jungle, as "the most political moment in the film—a fine, strange scene."[10] In its collision of cultures and psychological priorities (the deathly danger of the labor demanded by the bosses versus the carefree attitude of this lone and happy native), the scene, as well as the repeating iconography that we glimpse throughout the film (the opening titles unfold over a still of an indigenous carving, and the oil company uses a similar-looking pre-Columbian icon in its insignia) encapsulate much of the Western suspicion of what the modern world was doing to humanity and nature, what modern man had "won" in his domination of and separation from nature: a job that can kill you for just enough money to merely survive another day.

In Ridley Scott's *Alien*, these same issues of colonialism, extractive economics, the liminal zones on the fringes of empire where "cargo" is of great importance, and the ordinary Joes who do the work to keep the machine running all come to a head in a crucible of sudden and shocking violence and body horror. Scott and screenwriters Dan O'Bannon and Ronald Shusett transpose the action to the near-future in outer space, but the problems and challenges facing the crew of the freighter *Nostromo* are straight out of a late-Seventies economic milieu that moviegoers would recognize on a gut level. *Alien*, in fact, collects a number of signifiers of the past century-plus of colonial plunder and war-making on planet Earth, combining them with thematic hints of both the cargo cult and then in-vogue theories about ancient astronauts visiting Earth in the distant past and leaving behind signs and wonders we moderns cannot understand. The famous opening sequence of the film spells out everything about the material and economic web that enfolds our cast: "Commercial towing vehicle *Nostromo*. Crew: 7. Cargo: Refinery processing, 20,000,000 tons of mineral ore. Course: Earth." *Nostromo* is, of course, a reference to Joseph Conrad's 1904 novel *Nostromo: A Tale of the Seaboard*, in which an Italian adventurer of the same name ("Our Man" or "*bosun*" in Italian) tries to capture a fortune in silver from a forbidding South American island and ends up a victim of his own greed and hubris. The starship *Nostromo* carries ore as well, but this is no trading vessel; it's purely a gargantuan tug and refinery, processing vast quantities of raw material extracted from a distant planet (or planets) on civilization's edge, now on its way back to the imperial core. Underlining how far from home the *Nostromo*'s mission has taken it, we watch the ship's crew waking from deep-sleep hibernation, a necessity only if the distances involved are beyond the human capacity to survive without dying of old age. Once again, science and reason allow humanity to defy nature in the name of profit.

Prematurely and mysteriously woken from this "hypersleep" by the receipt of a "distress" signal, the crew is called upon to interrupt their largely automated journey (ship's captain Dallas [Tom Skerritt] is directed by central computer "Mother") to personally investigate the signal, as per company directives and contractual obligations pointed out by Science Officer Ash (Ian Holm). In these early sequences, as they try to figure out where the signal is coming from, we hear references to planet Earth: Ripley says in her hail to the signal's senders that she is calling from "Commercial towing vehicle *Nostromo* out of the Solomons." Whether this refers to Earth's own Solomon Islands, one of the centers of the aforementioned World War II Pacific theater and home to the original cargo cult (Harry Dean Stanton's Brett wears a Hawaiian shirt, another echo of World War II and the GI Generation's vogue for South Pacific "Tiki" culture[11]), or some far-flung star system isn't spelled out, but Ripley's mention of it and her call to "Antarctica Traffic Control" evoke these remote outposts of contemporary postwar Western civilization.

The discovery of the alien eggs, the film's equivalent of *Sorcerer's* nitroglycerine-soaked dynamite, is an eerie experience, the homeliness of the *Nostromo's* crowded dining room and the detailed realism of the ship's compartments and corridors eclipsed by the aura of an intelligent alien-designed structure or ship (a giant ring) filled with majestic horrors. Outsider artist H.R. Giger's designs meld the hyper-technological with the messily organic, another pertinent juxtaposition of modern with primordial. Early in the film, Lambert observes that the *Nostromo* is seriously off-course, "just short of Zeta II Reticuli. We haven't reached the outer rim yet." This star system was central to one of UFO lore's most famous cases: it was home to the aliens who interracial New Hampshire couple Betty and Barney Hill claimed abducted them in 1961.[12] In directly referencing it, O'Bannon, Shusett, and Scott nod to one of the Seventies' most popular esoteric beliefs: the ancient astronaut popularized by Erich von Däniken's 1968 international bestseller, *Chariots of the Gods?* In the book, von Däniken, an amateur scholar and convicted fraudster,[13] asserted that the great engineering works of ancient and "primitive" humanity—the Easter Island moai, the Nazca lines, the Egyptian pyramids, ancient calendars both monumental (Stonehenge) and inscribed (the Mayan calendar), and many more besides—were the result of the influence of alien visitors with advanced technology. These visitors left behind their works—their "cargo," if you will—for von Däniken's ancients, who are often explicitly racialized and thus, it is implied, inferior: "It is difficult to believe that [the Mayan calendar] originated from a jungle people."[14] Von Däniken and his successors' theories recapitulate the colonialist "cargo cult" lens for viewing pre-modern cultures on a cosmic scale—cosmic in terms of both space and time. And just as the cargo cult concept insulated the postwar Western world from its responsibilities for the traumatic clash of cultures on a geopolitical level, so too do ancient astronaut theories insulate our modern world from continuity with both ancient and pre-modern peoples who accomplished so much technologically without the benefit of Enlightenment reason.[15]

Upon touchdown on the alien planet, Ash analyzes the atmosphere, saying that "It's almost primordial": the conditions of ancient Earth. Kane (John Hurt) and Ash, the only two British members of the cast, with accents and attitudes that might signify "true" colonialism for many of the Americans viewing the film, encounter the ancient astronauts' magnificent works with the glee of discovery and a lust for power, respectively. The giant "space jockey" left behind on this seemingly colonial outpost merely slumbers, surrounded by thousands of eggs nestled like *Sorcerer*'s dynamite, or gold in some distant "native" temple. (Steven Spielberg's first film of the 1980s proper, 1981's *Raiders of the Lost Ark*, was about a doughty adventurer who raids ancient ruins; unlike *Sorcerer*, it made hundreds of millions of dollars.) But in *Alien*, this nest of eggs is a symbolic reversal of the disease and pathogens that

European colonists brought to the New World, with equally deadly results. It is pilot and executive officer Kane, the soon-to-be incubator of the alien threat, who is most intent on surveying the scene of weird yet alluring alien treasures: "We've come this far, we must go on! We have to go on!" Meanwhile, Ash, under secret direction from the company, encourages the exchange of pathogens, just as Europeans did for their various colonial enterprises.[16] When, after the deaths of Dallas and the other crew members, she discovers the truth—"Insure [sic] return of organism for analysis. All other considerations secondary. Crew expendable"—Ripley is forced to confront Ash, who is revealed to be an android. After being brutally dispatched by Parker (Yaphet Kotto), Ash's decapitated head sits like a pagan idol in a pool of the white fluid that runs through its artificial veins, speaking the giddy prophecies of the company's capture of the priceless specimen. Ash calls the alien he's midwifed into being "a survivor, unclouded by conscience, remorse, or delusions of morality": the perfect capitalist tool for war-making, bestowed upon the company thanks to its relentless penetration into the distant frontier, a jungle filled with ancient temples, idols, and magic.

Sorcerer ends with Scanlon the lone survivor, after rebels in the mountains take out Nilo and a blow-out on a dangerous cliffside road kills Kassem and Victor. Scanlon escapes the rebels, but Sorcerer the truck dies, leaving him to tote the dynamite by hand across an uncanny, forbidding landscape full of petrified features that looks an awful lot like an alien planet. Friedkin chose the Bisti Badlands in New Mexico, in fact, for their resemblance to a "place of ancient magic... a landscape of dreams."[17] Scanlon staggers, desperate to survive the quest upon which he has lost every companion to the implacable jungle. As the oil company workers mob the last man standing, careful to relieve him (gently) of his precious cargo, he collapses: mission accomplished. After he recovers, the company holds up its end of the bargain, giving him papers and pay to escape Porvenir finally and forever. But the web of money and corruption and crime that he thought he left behind in the States catches up to him: as Scanlon dances away with an elderly waitress at the cantina, the Mafia chieftain's hitmen and Vinnie (Randy Jurgensen), the man who sold Scanlon his escape in New Jersey, coolly exit their vehicle and approach the bar. The camera does not follow them inside, but we hear the faint pop of a gunshot. The cinematic audience, who has traced every drop of sweat, every scream of terror, every frantic glance for the past two hours, is denied even the satisfaction of seeing him die like a movie hero of old—with his dignity intact. Like an industrial process behind the closed doors of a factory, Scanlon is merely eliminated, surplus to requirements.

Ripley, too, is trapped and alone, the company's dangerous living cargo trying to break into her escape pod and destroy her. She destroys it instead, but her fate, like Scanlon's, is profoundly ambiguous (until, that is, the big-budget Jim Cameron-directed sequel that *Alien*'s profitability made inevitable). She dictates the final ship's log of the *Nostromo*: "The other members of the crew," whom she honors by naming, even Ash, "are dead. Cargo and ship destroyed. I should reach the frontier in about six weeks." The language of colonization rises up one last time, the mention of "frontier" intimating that the actions the company commits beyond the empire's boundaries are not crimes but simply the price of doing efficient global (or interstellar) business, cutting losses and maximizing profit at the expense of human lives. Ripley's and Scanlon's mutually fatalistic and final "fuck you" to the bosses is a declaration that they are more than just cogs in the machinery of capital. Sole survivors, in this brief defiance they have regained something of their humanity before settling into an uncertain sleep.

7. "PLEASE DON'T BLOW UP THE DOMES": *SILENT RUNNING* AND *PHASE IV*

To the sound of an elegiac score, 1972's *Silent Running* begins with a series of slow close-up shots of lush flora and fauna. Snails crawl over leaves, turtles peer up out of streams, toads squat on damp rocks—and the camera eventually encounters a naked man with long hair swimming blissfully in what appears to be a natural pool. Played by Bruce Dern, at the time best known for his portrayals of wild-eyed psychos, this is the film's protagonist, the subtly named Freeman Lowell. But Lowell isn't another free-spirited cowboy communing with the wilderness, as the next shot makes clear. Anticipating the evangelizing mood that hangs over the whole film, he now appears clad in a long-hooded robe, engaged in conversation with a rabbit like some hippy Saint Francis. The camera pulls back, revealing that the idyllic forest is not actually untamed nature at all; it's surrounded by a massive geometric frame, beyond which we can see only stars. Lowell's prelapsarian idyll is soon shattered by the arrival of three other humans who, racing "Cyclops" buggies, tear up his beloved turf and flower beds. "Do I have to put signs up here to keep you guys the hell off my grass?" shouts Lowell, as enraged as if they'd committed an act of sacrilege.

Later, as he prepares himself a meal of foraged vegetables

in a futuristic-looking kitchen, Lowell presses a button that opens a hatch in the wall. The viewpoint switches to outside looking in and, accompanied by stirring martial music, a voice solemnly intones,

> On this first day of a new century, we humbly beg forgiveness, and dedicate these last forests of our once beautiful nation, in the hope that they will one day return and grace our fouled Earth. Until that day, may God bless these forests, and the brave men who care for them.

The camera pulls further and further back, revealing that the window Lowell is looking out of is in fact set in the hull of a vast spacecraft, its flank decorated with the United States flag and the American Airlines logo.

This scene introduces the future *Silent Running* inhabits—a future where, for its protection, the scant remaining plant and non-human animal life on Earth has been gathered up and packed off into interplanetary space aboard a fleet of space freighters, each named after a United States national park. It's an absurd conceit that immediately tells us the film is far closer to being a tonal poem than anything resembling scientific possibility. In fact, practically nothing in *Silent Running* makes any sense at all on a rational level, the film's undeniable power generated almost entirely by the surreal aesthetic world it's set in, which plays out like a fever dream of techno-fetishism and cosmic ecology colliding.

Lowell and the three other men we've met crew the *Valley Forge*, a descendant of the real-life *Essex*-class aircraft carrier of the same name (decommissioned during the Vietnam War) in which most of the film's interiors were shot as a way to cut costs. The spaceship's exterior is clearly inspired by the Expo Tower at the 1970 Osaka Expo, the work of Japanese architect Kiyonori Kikutake, one of the founders of the postwar architectural movement called Metabolism, which aimed to fuse ideas about architectural megastructures with ideas about organic biological growth. Resembling "horizontal Eiffel Towers attached to gigantic oil tankers," as Vincent Canby described them in his review in the *New York Times*,[1] this folding of battle-scarred and mothballed military-industrial-complex power inside a superstructure of nominally progressive architecture feels peculiarly apt. The reveal of the ship is an astonishing moment, and introduces the audience to the structures housing the forests: vast transparent domes attached to the terminus of the *Valley Forge*'s superstructure.

A potent symbol of both domesticity and institutional power across many cultures, domes had sprung up across North America in the preceding decade like the sleek caps of psychotropic mushrooms. Before that, architects like Wallace Neff proposed domed "bubble homes" in the 1940s,[2] and one of the first completed works of Italian-born architect Paolo Soleri, creator of the proto-hippy concept of "arcology" (described as "the fusion of architecture with ecology"),[3] was the 1948 dome house he built in the Arizona desert. In the late 1950s, ufologist George Van Tassel built his domed "Integratron" near Joshua Tree in California, which he claimed could cause cellular rejuvenation and allow research into anti-gravity and time travel.[4] The geodesic dome, however, popularized by the unlikely countercultural guru and self-promoting quasi-grifter R. Buckminster Fuller in his 1969 book, *Operating Manual for Spaceship Earth*, was of a different domain: a restless generation began to see in the shape a symbol of a new kind of future.

Fuller's signature design was built using a three-dimensional framework of regularly repeating forms made out of strong, lightweight construction materials that were cheap and ideal for rapid assembly. He had originally designed it after World War II along lines laid down by German engineers and architects of the interwar period,[5] and it was rapidly integrated into the defense complex and used for structures like the radomes of the US Air Force's Distant Early Warning Line in the Canadian arctic.[6] Over the years, Fuller lived two parallel existences, the first consolidating his creation's totemic position in the burgeoning counterculture, the second brokering its usage within the Establishment. As his ideas began to gain traction among college students in the second half of the Sixties, hundreds of back-to-the-land hippies started using his elementary architectural example as the basis for homes and gathering places. One of the many venues that helped aficionados and utopians figure out how to build their own domed spaces was a guidebook assembled by a group of students and facilitators at a freeform California high school.[7] Inspired by their own experimentation with building geodesic structures, and directly assisted by the runaway success of Stewart Brand's *Whole Earth Catalog*, these DIY builders and educators released a pair of "Domebooks" in 1970 and 1971 for sale to the general public, with *Domebook One* more of a straight-ahead how-to construction guide and *Domebook 2* acting as a clearinghouse for correspondence from a panoply of counterculture builders. To them, the dome was democratic, unthreatening, un-square, mystical, and, despite often being made of aluminum and plastic, somehow innately *natural*.

And things being natural was increasingly becoming an issue. By the onset of the Seventies, anxiety about the side effects of industrial culture was peaking, and the dome fetish was part of the larger ecological movement driven by a growing awareness of the environmental damage the Western way of life was wreaking on the planet. Bestsellers like marine biologist and conservationist Rachel Carson's 1962 *Silent Spring* and Anne and Paul Ehrlich's 1968 *The Population Bomb* had shunted previously marginal ecological concerns into the mainstream, and events like the oil well blowout that killed huge amounts of animal life off the Santa Barbara coast in 1969 led to 1970's Environmental Rights Day, with the first Earth Day taking place in the spring of the same year.[8] Nixon's 1970 Reorganization Plan No. 3 added the Environmental Protection Agency to the federal roster with the mandate of consolidating efforts to protect America's air, water, and soil, and giving environmental protection efforts a fiercer executive independence.[9] Increasing numbers of environmentally themed public service announcements started appearing on TV screens and featured characters ranging from Smokey the Bear to the "Crying Indian," a lone Native American warrior (in reality an Italian-American character actor who called himself Iron Eyes Cody) traveling across a majestic American countryside soiled with the symbols of twentieth-century "progress"—factories, smokestacks, highways, and gargantuan late-Sixties automobiles—with the aim of encouraging Americans of all ages to think about their impact on the physical and natural environment.[10]

Silent Running's unlikely parent was Douglas Trumbull, a visual effects prodigy who, while still in his early twenties, landed the gig of special effects supervisor for *2001: A Space Odyssey* after *To the Moon and Beyond*, a space travel film he worked on for the 1964 World's Fair in New York, caught Stanley Kubrick's eye.[11] *Silent Running* was produced under the aegis of the unit Universal Studios set up in the aftermath of 1969's incredibly successful *Easy Rider* to fund its own "independent" films, hoping to connect with enthusiastic and repeat-viewing young cinemagoers. The unit commissioned five features, each of them given a budget of a million dollars and freedom from the interference typical of studio movies.[12] Written by Deric Washburn and Michael Cimino with Steven Bochco, *Silent Running* had originally been conceived of by Trumbull as "a straightforward, simple story about a guy who runs a space shuttle, who gets fired from his job, and out of revenge takes off with the ship," as Cimino put it in a 1977 interview.[13] Over the course of pre-production, though, the film's focus shifted repeatedly, first to include alien contact and then, thanks to Cimino, landing on the ecological concerns that were increasingly seen as one of the defining issues of the day. "My contribution to *Silent Running*," said Cimino, "was in providing the notion of [...] saving the forests."[14] The script was one of the first two that Cimino co-wrote after abandoning a career in advertising, the other being 1973 Clint Eastwood vehicle *Magnum Force*, a telling nod to the confusing overlap between the environmental movement and the deeply embedded mythology of the saintly lone frontiersman who enjoys a sacred bond with nature—and has a penchant for blowing holes in the things that trouble him.

That Cimino's take would be shallow is unsurprising, especially given his admission in 2005 that he found the science fiction genre boring: "most people who write science fiction are running away from life to create a fictional world. I'd rather have real life."[15] Cimino's idea of what constitutes real life is probably better captured in what was his most successful film, 1978's *The Deer Hunter*, which, though in many ways deeply affecting, was also ferociously criticized upon release for what many saw as the racism inherent in its portrayal of the Viet Cong as crazed sadists, a charge Cimino attempted to sidestep by claiming the film wasn't even really about Vietnam anyway.[16] His reluctance to engage with the opportunities offered by science fiction is especially galling given that *Silent Running* was released the same year as Ursula K. Le Guin's *The Word for World is Forest* and John Brunner's *The Sheep Look Up,* both vastly more mature and nuanced works of eco-sci-fi than *Silent Running,* and both proof of how well-equipped science fiction actually was and is at engaging with the issues at hand.

Lowell, we find out, is the ship's botanist and ecologist, and spends most of his time caring for the plants and animals in the *Valley Forge*'s domes until their hypothetical return to Earth and the reforestation of the planet. The three other members of the crew, on the other hand, regular working Joes, are happy to spend their twelve-month tour strutting about in their dapper uniforms (actually Bogner ski suits), racing their buggies, and hanging around the rec room with its robot arm-equipped circular pool table, trying to forget how bored they are. All they want is to return to an Earth where the temperature is a constant 75 degrees and unemployment has been eliminated—a comfortable conformity that Lowell, predictably, despises. The *Valley Forge*'s crew is completed by three robotic "drones": little two-legged robots resembling animated television sets with enlarged speakers and shrunken screens that handle the drudgery of running the ship. Played by Mark Persons, Steve Brown, Cheryl Sparks, and Larry Whisenhunt, all bilateral amputees, the drones—along with the domes—are the real heart of the film, and provide what is by far its most resonant motif. Like *2001*'s HAL 9000, they feel far more alive than the human characters who are nominally the center of the narrative. In fact, in many ways, *Silent Running* would probably have been a far better and more honest film without the humans altogether.

The conflict is thus established between the nature child and a soulless, uncaring humankind that has allowed its relationship with nature to degenerate to the point that it prefers "synthetic" food to the real vegetables Lowell grows in the domes. It's no surprise, then, that orders soon arrive to jettison—and, for no clear reason, destroy—the domes and return the freighters to commercial service. The market's profit imperative will not be denied. Lowell's crewmates are overjoyed, but, after four of the six domes have been jettisoned and blown up, Lowell snaps. He kills the affable Potts (John Keenan), the crewmate who shows up to plant nuclear explosives in Lowell's favorite dome, then jettisons and detonates the other remaining dome after trapping the remaining two crewmen inside it. After sending out an SOS saying that the *Valley Forge* is in trouble, Lowell pilots the ship through the rings of Saturn, jettisoning cargo containers from the hold in the hope that they will be interpreted as debris and convince American Airlines that pursuit is pointless. Inexplicably, the captain of the *Berkshire*, the ship sent in pursuit, suggests that Lowell might want to consider suicide, but Lowell demurs. "No… I just don't think that I'd ever be able to do anything like that." "God bless you…" replies the other man, "you're a hell of an American," to which Lowell thoughtfully whispers to himself: "I think I am." What exactly the admirable qualities of "an American" are supposed to represent in the logic of the film remains a mystery, given that it seems to be America that is behind launching the remains of the Earth's ecosystem into space, and American Airlines that has decided to incinerate Earth's remaining flora and fauna. But despite Lowell's attempts to convince the *Valley*

Forge's owners that the ship has been destroyed, the company, reluctant to lose a valuable asset, continues the pursuit, and the film ends with Lowell ejecting the final remaining dome into space—with the final remaining drone left aboard to tend to the forest—before blowing up the *Valley Forge* and committing a thoroughly pointless and un-American suicide.

Though purportedly the hero of the piece, the prickly Lowell is a less than sympathetic character, the vintage Smokey the Bear conservation pledge tacked to the wall above his bed hinting at an emotional development stuck in the simple binaries of pre-pubescence. By turns hectoring and sulky, he's the worst kind of smug, sanctimonious hippy: yes, in this case Lowell definitely has moral right on his side, but it seems like that might just be a coincidence. There's a Freeman Lowell for every situation, after all, and some of them would just as happily bump off anyone opposing the causes dear to them that *aren't* as justified as saving the planet's plant and animal life. Despite reminiscing on how fond he was of his crewmates after he's killed them, we never see him displaying towards them, when they're still alive, the patience and affection he lavishes on the non-human life that fills the domes—perhaps because, like the drones, the plants and animals can't answer back.

And Lowell's relationship with the drones is ambiguous too: what does it say about him that the only "people" he gets along with are the ones he programs to obey him? In the latter part of the film, it's almost as though Lowell has created his own little eco-cult, with its isolated compound and brainwashed members following his orders as they prepare for the inevitable Kool-Aid moment. Perhaps this is, in its way, Cimino's unwitting commentary on families and the self-obsessed, controlling father figures who sometimes program their mental and social circuitry? After he has murdered the human crew, Lowell decides to give the little robots names in place of numbers, taking inspiration, despite his freethinking credentials, from another behemoth of American industry and settling on Huey, Dewey, and Louie. What do they represent to him? Friends? Children? Servants? When one of the little robots is swept off the hull into space while the *Valley Forge* is flying through the rings of Saturn, Lowell's reaction is surprisingly cold, sounding more like a jaded factory foreman or resigned platoon sergeant than an eco-warrior: the robot "got careless—and you see what happens when you get careless?" And later in the film, after Lowell accidentally drives into and fatally damages Huey, one of the two remaining drones, while racing through the hold in a buggy, he tells it, "You have to come with me because you're just not working well enough to help Louis," before promptly whisking Huey off to be euthanized for the crime of being unproductive. For someone as manically committed to life as he presents himself as being, he's not too sentimental about the deaths of those around him.

Silent Running might make little sense, but some aspects of the film are strangely prescient: like *Alien* (1979) seven years later, it posits a future that is inhabited by normal working people who are neither heroic astronauts, heroic scientists, nor heroic military elite—albeit (in the case of *Silent Running*) normal working people who aren't women, or, for that matter, anyone who isn't white. It's also a future in which humanity's engagement with nature and the cosmos must inevitably take place through profit-hungry private corporations, as opposed to a public-minded body working for the good of all: private industry given custodianship of public services. All of these ideas have a long history in science fiction literature, but they find some of their first critical visual representations here.

Though clearly a well-intentioned film whose heart is in the right place, *Silent Running* often seems to be trafficking reactionary ideas hidden in swathes of cathartic emotion and sentiment, and in the process captures something about how approaches to hugely complex issues like safeguarding the natural environment have often developed: through the lens of individual, as opposed to collective, action. Like many films of its time (1970's *Five Easy Pieces*, 1971's *Dirty Harry*, 1976's *Taxi Driver*, 1979's *Apocalypse Now*), the "heroic" human here is a borderline psychopath—a wild-eyed, solipsistic man-child driven over the edge by the stupidity and venality of the people he is forced to share the world with. And the film's vision of nature too is oddly regressive: as perfect and fake-looking as some greenery display in the mall, there's none of the dirt and decay of real nature, no tetanus or shit, only a romanticized, sanitized version invested with a glow of inherent goodness. At the same time, the film radiates an oddly reassuring faith in technology that seems to run counter to its principal message— after all, the care of the last remaining shreds of nature is left in the hands of a robot. In fact, *Silent Running*'s abiding image is perhaps not the film's mawkish (though incredibly effective) finale, where we see Dewey, small and alone, tending to the space garden with Lowell's little watering can as the surviving dome drifts off into space, but the poignant shots from earlier in the movie of the little drones dutifully going about their daily business—a strangely powerful and haunting metaphor for us humans struggling through our own lives on our own satellite of the sun.

A fake indie film co-opting eco-cred, yet that hums with dissonant techno-utopianism, what is *Silent Running*'s point, if indeed it has one? Perhaps the best illustration of the contradiction at the film's heart comes during an argument with his fellow dome-tenders, the same ones he tells at the beginning of the film to get off his lawn, when Lowell opines that "There is no more beauty, and there's no more imagination. And there are no frontiers left to conquer." Beneath the rhetoric is a vision of the world where ecology and self-realization are inevitably tied to conquest and colonization. Despite its science fiction trappings, at the end of the day, *Silent Running* is a Western after all; Lowell isn't saving the forests for humanity, he's saving them for himself: a private (and privatized) place he can hoard and monopolize to get away from the rest of the human race.

The dome in Saul Bass's *Phase IV* (1974) is designed to keep nature out, not in. Released the year before 1975's *Jaws* pushed the "nature taking revenge" genre into overdrive, and despite posters for the film that featured giant ants and slogans like "The day the earth was turned into a cemetery," and "ravenous invaders controlled by a terror out in space… commanded to annihilate the world," *Phase IV* is less creature feature than existential horror film—a philosophical reflection on humankind's lack of primacy in the universe and the arbitrary events and conditions that have, for the moment, given us control of our planet. The film posits what might be called a post-human perspective, in which a suddenly out-evolved human race finds itself on the receiving end of natural selection: a vision that puts it at odds with the paternalistic and androcentric worldview of *Silent Running*, with its Christ-like savior of the natural realm immolating himself with holy fire as he dispatches the last remaining trace of the garden of Eden into the void.

Director Saul Bass and writer Mayo Simon conceived of

the film as a riposte to *2001: A Space Odyssey*, except here it would be ants, not humans, who receive the fateful signal from outer space.[17] Unlike the enemy in *Phase IV*'s ant-attack ancestor, 1954's *Them!*, the ants in *Phase IV* remain as tiny as ever, their menace deriving from their newfound intelligence. The film begins with an unexplained cosmic event that sparks the rapid evolution of a group of ants in the Arizona desert, triggering a completely unprecedented situation: the ants begin communicating and cooperating across species and organize to rid the area of threats to their welfare. These threats include the inhabitants of Paradise City, a now-abandoned tract development whose signs for a country club and golf course still loom out of the emptiness, and whose disintegrating houses may be a nod to the scene in *Them!* where the ants, grown huge after exposure to radiation from atomic bomb testing in the New Mexico desert, tear apart dwellings in search of sugar.

The ants' antagonists are scowling middle-aged scientist Ernest Hubbs (Nigel Davenport), who has come to the area to investigate the situation, and James Lesko (Michael Murphy), the young expert in computers and game theory he has brought along to help. Clad in jeans and sneakers, Lesko is an easygoing, relaxed, vaguely Jimmy Carter-esque young American, while Hubbs is an intense and supercilious Brit. They are introduced to us while driving along the roads between the now never-to-be-developed lots of Paradise City, a scene that immediately creates a mood of impermanence and emphasizes humanity's tenuous grip on the Earth. The two set up their headquarters—an air-conditioned silver geodesic dome packed with computerized technology—near the five tall columns of dried mud, each with a slit-like mouth at the top: the watchtowers of the ant colony. While

Trumbull's domes are transparent and glowing, their bounty of life visible from outside, Bass's is designed to hide what it contains. It's just as mute and inscrutable to the outside world as the ants' towers seem to Hubbs.

Hubbs and Lesko visit the sites of the ants' increasingly frequent sorties into the human world: a cornfield where (anticipating a motif that Steven Spielberg would develop in *Close Encounters of the Third Kind*) the ants have carved a vast crop-circle-like square-within-a-circle symbol out of the plants, killing any sheep that got in their way, and a nearby farm whose owner, Mr. Eldridge (Alan Gifford), is planning to defend his homestead with a moat of burning gasoline. While they carry out their studies of the ants, who at this point have been silent for several weeks, Hubbs is also forced to fend off the increasingly pressing demands of the university's accounts department, which threatens to cut the project's funding unless Hubbs and Lesko start to produce results. Rattled into recklessness, Hubbs blows up the ants' observation towers in an attempt to provoke them into making an appearance, but instead provokes an offensive from the enraged insects as they attempt to defend and secure their territory. The scene resonates like some strange, topsy-turvy foreshadowing of the grim events of 9/11, and the violent American reaction that followed them.

The ants attack the Eldridge homestead, forcing the elderly couple and their orphaned teenage granddaughter, Kendra (Lynne Frederick), to flee in the family pick-up, but the escape attempt ends in disaster when Mrs. Eldridge (Helen Horton) reacts hysterically to the appearance of ants in the truck's cab, causing the vehicle to come off the road. The family tries to make its way on foot to the dome, but a battle is underway between the ants and Hubbs, who has retaliated with "Yellow," one of the facility's three color-coded pesticide sprays—a plot device clearly meant to evoke the "Rainbow Herbicides" (like Agent Orange) used in the Vietnam War, and by extension the links between university research and the war machine. The war is also brought to mind by the collectivist nature of the ant society itself: tunneling guerillas attempting to protect their culture and territory.

Caught in the toxic chemical snowstorm, Eldridge and his wife are killed. The following morning, the two scientists emerge from their dome clad in silver hazmat suits. Before them, cloaked in yellow scum, is a surreal battlefield strewn with everyday objects like strollers, birdcages, coffee cups, as well as the huddled corpses of Mr. and Mrs. Eldridge. A dazed Kendra emerges from a storm shelter and collapses to the ground. They carry her into the dome where, despite Lesko's insistence that the girl needs medical help, Hubbs refuses, replying that it would bring about the failure of the project. As the two argue, a hysterical (of course) Kendra smashes a container, releasing ants into the dome. One of them bites Hubbs.

After samples of "Yellow" have been dragged down through the beautiful geometries of their city into the depths of the colony and fed to a queen ant, who begins producing yellow larvae that will be resistant to the pesticide, the ants resume their attacks on the dome by building a series of reflectors around it that concentrate the hot desert sunlight on its surface. Hubbs and Lesko retaliate by blasting the reflectors with high-pitched sound, causing them to collapse and dealing catastrophe to the ant world. The scenes that follow, where we see the ants laying out the bodies of their dead in their underground chambers, are mesmeric, and far more emotionally charged than anything we see in the human world (testimony to the talents of Ken Middleham, the expert in insect close-up photography who shot the film's beautiful and compelling ant society). The ants short-circuit the dome's communications, cutting off the humans from the rest of the world, and their reply to the geometric message Lesko gets off prompts him to wonder who is actually studying who.

Kendra sneaks out of the dome and Hubbs, his arm dangerously swollen from the ant bite and his behavior erratic, follows her, only to be swallowed up by a trap and devoured as Lesko watches in horror. Convinced now that the only way of stopping the ants is to kill their queen, Lesko climbs down into the nest with a canister of "Blue" pesticide. In an underground chamber, Kendra emerges from beneath the sand that covers the floor and holds out her arms to him. Over the trippy montage sequence of surreal images that follows, a voiceover from Lesko says, "We knew then we were being changed and made part of their world. We didn't know for what purpose, but we knew we would be told." Gnomic as it is, with its implication of humanity's now passive role before the evolutionary dictates of the ants, the ending is less strange than Bass's original finale, a much longer montage that shows Kendra and Lesko traversing the strange, labyrinthine new world of the ants, intercut with images of faceless people, burning hands, and humans laid out like butterflies in display cases, and which seems to end with humankind moving to a new stage of evolution under the ants' supervision.[18] Cut by the studio, it's a far cry from the bellicose ending of *Them!*, where the US Army slaughters the mutant ants with flamethrowers.

In Lowell and Hubbs, both films share to some extent a vision of man that, intentionally or unwittingly, is deeply unflattering: self-obsessed, manic, petulant, and dangerous, they are driven to the edge of madness when their worldview is challenged.

WE ARE THE MUTANTS

One of the two may be "right," and the other "wrong," but their positions spring from the same self-referential matrices. And given the central role masculinity plays in both films, it's instructive to look at the way women are portrayed in them—or rather, how they are portrayed in *one* of them: the only traces of women in *Silent Running* are Joan Baez's singing voice and a photograph of a little girl tacked to a wall. The women in *Phase IV* are consigned to one of three reductive modes: diffident shrews who become hysterical at the sight of ants; nubile, sensitive ingenues who do the same; and alluring physical scenery, as in the beautifully shot but unambiguously lecherous sequence showing an ant climbing Kendra's body beneath her clothing. A sympathetic reading might be that these female characters are at least engaging emotionally with the world around them, even if that engagement takes the form of hysteria, instead of closing themselves off in stoic machismo like Hubbs or juvenile glibness like Lesko.

And what about the domes? Two domes, one built to protect nature from the rapaciousness of humankind, the other built to protect humankind from the realization that it too is a part of nature. In *Silent Running*, humanity is the literal savior of nature, the center of everything, while the humanity of *Phase IV* is no hero, its self-aggrandizing pettiness triggering an inter-species war that hands control of the planet over to other creatures—demonstrably collectivist creatures. Both films are, in their way, religious. Dern's sainted holy fool uses explosive force to martyr himself (as well as several other people) for the cause of non-human nature, while *Phase IV*—clearly the more "ecological" of the two, with its emphasis on decentralizing the position of *Homo sapiens* in the natural world—hints at humanity being given an opportunity to transcend itself thanks to the intervention of (literally) heavenly forces. Or maybe the humanity of *Phase IV* will turn out to be nothing at all—just another superseded species on its way to extinction or transformation.

A poignant detail emerges from the stories in *Domebook 2*: for all the hopes the structures inspired of a new life outside a reactionary, oppressive society, ultimately the domes weren't very good at keeping their inhabitants all that warm, dry, or safe. "Probably the main reason there are not more dome homes," says someone in the "Sealing" section, "is the problem of leakage."[19] Beneath the two-dimensional narratives of *Silent Running* and *Phase IV* is the implication that, despite their builders' good intentions, the cracks in the domes, along with the rain and the wind, also let in the inevitable human defects that doomed them.

8. "A LITTLE HUMAN COMPASSION": *DEATH WISH* AND *ESCAPE FROM NEW YORK*

John Carpenter wrote the original script for 1981's *Escape from New York* in 1974, inspired by the same year's *Death Wish*—specifically, director Michael Winner's seedy portrayal of New York "as a kind of jungle."[1] Both films did extremely well commercially and, along with *The Taking of Pelham One Two Three* (1974), *Taxi Driver* (1976), and *The Warriors* (1979), are representative visions of late-twentieth-century New York as a contemporary Sodom and Gomorrah, the cosmopolitan verve and neon lights of Broadway snuffed out by carnivalesque decadence and sweeping material decay. Beyond the sharing of a storied setting, however, the films are sure ideological enemies: Winner's starkly violent world is the product of rampant criminal evil that is innate and therefore incorrigible, while Carpenter's hangs on "the man": a belligerent, fascist American police state.

Death Wish follows a liberal pacifist architect, Paul Kersey (Charles Bronson), who turns to vigilantism after his wife (Hope Lange) is killed and his daughter (Kathleen Tolan) is raped by street thugs. Though Kersey says little during the course of the film—his gun, we're to understand, becomes his voice—we find out what we need to know very early on. Kersey has just returned to New York's Upper West Side after vacationing in Maui, the gridlock, grime, and bluster of the former set against the latter's breezy paradise of noble savages untroubled by the strictures of urban civilization. On his first day back to work, Kersey's colleague Sam (William Redfield) immediately hits him with an account of violent crimes committed during his absence: "there were 15 murders the first week and 21 last week in this goddamn city." Sam laments that "decent people" are going to have to move away, and Kersey chastises him, noting that not everyone is wealthy enough to escape to greener pastures. Then comes the following exchange:

SAM: Christ, you are such a bleeding-heart liberal, Paul.

PAUL: My heart bleeds a little for the underprivileged, yeah.

SAM: The underprivileged are beating our goddamn brains out! You know what I say? Stick 'em in concentration camps. That's what I say.

This Gestapo proposition is exactly what we must come to accept, on some level, for the logic of *Death Wish* to work, and it's exactly this absurd what-if that Carpenter and co-writer Nick Castle exploit in *Escape from New York*. Carpenter's film opens in 1997, nine years after the US crime rate jumped 400% and "the once great city of New York" became "the one maximum security prison"—a concentration camp, if you will—"for the entire country." The United States Police Force (USPF) surrounds Manhattan Island Prison, but there are no guards or soldiers inside. Airborne suppression of escape attempts, as well as the occasional food drop, are as close as the authorities get to the prisoners. It's like the desert survival course of Peter Watkins' *Punishment Park*, except here there is not even the suggestion, however hollow, that there's a finish line, and freedom beyond.

That the New York of *Death Wish* could inspire a science fiction or fantasy film is not as counterintuitive as it sounds. In Winner's hands, the city resembles a paranoid phantasm: the streets are nearly derelict after dark, save for prowlers and ominously costumed revelers swinging balloon bouquets; the shadows are all-consuming abysses; the cops turn their backs on obvious criminals about to commit bodily harm; and the "underprivileged" are everywhere—murderous vermin scuttling from gutter to gutter when they're not attempting to maul the one man foolhardy enough to challenge them. The atmosphere is so unreal that Roger Ebert makes the connection to a future dystopia in his positive review of Winner's film, which

> gives us a New York in the grip of a reign of terror; this doesn't look like 1974, but like one of those bloody future cities in science-fiction novels about anarchy in the twenty-first century.[2]

Escape from New York simply follows through on Winner's glorification of frontier justice. The lone vigilante becomes the autocratic USPF, and Manhattan, bereft of any rule of law or controlling authority, becomes an anarchic state controlled by rival gangs. We see the same shadows, the same empty streets, the same sprawling rust and graffiti, and we feel the same imminent peril, only more exaggerated: overturned cars, burned-out buildings and crumbled masonry, severed heads mounted on parking meters, all passingly lit by the blaze of rubbish fires. It's not so much the "ordinary" prisoners of

Manhattan who resemble the villains of *Death Wish*, but the "crazies," mindless cannibals who emerge from the sewers after dark to feed.

Though both films are rooted in fantasy—Carpenter's explicitly, Winner's surreptitiously—the soaring violence in urban America at the time was a reality. Violent crime in the US shot up by 270% between 1960 and 1980[3], the "biggest single jump [...] occurring in 1974," the year *Death Wish* came out.[4] Not quite 400%, but still pretty grisly. The brutality would metastasize in the cities between 1984 and 1991—the historical peak year—largely because of the crack cocaine epidemic. New York City itself was so close to bankruptcy in 1975 that police officers were poised to serve the papers on the city's banks.[5] The politicians chose austerity, and public services were cut drastically: the Department of Health budget was slashed by 20%, while the NYPD "lost 20% of its workforce, eliminated the youth unit and the organized crime squad, and cut the narcotics squad by 33%."[6] (Cops were pulled off of subway duty to cover the streets, making the only means of transportation for most residents particularly dangerous.) Community health and psychiatric clinics were scrapped, as were youth centers and job training programs. Meanwhile, unemployment stood at almost 10%, then an all-time high. It's into this gutted, lawless town that Paul Kersey rides, the mad as hell "ordinary" guy who would single-handedly exterminate the Big Apple's rotten inner core. A week into his rampage, muggings go down by half, and the humiliated district attorney (Fred Scollay) and police commissioner (Stephen Elliott) tell the police inspector (Vincent Gardenia) not to arrest Kersey ("I don't want a martyr on my hands," says the DA), but to "scare him off": a city full of vigilantes, and the presumptive lack of non-vigilante-related crime to follow, would put both of them out of office. At least some audiences, their fears and frustrations pinned squarely to the malignant faces of the underclass, cheered in the theater every time Kersey gave a bad guy a taste of his own medicine.[7]

If Winner's metropolis rots from the inside out and the bottom up, then Carpenter's poison moves in the other direction. The criminals are endemically corrupt because the state is endemically corrupt—because the *global* state, the reigning superpowers, are endemically corrupt. Part of the thrill of *Escape from New York* is anticipating the Biblical comeuppance we know the world deserves, the proverbial "flood of waters upon the earth." And if the ruinous landscape of *Escape from New York* looks a little *too* apocalyptic, that's because most of the film was shot for cheap in a section of downtown St. Louis that had been ravaged by fire in 1976, a section so devastated by urban blight to begin with—amidst the general decline of the Rust Belt, St. Louis lost nearly 30% of its residents between 1970 and 1980—that the city never bothered to clean it up.[8] As bad as the prisoners of 1997 have it, at least they're not beholden to slumlords and gerrymandering, and they're essentially as free as they can be (no one who lives in Manhattan wants to go to the Bronx or Queens, anyway). All they have to do is stay alive in "the worlds they have made."

As *Escape from New York* begins, leftist terrorists have hijacked Air Force One en route to a "peace summit" with China and Russia. They announce, in rhetoric that's not unlike something from a Weather Underground or Symbionese Liberation Army communiqué, that the President "will perish in the inhuman dungeon of his own imperialist prison" before crashing the plane into Downtown Manhattan (an uncomfortable scene in 1981, shortly after the Iran hostage crisis ended; an eerily chilling sequence now). The President

(Donald Pleasance) ejects in an escape pod seconds before the crash, but is taken hostage by the prison's most powerful gang, the Gypsies. The police commissioner, Bob Hauk (Lee Van Cleef), offers new Liberty Island arrival Snake Plissken (Kurt Russell), a legendary criminal and former war hero who has been arrested after attempting to rob the Federal Reserve Depository, a full pardon in exchange for finding and rescuing the President, who has a tape recording in his possession vital to the "survival of the human race." Plissken reluctantly agrees because he's going into New York "one way or the other," and stays motivated when things go sour because he's been injected with two microscopic capsules rigged to explode unless he's back on Liberty Island—with the President and the tape recording—in less than twenty-four hours.

We're told almost nothing about Plissken or his wider world during the course of the film, but the *Escape from New York* novelization, written by Mike McQuay and based on the script by Carpenter and Castle, fills in the gaps and reveals quite a bit of subtext. We find out that World War III, still being "fought heavily in the West"[9] as the story opens, started with mass chemical warfare, and that the nerve gas, still coursing through the atmosphere, is making everyone who breathes it violently insane. The soldiers who came home from the war's first campaign, already demented by the gas, were recruited into the fledgling USPF and deployed to wipe out the escalating poor, "who were going crazy with gas madness" and turning to crime to survive.[10] (The violent crime epidemic of the 1970s and beyond, goes one theory, may have been caused by exposure to lead emissions.[11]) Plissken refers to the USPF as "blackbellies": "Kevlarred killers, crazies with guns… judge, jury and in more cases than not, executioner," an obvious allusion to the Blackshirts, Mussolini's National Fascist Party militia. The Battle of Leningrad mentioned during Hauk's interview with Plissken was a nominal rescue mission, but in reality a ruse by US military leadership to confuse Russian intelligence. Plissken lost his squad and his eye in the battle, and was afterwards decorated by "a President who thought he could buy his love and loyalty with a cheap slug of bronze and a bit of colored ribbon"—just one of many parallels to the disillusioned, disenfranchised Vietnam veteran. The betrayal deepens as, back home, Plissken's mother and father are taken hostage by crazies. The USPF burns down the family house indiscriminately, killing everyone inside. His parents are buried alongside the criminals in a "paupers' grave," their savings appropriated by the state in the name of "restitution." Plissken's break with his country and every authority therein—*all* authority—is violent and absolute.

Paul Kersey is also a veteran, having served in a medical unit in the Korean War as a conscientious objector. He "grew up with guns," however, "all kinds of guns," his committed pacifism the result of a hunting accident in which his father was killed by another "gunman." Kersey's grieving mother—women are portrayed as deeply feeble and enfeebling in the film—asks him to renounce firearms, and he submits. His turning to vigilantism, then—"if the police don't defend us, maybe we ought to do it ourselves"—is a conversion narrative, told in near religious terms. The epiphany comes during a Wild West gunfight reenactment in Tucson (where, like Hawaii, there is "space for life") while visiting a gun-nutty client (Stuart Margolin). Kersey says nothing during the scene, but, as the camera zooms in, his face registers the transformative moment: America has always been violent, will always be violent, and, as the narrator concludes at the end of the stunt show, it was the gunslinging lawmen of the Old West who dispensed justice, who ultimately "were to plant the roots that would grow into a nation."

Death Wish was adapted from the 1972 novel of the same name, written by Brian Garfield. The book is a thoughtful if slow character study of middle-aged accountant Paul Benjamin who, after his wife is murdered and daughter rendered insane by a criminal assault, realizes not only how unhappy and empty he is, but how unhappy and empty he has always been. His attempt to reestablish some emotional connection to the world by gunning down muggers, and his belief that he's a martyr, establishes the conversion format followed in the film, with an important caveat. Said Garfield:

> The essential difference, to me, between the book and the movie, is that the book suggests that this kind of thing could happen and that it's a dangerous possibility. The movie suggests not only that it could happen but that it ought to happen.[12]

"In the novel," Garfield went on, "Paul was psychotic. In the movie, he becomes a hero."[13]

A psycho who becomes a hero is, in fact, the basic plot of Martin Scorsese's *Taxi Driver*. Travis Bickle (Robert De Niro)—the quintessential vilification of the Vietnam vet as a "walking time bomb"[14]—undergoes his own conversion. Assaulted by loneliness and insomnia, the result of his own profound stupidity and megalomania, Bickle decides that he is the avenging messiah who must bring about the "real rain" that will "wash all the scum off the streets." This New York, instead of evoking a bloody future city, resembles the Book of Revelation's "great whore" of Babylon, oozing apart at its "sick" and "venal" seams. "There's an atmosphere at night that's like a seeping kind of virus," Scorsese said of the city during the shoot. "It reminds me of a scene in [1956's] *The Ten Commandments* [...] where a cloud of green smoke seeps along the palace floor and touches the foot of a first-born son, who falls dead."[15] When slimy liberal Senator and presidential candidate Charles Palantine (Leonard Harris) makes an unexpected appearance in Bickle's cab, he asks Bickle what "bugs" him most about his country. Bickle only cares about "this city here [...] full of filth and scum." The next president, Bickle says, "should just clean up this whole mess here—he should just flush it right down the fuckin' toilet." Real-life slimy President Richard Nixon agreed. "Goddamn New York," he railed in the Oval Office in 1972, deriding the East Coast liberal stronghold's "Jews and Catholics and Blacks and Puerto Ricans." There's a "law of the jungle, where some things don't survive. Maybe New York shouldn't survive. Maybe it should go through a cycle of destruction."[16]

Much of John Carpenter's work concerns the inherent antagonism between freedom and authority, and the moral necessity of the responsible exercise of both. The Western genre is famous for exploring this primal territory, and *Escape from New York* is, in many ways, a noir Western: it's hard to tell the good guys from the bad guys, the winners from the losers, and right from wrong. Carpenter cast Lee Van Cleef ("the Bad" in 1966's *The Good, the Bad and the Ugly*) and Ernest Borgnine (1969's *The Wild Bunch*) largely because of their influential roles in the genre, and Plissken's character was modeled after Clint Eastwood's "the man with no name" from Sergio Leone's *Dollars Trilogy*. (In fact, Clint Eastwood was the studio's first choice for the role of Snake. The second choice was Charles Bronson, then fifty-nine years old.) The running joke in *Escape from New York* is that everyone who meets Snake says much the same as Cabbie (Borgnine): "I thought you were dead." It comes from 1971's *Big Jake*, a Western starring John Wayne as the titular gunfighter who must reconcile with the grown sons he's estranged to rescue the grandson he's never met. "Not hardly," Jake replies in each case.

The President is being held by the Duke of New York (Isaac Hayes), the de facto president ("A-number-one, the Big Man") of Manhattan Prison, and the Duke, we find out, is planning to unite the city's gangs and lead them across the Queensboro Bridge to freedom, holding the President as insurance. The plan, though no one knows it, is dead on arrival, because the tape recording in the President's briefcase is not exactly a McGuffin: it contains detailed information on what McQuay's novel calls a "Super Flash," a clean nuke that would "zap out the Ruskies and the Chinks and not leave so much as one particle of radiation in the atmosphere." (When Plissken briefly plays the cassette in Cabbie's radio, we hear that "the discovery of the tritium creates only one one-millionth of the biological damage of iodine-1..."—presumably iodine-131, a component of nuclear fission.) The President plans to present the tape at the "peace" summit and give his enemies twenty-four hours to surrender; if they don't comply, he'll "turn the entire eastern world into a giant firestorm." Even though the film doesn't reveal the President's plan, we instinctively know he's a contemptible shit. Such was the effect of Watergate, the Nixon tapes, the Pentagon Papers. Carpenter's repeated use of the counterculture phrase "the man"—"Workin' for the man now, huh?" Brain (Harry Dean Stanton) goads Snake— is a reminder that a thoroughly rotten future is not exactly the stuff of fantasy: it's just one more brazen power grab (or

Capitol riot) away. That's why, when the President grabs a guard's gun and frenziedly mows down the Duke at the end of the movie, saving Plissken in the process, we feel a little sorry for the Duke. He may have been cruel in his application of jungle law, but he didn't grow the jungle—and he's not a genocidal maniac.

Snake Plissken, the deadly capsules in his bloodstream quickly dissolving, has become one with the escalating world disorder that spawned him: if he survives, so does the human race—"something you don't give a shit about," Hauk chides him during mission prep. The most revealing moment of the film comes when Plissken finds the President's life-monitor device on a city drunk. He radios Hauk, telling him that he's abandoning the mission and coming home. Hauk threatens to "burn [him] off the wall" if he shows up without the President. "A little human compassion," Plissken pleads— crucially, without pressing the talk switch on his radio. Who would listen? During the final escape scene, after the cab hits a mine on Queensboro bridge and Cabbie is killed, Brain, Maggie (Adrienne Barbeau), the President, and Plissken run for the Liberty Island wall. Brain trips a mine, dying instantly. The President pauses for a heartbeat to register the blast, then keeps running. Maggie, Brain's girlfriend, stops, heartbroken. With less than five minutes left to live, Plissken stops too, pleads with Maggie to "keep moving." Maggie defiantly holds out her hand for his last gun: she wants to kill the Duke, who's pursuing them in his Cadillac. Snake gives it to her, along with a look of admiration, and chases after the President. Inside the "inhuman dungeon," there is not only compassion, but loyalty.

As already mentioned, Winner also makes extensive use of the Western mythos, or at least its Lone Ranger phase, not being overly concerned with moral complexities. Paul Kersey—like Hauk, like the President, like the Duke of New York, like the crazies—is beyond the sway of compassion, and he is loyal only to his higher calling, more or less abandoning his only child, who was reduced to a state of catatonia following the assault and eventually institutionalized. Kersey is the only good guy in *Death Wish*, and there are only two sets of bad guys: the street criminals and the cops. There is no in between. After the cops tell him that there's little chance of catching the thugs who killed his wife, Kersey never asks them about it again, attempts no private investigation into the matter, and hires no private investigator. He simply prowls the streets and pulls the trigger when a lowlife attacks—and lowlifes always attack. For Kersey, all criminals are the same, and they will never stop being criminals. (Ronald Reagan to the International Association of Chiefs of Police, 1981: "for all our justified pride in intellectual accomplishment, we must never forget the jungle is always there, waiting to take us over."[17]) They are not individuals so much as willing extensions of the substance of evil. And while evil itself is indestructible, its human hosts are not. (Reagan again: "Only our deep moral values and our strong social institutions can hold back that jungle and restrain the darker impulses of human nature."[18]) If he keeps fighting the good fight, he seems to believe, he will eventually lop off the particular malignancies that dealt him personal tragedy.

Keeping in line with the ingeniously manipulative narrative, Kersey's murdered wife is never mentioned in the press, but when Kersey kills his first would-be mugger, a junkie, the next morning's front page reads, "Ex-Con Killed; Motive Unknown." Once it's clear that a vigilante is loose, the entire police force immediately mobilizes, spurred by the

Mayor. The newspapers and billboard-advertised magazines are aflutter with vigilante controversy ("Vigilantism: Can It Stop Urban Crime?" a faux *Newsweek* cover reads). There's a televised press conference, covered internationally, in which the commissioner asks the vigilante to turn himself in: "Murder is no answer to crime in the city. Crime is a police responsibility." The beat cop (Robert Kya-Hill) who showed Kersey some compassion at the beginning of the film betrays him, pegging him for the vigilante; the police inspector has everyone in the precinct working the case, staking out and routinely harassing Kersey; and, when Kersey is shot at the scene of his last showdown, another beat cop (Christopher Guest) gives Kersey's gun to the inspector on the sly, fishing for a professional quid pro quo. The inspector is more than happy to reciprocate. If the vigilante's capture is made public, the "underprivileged" would resume their uncontested molestation of taxpaying citizens, and taxpaying citizens would further question the legitimacy of the NYPD. So the law enforcement establishment, when its various officers are not corrupt, craven, or both, are entirely motivated by saving face. They protect and serve only themselves. Which is not far from the truth, given the systemic corruption then tearing through the NYPD: "Who can trust a cop who don't take money?" undercover man Tom Keough (Jack Kehoe) warns his righteous hippie partner Frank Serpico (Al Pacino) in Sidney Lumet's truc-life *Serpico* from 1973.

At the end of *Death Wish*, the cops chase Kersey out of town. He lands in Chicago, and the last shot of the film has him making a gun out of his hand and pointing it at a group of unpoliced (every city is the same) lowlifes in the train station. (*Taxi Driver*'s Bickle, after he's blasted his way through the brothel, points the hand-gun at his own temple: he knows now that he's no better than the "filth and scum" he despises.) Kersey's evangelism, we know, will continue unabated, will escalate even. Plissken, as *Escape from New York* concludes, destroys the all-important tape recording, likely consigning the human race to what he believes is a well-deserved oblivion. After giving the President a chance to atone for the inhuman America he has fed and nurtured, a chance to show "a little human compassion"—a test the President, smug in his reinstatement, predictably fails—Plissken essentially completes the mission the terrorists began. The difference between Snake and Paul, though, is that Snake knows he's a sinner no matter what he does, because the moral high ground has been forcibly removed by people like Paul, who thinks he's God.

PART THREE

WORLD WITHOUT END
1981–1987

SHEPPARD: If you're looking for money, you're smarter than you look. If you're not, you're a lot dumber.

O'NIEL: Then I'm probably a lot dumber.

SHEPPARD: That could be very dangerous.

Outland, 1981

9. "THE SLUMS OF THE FUTURE":
POLTERGEIST AND *SUBURBIA*

What's peculiar about 1982's *Poltergeist* is that the thing advertised in its title never appears. The film presents plenty of noise and disruption, yes, but not much sign of anything resembling the unsettling but invisible "noisy spirits" that had increasingly roamed the supernatural-saturated media of the previous decade. This prudish reluctance to engage with the confusing and frightening "realities" of the supernatural captures something about the film—a literal and figurative lack of spirit at its heart that inevitably evokes its setting.

How do you speak about the suburbs without descending into cliché, given that an all-consuming, all-enveloping cliché is precisely what the suburbs were designed to be? One of the most pervasive tropes of postwar American life and popular culture, the 'burbs taught the entire world an immediately recognizable iconography for sedate middle-class comfort: the wide streets flanked by large detached houses with double garages and immaculate lawns kept moist by the persistent hissing of sprinklers (persistent and catastrophic droughts be damned), children riding bikes and Big Wheels, joggers and dog-walkers, station wagons gliding back and forth, no shops, no litter, no crowds, no unpleasant surprises that can't be averted by prudent planning. The word "suburb" has its origins in *suburbium*, Latin for a peripheral part of a city, but the North American version, made possible, or necessary, by the *real* animating spirit of twentieth-century American culture—the automobile and 41,000 miles of a new Interstate Highway System—had developed into a new kind of autonomous settlement: one that explicitly rejected the city's confusing accretion of humanity and unmediated spaces that purportedly made the country a melting pot of races, ethnicities, and beliefs. In short, middle-class whites built walls around themselves, and took their tax dollars with them. Black and non-white families, pointedly kept out of the suburbs for decades by "restrictive covenants" and a federal refusal to insure mortgages,[1] inherited the suddenly disinvested cities, some of which stood in for future dystopias in films like *Escape from New York*.

The fact that *Poltergeist* was helmed by Tobe Hooper, whose gift for skewering a certain kind of curdled Americana had been evident since *The Texas Chain Saw Massacre*, suggested that *Poltergeist* would subvert the stereotypes and expose the inchoate fears lurking beneath the green belts and sun-spangled swimming pools. If so, it wouldn't be the first time: the suburbs had been trite shorthand for the various existential malaises plaguing the middle-class psyche in any given moment for decades, from 1955's *Rebel Without a Cause* to the 1964 *Twilight Zone* episode "The Monsters Are Due on Maple Street," 1968's *The Swimmer*, 1975's *The Stepford Wives*, 1978's *Halloween*, and 1979's *Over the Edge*, which took inspiration for its story of kids rebelling against the boredom of their planned community from real events in Foster City, California.

Famously, *Poltergeist* opens with the sound of "The Star-Spangled Banner" playing over a black screen, upon which the film's title appears in stark white outline text—the implication being that the noisy spirit of the title might actually be America itself. It's one of the film's few genuinely inspired moments. The camera slowly pulls back from a close-up of a TV screen as the images of the US Marine Corps War Memorial signal the day's close of broadcasting—when there still was a close of broadcasting—and give way to static. We glide past the body of Steve Freeling (Craig T. Nelson), slumped inert in an armchair, and take a tour of the bedrooms where the rest of the Freeling family are asleep: spunky housewife Diane (JoBeth Williams) and the three Freeling children, teenager Dana (Dominique Dunne), pre-teen Robbie (Oliver Robins), and little Carol Anne (Heather O'Rourke). The Freelings live in Cuesta Verde, a vast, anonymous, and seemingly entirely white suburb somewhere in California, built by the same real estate development company where Steve is a hotshot salesman. When one potential client protests that he can't tell one house from another, Steve doesn't argue but simply points out that "our construction standards are very liberal": the chance to indulge yourself with an outdoor jacuzzi or swimming pool, it's implied, is a worthwhile trade-off for the production-line uniformity and lack of character.

The origins of *Poltergeist*'s story nominally lie in the 1958 events that plagued the Herrmann family of Long Island, who claimed they were being tormented in their recently built suburban home by an entity that confounded the efforts of an investigating team of scientists from Duke University's Parapsychology Laboratory.[2] In the case of the Freelings, the problems begin when little Carol Anne descends the stairs to the living room in the middle of the night and begins to talk to the "TV people" she claims live inside the static, unnervingly responding to questions that only she can hear. Scored with nursery rhyme music that highlights the reassuring, family-friendly nature of the setting but also provides an unwitting critique of this infantile and reductive version of the world, a montage of scenes of suburban life follow that concludes with Steve and his friends yelling and jeering at a football game on the screen of the same TV we saw in the opening scene. The boorish show of performative aggression is cut short when the game is interrupted by a children's show, the soothing *Mister Rogers' Neighborhood*, triggering an argument between Steve and his next-door neighbor: their TV remotes are tuned to the same frequency. Encouraging seclusion and intensifying the suburbanites' reluctance to share spaces, TV clearly sits at the heart of this unmoored existence, and the spat concludes with a mock gunfight—American men of a certain age always a hair's breadth away from acting out the deathless archetype of the cowboy—to decide which of the images flying about like bullets will dominate the screens. Meanwhile, Diane is stopped from flushing the corpse of the family's pet canary down the toilet by Carol Anne—it's left to the youngest Freeling, who has not yet been indoctrinated with the pain-free pragmatism of the suburban adult mindset, to insist on the need for ritual and a little respect for the dead. Before long, though, Tweety's grave will be desecrated by the bulldozer digging the swimming pool that, naturally, the upwardly mobile Freelings want to add to their home.

Despite their boomer lifestyle pretensions, Diane and Steve spend their evenings smoking pot in bed like a couple of college kids. She reads about Jung and he reads about Ronald Reagan, opposing ideologues with a common gift for engaging with their respective followers' dreams. But the domestic idyll is shattered when Diane discovers a strange force manifesting in the kitchen that stacks the chairs and slides family members across the floor like a theme park ride. Initially, she's enthusiastic about the novelty, but after Robbie has been attacked by the tree outside his bedroom window and Carol Anne is sucked into the walk-in closet, her voice calling out from the TV set, she and Steve turn to the "Popular Beliefs, Superstitions and Para Psychology" department of the local university to investigate. The team of researchers, including the maternal Dr. Martha Lesh (Beatrice Straight) and Dr. Ryan Mitchell (Richard Lawson), are shocked at the supernatural chaos that now reigns in Carol Anne's bedroom: a hurricane of special effects work that functions as a metaphor for the film as a whole—a meaningless storm of costly nonsense in a space devoid of any human presence.

Unaware of the paranormal events and worried that Steve's absence from work might mean he's thinking of changing companies, his boss Teague (James Karen) takes him for a stroll up in the nearby hills, offering him the chance of a "phase 5" home near the graveyard overlooking the already outdated original Cuesta Verde development. (In his 1964 book *God's Own Junkyard*, architecture critic Peter Blake compared the suburbs to automobile graveyards and military cemeteries.[3]) "We've already made arrangements for relocating the cemetery," explains Teague when Steve expresses unease, adding, "It's not ancient tribal burial grounds [...] it's just... people." He pauses. "Besides... we've done it before." It's one of the film's more egregious sleights of hand, not only sidestepping the issue of whose cultural sites actually *had* been desecrated historically to make way for the American built environment, but also appropriating that frisson of feeling wronged and transplanting it onto the white population— which is admittedly less offensive than the original version of the screenplay, then called *Night Time*, where the source of the supernatural disturbances is a vast grave site resulting from a massacre of white settlers by Native Americans.

The baffled researchers call for backup in the shape of a medium called Tangina (Zelda Rubinstein). Unlike the conformist Freelings and the straight-laced researchers, Tangina, with her Southern accent, diminutive stature, rock'n'roll charisma, and unambiguous belief in a reality that transcends the kinds of materialism valued by suburbanites and academia, looks and acts like an outsider. Although in many ways as hackneyed as everything else in *Poltergeist*, she's also by far the most engaging character in the film, her working-class cred unwittingly highlighted by the well-spoken Dr. Lesh when she tells a skeptical Steve that Tangina has "cleaned many houses." Tangina explains that Carol Anne has been abducted by something called "the Beast," and a rescue effort ensues that involves sending Diane into the other dimension inside the closet, then pulling her and Carol Anne back out into the suburbs. (A little girl who disappears into another dimension inside her own house, unseen but clearly heard by her frantic parents, is the plot of 1962 *Twilight Zone* episode "Little Girl Lost," whose writer Richard Matheson says Spielberg asked him for a video copy while developing *Poltergeist*.[4]) In contrast to the haunted room scene earlier, the sequence dispenses with flashy effects and makes do with strobes, spotlights, and a smoke machine—a de-escalation of production values that results in some of the film's most memorable imagery.

Once an ectoplasm-smeared Diane and Carol Anne have reemerged, Tangina announces that the "house is clean," and, like the entrenched-in-denial boomers they are, Diane and Steve promptly go back to acting almost as if nothing has happened, the irruption of the irrational that only hours before threatened the lives of their children resolved by a psychic "cleaner" as decisively as an infestation of roaches might be resolved by an exterminator. After they decide to stay in the house one last night while preparing to move out, Steve absents himself to the office, naturally, and the children are sent back to their bedroom, which only hours before was the locus of hell. Diane, meanwhile, indulges in a long bath. This nonchalant parenting approach might almost be a deliberate poke at boomer child-rearing if it weren't so clearly of a tonal piece with the mindset of the rest of the film: whether it's sending traumatized kids off alone in taxis, smirking indulgently as lecherous workmen catcall their teenage daughter, or, again, thoughtlessly putting their children to bed in the same room where they have narrowly escaped being killed by an evil ghost called the Beast, they aren't callous, just completely, devastatingly oblivious to the potential effects of their decisions on their kids' lives. At the same time, they themselves are profoundly infantile, as when they're goofing around in the bedroom like a couple of teens, or when Steve duels with his neighbor over control of the TV, or in the scene where Diane sits on Dr. Lesh's knee and puts her arms around her neck like a child seeking comfort.

Inevitably, as the parents are off attending to their own needs, the supernatural forces reappear to claim their kids. While Diane is drying her hair, oblivious to the fact that Robbie is being choked by a possessed toy clown, she is attacked by demonic forces that yank up her top to reveal her panties before throwing her around the room (even though the scene only lasts a moment, it's a disconcerting tonal switch from childishness to something even more unpleasant). Diane rescues the kids from another attempt at dimensional-closet-sucking, and Steve returns home to find corpse-filled coffins blasting up through the ground. When Teague appears, Steve suddenly realizes what's going on: "You moved the cemetery but you left the bodies, didn't you? You son of a bitch, you left the bodies and you only moved the headstones!" The film ends with the neighborhood hemorrhaging market value as water mains burst, gouts of flame erupt from the sidewalks, and the Freeling house is sucked into oblivion in a scene that echoes the finale of 1976's *Carrie*: homes that have witnessed an injustice annihilated by supernatural forces; malignancies lopped off the perfect suburban body. Their home taken from them by forces beyond their control, the Freelings check into a motel, foreshadowing a reality that growing numbers of middle- and working-class families would experience over the decades to come as they paid the price for cheap mortgages and a lack of financial regulation. Steve's one concession to the gravity of the events that nearly cost him his wife and children is to put the room's TV set out onto the balcony—though we sense it probably won't be out there for long.

An attempt to reconcile two profoundly disparate visions of America—with writer-producer Steven Spielberg's bratty, cloying embrace prevailing over Tobe Hooper's tense worrying at the scabrous underpinnings of the nation's life and culture—*Poltergeist* is, then, a pretty accurate avatar of its setting: phony, unprincipled, and not what it claims to be. With its wearying atmosphere of Halloween phoniness, *Poltergeist* turns something that should be frightening into something by turns wheedling and hectoring: a detached postmodern freak show that wants you to both love it and fear it, and whose desire to be all things to all people means it ends up being nothing more than a safe, fundamentally reassuring ride through the greed and ruthlessness the film pretends to critique with its "ghosts as victims of capitalism" schtick.

Could *Poltergeist* also, at least in part, be about the chaos of the city bursting into the drowsy calm of the suburbs? 1983's *Suburbia* looks at the thing from the perspective of the noisy spirits, turning the haunting inside out and taking as its protagonists the broken teens haunting empty houses. It begins with runaway Sheila (Jennifer Clay) thumbing a ride with a mother and her toddler down a desolate Los Angeles highway as night falls. "Where are you going?" asks the driver (Dorlinda Griffin). "The end of the highway," the girl replies. When the station wagon gets a flat tire, the three go looking for a phone booth, and while the mother is calling for a tow truck, the unattended child is savaged by a wild Doberman that appears out of the darkness, the scene no less shocking for the obviousness of the doll between the dog's teeth.

Director Penelope Spheeris came up with the idea for the movie after the niche success of her 1981 punk documentary, *The Decline of Western Civilization*, had convinced her that only narrative film would get her work into theaters. She pitched it to Roger Corman, who agreed to fund it on the condition that she include enough lurid sensationalism (to which we've already been introduced) to guarantee box office viability.[5] Despite this proviso, Spheeris—who had her own challenging upbringing to draw on when writing the script—treats the damaged young people who populate *Suburbia* with compassion and empathy, even when they're pretty unsympathetic and lacking in compassion themselves.

A toy rifle on his back, a little boy (Andrew Pece) rides a Big Wheel in circles outside a bungalow that looks like it has seen better days. We're in smaller, older suburbs than those in *Poltergeist*—the kind whose garages can only accommodate a single car. Inside, Evan (Bill Coyne), the kid's teenage brother, is reading comic books while war footage plays out across the TV. "Any more groceries out in the car?" he asks, when his mom comes home from the store. "No, I couldn't afford any more groceries!" Evan: "How come you're so late?" Mom: "Stopped by for a couple of drinks with someone from work. Any objections?" Their exchange neatly captures the eroding quality of the lives of the once optimistic lower middle-classes. Mom's relaxant is vodka, not the weed of the upwardly mobile Freelings, so when she finds her hidden stash depleted, she slaps her son. "I can see your father in you, it makes me sick!" "*I* didn't choose him to be my father," Evan snaps back, as tanks and airstrikes fill the TV screen, "*you* did!"

Weary of dealing with the fallout of his parents' choices and his down-at-heel suburban existence, Evan stuffs his belongings into a trash bag and heads into the urban realities of LA. His curiosity piqued by a passing gang of punks—one of whom sarcastically tells him to "Get a job"—Evan tags along after them to a gig, where he finds what seems to be a happy, relatively functional community. But one that still has its problems: there's theft, drugs (some of which are slipped into Evan's drink), violence, and misogyny. We watch a skinhead accost a pretty poser punk girl—"I think I'd like to fuck your brains out [...] but it doesn't look like you have any"—before initiating a pile-on where sundry punks tear the girl's clothes off while, onstage, punk band D.I. reaches the crescendo of "Richard Hung Himself." As per Corman's orders, the camera lingers on the girl's naked body, onto which one of the club lighting guys swings a spotlight. For all its intended titillation, it's an uncomfortable scene, and its protracted length feels almost as if Spheeris is rubbing our noses in our own discomfort for demanding that our entertainments contain this kind of sleaze. It's also completely out of character with the way we see the punks behave throughout the rest of the film. Equally jarring is the reflex-level bigotry, as when D.I.'s singer shouts "Come on, you homos!" as he tries to break up the altercation, a précis of the strange tensions between punk's transgressive mindset and the reactionary thinking that lurked beneath the surface. "Give 'em the muzak!" shouts the club's manager as he shuts down the show. The punks file out, hands over their ears to block out the Herb Alpert-esque sounds that fill the hall, the soothing and anodyne tones so beloved by their boomer parents more grating to their ears than discordant punk could ever be.

Peroxide-haired Jack Diddley (Chris Pedersen) takes pity on Evan after finding him on the ground outside, rendered unconscious by whatever was slipped into his drink. He lets the young runaway sleep in his car, safe from the "acid rain that comes down every night about this time." The next day, as the two drive past decaying homes and unmown lawns, Evan reads out a page from his mother's diary, which sounds almost like something *Poltergeist*'s Diane might have written:

May 10th, 1968. Dear diary, Mark and I are going to be very happy here, the air is clean, the skies are blue and all the houses are brand new and beautiful. They call it suburbia and that word's perfect because it's a combination of suburb and utopia.

"They didn't realize they'd be the slums of the future," smirks Jack. The two arrive at a condo where Jack's friend Joe Schmoe (Wade Walston) lives with his dad and his dad's male partner, who are sunning themselves by the pool while watching TV and drinking drinks. It's hard to tell if Joe's antipathy is the result of homophobia or familial strife or both, but though he's clearly not making much of an effort to understand his father, his dad's blasé response to seeing his son's departure—"Movin' out again, huh, Joe?"—implies he's too narcotized by his boomer comforts to try and salvage their relationship.

The three head off to a derelict bungalow "out by the 605" that a group of punks have squatted, driving through a landscape saturated with a sense of impermanency and danger: walls are covered with graffiti saying things like "Love is murder" and packs of wild dogs roam the streets. "I heard that when people were forced to move from their houses some of them left their dogs behind and coyotes came down from the hills and fucked them," explains Jack. "After a while—wild dogs!" They pull up outside the squat and, to the "I want to be a cowboy" refrain of the Vandals' "Urban Struggle," we meet the inhabitants of "T.R. House"—including Sheila, whose thick blond hair is now being shorn. The mood is confrontational but accepting: one punk (Flea, as Mike B. The Flea) kills a cockroach with a catapult, then turns to Evan and asks provokingly, "You wanna be next?"—though it turns out he's only talking about a haircut. In the next room, a dozen punks—one of them Skinner (Timothy Eric O'Brien), the skinhead from the show—are sprawled about watching a TV propped on a crate while a commercial asks, "Are you experiencing feelings of alienation or depression or loneliness?" The kids laugh numbly about the $800 a week the clinics charge to help ("If you had 800 bucks a week, you probably wouldn't be depressed in the first place"). Evan finds out that T.R. stands for "The Rejected," and that he'll need to brand his arm with the house's initials if he wants to stay: "If we didn't do that, we'd have all kinds of flakes hanging around." Disgusted (or perhaps intimidated) by the barbaric ritual, Joe returns home, but soon gravitates back to

T.R. House where, as he heats the brand, Sheila shows him the other kind of scars that cover her back. When Joe asks where they're from, Sheila declines to say: "I'll tell you about it someday if I ever get to know you better."

Early next morning, the punks are awoken by the sound of shots and the squeals of wounded dogs: it's "Citizens Against Crime," a gang of middle-aged white guys with rifles and pistols who want to clean up the neighborhood. Scared that the stray dogs they've adopted will be next, the punks confront them. "Where's the war?" asks one of the suburban rednecks at the sight of the ex-Army gear that's such a constant in punk style. "Up your ass," replies Skinner. Two cops arrive, one of whom, Officer William Reynard (Don Allen), is Jack's stepdad. ("What a drag," Evan says earlier, when Jack reluctantly divulges that his stepfather is a cop, and "worse," a Black cop.) After sending the "citizens" packing, he confides presciently to his partner, "I'm more worried about our vigilante sharpshooters than I am about a bunch of teenagers in a crash pad."

The punks live on the food they steal from the open garages of the more affluent suburbs—like Cuesta Verde—and, after one such raid, find themselves in another, slightly more down-market suburbia where a lawn sale is underway: it's the Citizens Against Crime boys and their families, who need the cash after being laid off from General Motors. Clearly, in a way, the vigilantes have something in common with the punks: they too are disenfranchised and looking for some kind of stability in their lives. But at least the punks have some— albeit shaky—idea of who's to blame for the state of the world and don't just project their frustrations onto the nearest easy target. The lack of a common language, or maybe just a shared aesthetic, means the two are destined to be eternally at odds.

Evan abducts his brother Ethan from his foster home, snatching the kid's Big Wheel too (perhaps a nod to *The Shining*'s [1980] Danny Torrance, another child riding his bike through the haunted territory of parental alcoholism and neglect), and takes him to T.R. House, where he's decked out with a mohawk and a child's size M-65 field jacket—a miniature Travis Bickle. Echoes of war and its generational traumas permeate the whole movie, from the mohawks (occasionally worn by American combat troops in WWII and Vietnam) and the hand-me-down military clothing to the Vietnam stories about the death of Jack's dad and Peg Leg (André Boutilier), who was born without a leg after his father was sprayed with Agent Orange. The Rejected are themselves living in something resembling a battlefield: Skinner and Jack warn Evan not to drink the water ("you never know where the toxins are going to creep in") and forecast that "by the year 2000 it'll all be one big chemical wasteland." "And all the mutants'll be roamin' around bumpin' into each other," predicts Joe.

After stealing someone's turf lawn, the kids take it to a closed mall, unroll it in front of a Radio Shack with a wall of live TVs in the window, and have a picnic while watching a documentary about the effects of nuclear fallout—their way of appropriating a slice of the peace and belonging of suburbia for themselves. Here, as in *Poltergeist*, TV plays a central role, but the punks of T.R. House use it as a vaccine to inoculate themselves against the hypocrisy and lies of the straight world; Steve and Diane use it as a soporific, not much different from the cigar box of weed they keep in the bedroom for when the kids are asleep. While a voice reels off statistics about radiation poisoning, Sheila and Joe get to know each other better, and Sheila admits that the scars that cover her back were put there by her abusive father.

Meanwhile, the conflict with the local community escalates until one of the club's security guys is killed by a couple of straights attempting to stab Skinner. After a meeting at the Elks Lodge, where the locals blame the punks for the problems afflicting the neighborhood and the GM boys discuss playing vigilante, Reynard warns the kids to go back to their homes until things blow over. Only problem is, most of the kids don't have homes to go to. "Families?" scoffs Evan. "Everyone knows families don't work! [...] This is the best home most of us ever had." "Besides," adds Skinner (who, despite his bent for violence and the out-of-character sexual attack earlier in the film, is the emotional heart of the group), "if we didn't have each other, we wouldn't have anything." That night, the two GM crackers return to the squat and creep inside, ripping Sheila's t-shirt off in another bit of gratuitous titillation: an invasion of domestic and physical privacy that echoes the supernatural Beast's lecherous attack on Diane in *Poltergeist*. But here, the brutal assault has consequences. Soon afterwards, Sheila is found dead, having killed herself by overdosing on the dope of T.R. House's resident junkie, the book of fairy tales she used to read to Ethan—and the other punks—on her lap.

The punks take Sheila's body to her wealthy parents' large house, but the family tries to kick them out when they turn up for her funeral. "We're sitting all the way in the back—can't you just ignore us?" protests Evan, bemused by the straight world's hypocritical refusal to tolerate transgressions, however slight, that challenge its dominance. The kids are "sitting all the way in the back" in a larger sense too: compelled to live in an abandoned house in an abandoned neighborhood that has literally gone to the dogs. A fight breaks out and Sheila's father ends up in the hospital, sending tensions to a breaking point, and Reynard warns the punks to get out of the house before they're attacked. Skinner convinces the rest of the kids that they need to stand their ground, though: "We're smarter than those assholes." T.R. House might be a roach-infested hovel but, for The Rejected, it's home, and who wouldn't put up a fight to defend their home? "Seems like if they run us out of this place…" say T'resa (Christina Beck) and Mattie (Maggie Ehrig), "they'll just run us out of the next place we find."

Sure enough, after an evening spent getting loaded and pissed off at a seedy strip club that feels like a throwback to the previous decade, the Citizens Against Crime boys turn up at T.R. House with guns in hand. The kids are ready for them and manage to send the attackers packing, but the humiliated boomers turn their car around and drive right at them, everyone diving out of the way except Ethan, who's playing on his Big Wheel. *Suburbia* is bookended by the deaths of children paying the consequences for the refusals of the adults around them—the dog-owners who abandon their vicious pets, the parents incapable of creating healthy relationships with their offspring, the angry men seeking scapegoats for the real sources of their unhappiness and frustration—to behave responsibly and look reality in the face.

The idea of home is at the heart of the film, as it is in *Poltergeist*. They're important in every culture, but in the US homes and home ownership possess an almost supernatural significance, as much an investment to protect their inhabitants psychically and financially from the mercenary realities of American life—and even from the neighbors of the communities they buy their way into—as they are a shelter. The scenes showing the punks' domestic lives as they gamble for matches, play rock-paper-scissors, read fairy tales to one another, interact lovingly with their pets, and take turns sleeping in the house's only "proper" bed repeatedly emphasize that the kids in T.R. House are just that: kids. Dumb and impulsive, yes, but also confused and trying to cope in their own way with difficult backgrounds and the increasingly confusing and fractured world that has been handed to them. What are they supposed to do, invest what they've been told are the best years of their lives in some dead-end job at a car plant, only to get laid off at forty-five and channel their rage against a new generation of kids they're too far gone to understand?

Spheeris cast real punk kids with no experience in acting on the grounds that it would be easier to teach a punk to act than an actor to be a punk, and the gentle, awkward behavior of the kids draws a vivid line between them and the "grown-ups." The film features plenty of the silly punk provocation Corman demanded—like the scene where a roadkill cat is dumped in a washing machine—and the punks are painted as being unable to avoid pressing people's buttons, even when they're treated with courtesy; but the abiding impression is that these youngsters are fundamentally lacking in the mean-spiritedness that is such a feature of the straight world, despite looking like captives of *Escape from New York*'s urban prison. At the same time, though, *Suburbia* isn't squeamish about highlighting the negative side of this adolescent society—the offhand racism and homophobia, the casual sexism (there's porn tacked to T.R. House's refrigerator), and the displays of machismo that resemble the regressive aggression of Steve and his peers at the beginning of *Poltergeist*. Yet despite all this, *Suburbia* genuinely captures something of the freedom to create a persona and a family and a home from scratch, and the dreamy aimlessness that was often at the heart of punk life.

Both *Suburbia* and *Poltergeist* share a feeling that it's the side effects of America's relentless drive to insulate and isolate itself from the confusions of real life, whether they're the horrors of history or the complications of today, that risk consuming it from within. There's a sense of foreboding that the suburbs and their eerie fantasy of a frictionless life are in some way haunted—in one by the ghosts of the marginalized living and in the other by the ghosts of the displaced dead. Beneath their undeniable appeal lurks an unhealthy contradiction: the suburbs are places where those families who can afford them feel safe, but also places where the forced disengagement from the wider world makes bad things happen; a safe haven inhabited by a generation of parents who, because of psychology or circumstance, are uninterested in or uncomprehending of the threats facing their children, be it acid rain and toxins in the water, existential ennui, or murderous toy clowns. And while the older generation lives in denial, refusing to think about who or what it is building its homes on top of, the children have been left to cope, alone, with the consequences: abandoned creatures, like the packs of wild dogs that haunt *Suburbia*, who for self-protection take on the wildness that surrounds them.

10. "WHAT IS IT YOU THINK YOU'RE BECOMING?": *DRAGONSLAYER* AND *MANHUNTER*

Sequestered away from the world, the peaceful life of a recluse is disturbed by the arrival of a delegation that has journeyed from afar in a desperate attempt to convince him to use his preternatural powers to prevent a ritual human sacrifice. This is the event that, in very different iterations, begins two films from the 1980s—1981's *Dragonslayer*, a fantasy story nominally aimed at children, and 1986's *Manhunter*, an adaptation of Thomas Harris's bestselling *Red Dragon*, a 1981 novel that did a lot to establish the concept of the serial killer in the landscape of popular culture.[1] As different as they are, both feel like attempts to metabolize the collective realization that the grim lessons of "the Seventies" would never really be going away, and were perhaps developing into something even more worrying.

When *Dragonslayer* was released in 1981, what Judith Martin identified in her *Washington Post* review of the film as "The Tolkien industry and the game of 'Dungeons and Dragons'" had given American kids and young adults a new lens through which to view, or avoid, reality.[2] In the mid-Sixties, J.R.R. Tolkien's *The Lord of the Rings*, a previously obscure epic fantasy, became a touchstone for the coalescing American counterculture, whose young dissidents found in it an antidote to what they perceived as their country's rush into turpitude, technocracy, corruption, and belligerence.[3] The novel and its many imitations spawned an even more pervasive form of escapism: the first commercially available role-playing games. The most successful of them—*Dungeons & Dragons*, originally released in 1974—sparked the fantasy boom that, by the early Eighties, had transformed the genre from an esoteric (and often scoffed at) pastime into a mainstream commodity. At the same time, much of the counterculture's radicalism turned inward, seeking to transform the individual and consciousness itself, and the products of this "New Age" thought developed into a cottage industry.

Made at a time when Disney was releasing uncharacteristically bleak fare like 1979's *The Black Hole*, 1980's *The Watcher in the Woods*, and 1985's *The Black Cauldron* (another attempt to capitalize on *Dungeons & Dragons*) to pursue more mature audiences, *Dragonslayer* begins with a very literal rendering of the Dark Ages in which it is set. Dim forms bearing burning brands make their way through the murk, gradually resolving into a group of petitioners seeking an audience with sorcerer Ulrich of Cragganmore (Ralph Richardson). Inside his keep, the aging Ulrich dons his snake-decorated cap and robe of office and examines himself in the mirror: "Looks forbidding enough, don't you think?" he asks his apprentice, the callow young Galen (Peter MacNicol), adding, "Balisarius wore this before he died." "You're not going to die!" protests Galen. "Oh, but I look forward to it," replies Ulrich. "All this magic—what has it accomplished?" The question goes to the heart of what *Dragonslayer* is about: is "magic"—the energies that the counterculture had liberated—enough to resolve the issues that plague the world? Or is it simply dress-up? Or worse still, does it risk replacing existing problems with new ones?

With Galen providing a tawdry little drum roll and flash of magnesium to awe the visitors, Ulrich presents himself to the delegation from Urland, led by a brusque young man by the name of Valerian (Caitlin Clarke). Every equinox, Valerian explains, a lottery is organized by king Casiodorus (Peter Eyre) to choose a virgin, who will be sacrificed to ensure that the dragon that once terrorized Urland doesn't incinerate the villages and crops. He produces some shabby dragon scales and a huge tooth as proof. "You want me to do battle with *that?*" asks an appalled Ulrich. "Who else can we turn to?" asks Valerian. Ulrich offers up some names, but Valerian cuts him short. "They're all dead. You're the only one left." Like Prospero in his island exile in *The Tempest*, Ulrich has all but given up on humanity: this is a world where the excitement and promise of the fantastic have died, leaving behind only resentment, exhaustion, and malaise—a world, in its way, not unlike the USA of 1981. "When a dragon gets this old, it knows nothing but pain," muses Ulrich. "It grows decrepit, crippled, pitiful—spiteful." Moribund and rotten with disease, heaving and convulsing as it attempts to crawl out of an age of defeat, yet still powerful enough to incinerate its enemies, came the perfect creature for the 1980s. "It's a long way to Urland," Ulrich concludes, unenthusiastically.

At the same time as the mythical dragon was asserting its presence in popular culture, another monster had reared its head. Many theories have been advanced as to why the Seventies and Eighties were seemingly so infested with serial killers. In *Extreme Killing: Understanding Serial and Mass Murder*, criminologists James Alan Fox and Jack Levin posit that the societal decay and atomization caused by the decline of cultural consensus during the 1960s, followed by the global economic shocks of the following decade, created "a culture of sociopathy"[4] that enabled the rise of a type of—seemingly overwhelmingly male—murderer who depersonalized and objectified his victims: "social responsibility" and "altruism quickly dissipated," they wrote, "leaving selfish individualism in its wake."[5] This is the world *Manhunter* inhabits: one full of humans who are narcissistic, predatory animals. Aesthetically, it occupies the opposing end of the scale to *Dragonslayer*: while everything around Ulrich and Galen is crumbling, worn, or handcrafted, *Manhunter* exists in a reality where everything seems new and gleaming, or at least freshly painted, each image as potent as a page out of a glossy sales brochure. It's a society bristling with repression—one committed to obsessively painting over the cracks in the walls in the hope they'll stop appearing. Following his 1981 debut *Thief* and his 1983 flop *The Keep*, *Manhunter* was director Michael Mann's third feature, and carried even further his trademark hallucinatory vividness: confounding the received criticism of the Eighties as a time when form gained primacy over substance, Mann frames the film's pristine surfaces with an intensity that implies surreal, dream-like depths—an aesthetic that couldn't be further away from *Dragonlayer*'s impoverished and shabby Middle Ages.

The petitioner in this case is FBI boss Jack Crawford (Dennis Farina) and the recluse Will Graham (William Petersen), a retired profiler of serial killers with a gift for entering into the thought processes of his quarries that borders on the supernatural. Physically and psychically scarred by his last case, the pursuit and capture of a serial killer named Hannibal Lecktor (Brian Cox), Graham has retired not to a crumbling tower but to the Florida Keys with his wife and son, who helps him build an enclosure on the beach to protect turtle eggs from predators. A new serial killer the police have dubbed "The Tooth Fairy" (due to the bite marks he leaves on his victims) has slain two suburban families over the previous two months, apparently following a lunar cycle, and Crawford needs Graham to stop him before he kills again. Though initially just as reluctant as Ulrich to leave his peaceful seclusion, Graham agrees to take part in the hunt after seeing photos of the murdered families, and the two depart for Atlanta.

As Ulrich is about to set off for Urland with Valerian's delegation, a group of armed men led by Tyrian (John Hallam), the captain of Casiodorus' Royal Guard, appears at the keep's door, blocking the way. "I've no more love for that creature than you lot, nor has the King," says Tyrian, "but before you stir things up, don't you think you should find out if he's the right man for the job?" Sorcerers, insists Tyrian, are charlatans, as evidenced by their reluctance to submit to any tests of their abilities: "Oh, conversation with your grandmother's shade in a dark room, the odd love potion… but comes a doubter, why, then it's the wrong day, the planets aren't in line, the entrails aren't favorable, 'We don't do tests'!" The world of *Dragonslayer* has grown diffident towards an institution—magic—that once played an important role in regulating society but has proved itself incapable of doing its job. The dragon, called Vermithrax Pejorative, is instead an objective reality: a frightening force of nature as tangible as hurricanes or earthquakes or war, which the stately old style of governance has only managed to keep in check by sacrificing its children. To prove that his magic is real, Ulrich bares his breast and orders Tyrian to stab him, proclaiming "You can't hurt me," before promptly slumping to the ground dead when Tyrian obliges. But when the ambitious Galen notices the late sorcerer's dragon foot pendant glowing, he decides to undertake the quest himself, and sets off in pursuit of the Urlanders.

Meanwhile, in Urland, a young woman in a flowing white robe and with flowers entwined in her hair—apart from the manacles on her wrists, she looks like something out of 1967 San Francisco—is being led towards the dragon's lair. "Now be it known throughout the kingdom," declaims Horsrick the Chamberlain (Roger Kemp), "that this maiden, having lawfully been chosen by a deed of fortune and destiny, shall hereby give up her life for the greater good of Urland... By this act shall be satisfied the powers that dwell underground and the spirits that attend thereto." It's formal and flowery language that belies the reality of the institutional sacrifice of young women, formalizing it into an abstraction as epic as the clouds of rhetoric surrounding the young men who were sent to their deaths in Vietnam and Korea. As the guards and assembled dignitaries flee the subterranean rumblings, the doomed maiden lubricates her wrists with spit and manages to wrench them free, her bloodied hands and subsequent incineration by dragon's breath testament to *Dragonslayer*'s deeply un-Disney-like mood, which continues in the following scene when, during a swim in a forest pool, Galen accidentally discovers that Valerian is not actually the boy she had been claiming to be. "Oh, I... I knew the moment I saw you," dissembles the gauche Galen. "You never knew a thing," snaps a scornful Valerian (who, from her first appearance, is clearly the film's most level-headed and astute character, and nothing like the optimistic, put-upon dreamers usually playing the female leads in Disney products). "No one's known, not since I was born." Casiodorus' lottery is corrupt, she explains, and the names of the wealthy never go into the pot for sacrifice, so she has spent her life hiding her real sex—another kind of draft evasion.

Graham too travels to the place where his own dragon has struck: the home of the most recent victims, where the camera—and Graham—lingers on the contrast between the thick, soft carpeting and solid, smooth fixtures of the house's curated interior and the chaotic despoilment of the crime scene. Graham returns to his hotel (the Atlanta Marriott Marquis hotel, built in 1985, one of the avatars of the Sun Belt's growing economic power[6]), an immense edifice whose futuristic atrium evokes a vast ribcage through which he ascends to his room, as if returning from the body to the brain, to watch the family's home movies. Unable to make headway, he calls home to his sleeping wife Molly (Kim Greist), and her somnolent voice seems to trigger the predatory relational instinct within him: "What are you dreaming?" Graham asks his quarry as soon as he hangs up, his face illuminated by the screen and suddenly attuned to the killer's thought process. "That's something you can't afford for me to know about, isn't it?" While he talks his way through his mental process, Graham stares at the TV set, huge in the frame, as though looking directly into the Tooth Fairy's mind: the film is saturated with ambiguity about whether the damaged Graham's affinity with his quarries goes beyond a desire to stop them and verges on a repressed desire to imitate them. In any case, his obsession clashes with, and prevails over, his desire to be a good husband and father. His identity as fluid and mercurial as Valerian's, his voice incongruously soft for the male lead of a 1980s action movie, Graham's radical empathy allows him to not only slide into the mechanisms of a serial killer's obsessions but also into their uniquely warped philosophies and aesthetic senses. With a sudden flash of insight, he realizes that the killer may have removed his surgical gloves and left his fingerprints on the victims' bodies and eyes while placing shards of smashed mirror upon them, snapping, "Did you open all their eyes so they could see ya?": being desired, being *seen*, is the killer's animating drive, a drive perfectly suited to a 1986 when appearance—magical *glamor* in its modern incarnation—was assuming ever increasing importance.

Galen sets his crusade in motion by using the amulet to cause a rockslide that seals the entrance to the dragon's lair. The ecstatic Urlanders immediately set about burning straw dragon heads while Galen enjoys his new-found local fame and, much to her father's anxiety, Valerian "comes out" as a female to the rest of the village, emerging from her hut dressed for the first time in women's clothes. To help break the awkward atmosphere, Galen takes her hand and leads her in a dance, and the others soon join in, but the presence of a holy man in the village spurs some—including Greil (Albert Salmi, with the voice of Norman Rodway), a member of the delegation to Ulrich's keep—to wonder if it's perhaps the new Christian god and not Galen who is responsible for burying the dragon. It's the first hint at the growing power of the evangelical newcomer that aims to supplant the pagan religions. Soldiers silhouetted like riot cops suddenly appear and take Galen off to the castle, where he attempts to impress the bemused Casiodorus with some feeble tricks. The king tells the story of how his late brother's attempt to kill the dragon not only led to his own death but sparked a vendetta from the beast that burned entire villages and destroyed the harvest. "How did you arrogate to yourself the role of savior?" he asks Galen. "Have you considered the consequences of failure?"

GALEN: But your children were dying!

CASIODORUS: Only a few... Does that sound cruel? It is better they die that others might live.

GALEN: You can't make a shameful peace with dragons. You must kill them as I have done.

CASIODORUS: The beast is dead? We shall see.

It's a dialogue that captures nicely the tensions between wary and cynical realpolitik and impulsive direct action, hinting, in this case at least, that neither is really suited to solving the problem. In fact, signs that the dragon's death may be less definitive than hoped soon appear, prompting the king to confiscate Galen's amulet and imprison him in the castle's dungeons, where he is visited by Casiodorus' daughter, Elspeth (Chloe Salaman), who, convinced of her father's even-handedness, is shocked when Galen tells her that she has never been included in the lottery. "Everyone knows how this choosing works," he says, explaining that the families with money and connections are protected from risk and prompting the shaken Elspeth to run away, while a roaring in the distance announces Vermithrax's escape from imprisonment.

In an attempt to "recover the mindset," Graham too visits a prison—the one holding Dr. Lecktor. In his all-white cell, Lecktor (who we first see from behind, lying on his bed clad in a white jumpsuit like a gargantuan baby) immediately recognizes Graham from his "atrocious" aftershave, before complaining about the university types who come to visit him, "second raters the lot." "You're very tan, Will," says Lecktor, using their shared talent for parsing other people's identities to seek a foothold in Graham's brain, like an advertising copywriter identifying his target. "Your hands are rough."

Graham asks Lecktor to help catch the Tooth Fairy, inevitably recalling their own history. "The reason you caught me, Will, is we're just alike," Lecktor tells him. "You want the scent? Smell yourself." Shaken by this reminder of the proximity of his own psychology to psychopathy, Graham flees the cell, running down the spiral staircase of the hospital and out into the bright light of day, where sleazebag journo Freddy Lounds (Stephen Lang) awaits to snap photos of him looking distressed.

After discovering that Lecktor has been communicating with the Tooth Fairy via newspaper ads, Graham organizes with Lounds to publish an article containing a taunting, derogatory description of the killer designed to provoke him into revealing himself. The Tooth Fairy is actually a man called Francis Dollarhyde (Tom Noonan), who works in the film lab in St. Louis that processed the murdered families' home movies. Dollarhyde's entry into their lives through their self-documenting carries an implication that it's our need to stop time and to see ourselves, in home movies just as in the shards of mirror Dollarhyde places in the eyes of his victims to reflect his image back at him, that make us visible to the monsters that wish to prey on us. Dollarhyde is obsessed with "becoming" the protagonist of the William Blake painting *The Great Red Dragon and the Woman Clothed in Sun*, and thinks that his murders are helping him achieve this aim, as he explains to abductee Lounds, who is duct-taped to a wheelchair and forced to witness a series of slides of the murdered families. After each, Dollarhyde asks him, "Do you see?" Once Lounds has played witness, Dollarhyde sets his body on fire and returns him to the parking lot where he was snatched, another incinerated dragon victim. Other people's visions of us—or not being seen at all—are no longer enough:

we need an image to aspire to so that, like Dollarhyde, we can "become."

In Urland, a guilt-ridden Elspeth releases Galen, who flees the castle, while the Christian priest leads a group of followers to confront the dragon. "Horns, tail, wings and clawed feet," he says, reframing their adversary like a TV evangelist, "this is no dragon—this is Lucifer!" As his followers flee, the holy man crawls to the edge of the beast's pit and, in another of the film's incongruously brutal scenes, is consumed by fire (like the fearless-in-faith priest who greets the Martian war machines in 1953's *War of the Worlds*), his hair burned away and clothes blazing like a victim of napalm, or even a nuclear attack: Vermithrax as atomic weapon, dwelling in its underground silo. Valerian is herded off to the women's enclosure to participate in the new lottery that Casiodorus has called, but to the king's horror, the idealistic Princess Elspeth has put her name on all the lots, a suicidal act she says "redresses an injustice." "Vermithrax is an old dragon," Casiodorus tells Galen, when he surprises him attempting to steal back the amulet. "That, I thought, was the beauty of my plan—time. We'd wait it out. I'd live to see the end of it…" But you can't outwait the flaws that you have allowed to fester in your society, and now that the injustice of his plan is revealed and his daughter is in danger, Casiodorus is all too happy to return the amulet to Galen and beg him to save her.

While collecting scales from the dragon's lair to fashion into a shield for Galen, Valerian is attacked by a baby dragon, revealing that Casiodorus' hope of outliving the creature's reign of terror was in any case doomed from the start. "You're going to be dead," she tells Galen when he arrives to face his foe. "[T]he dragon will be worse than ever, there will be more lotteries… and I'm not a boy anymore." And in yet another departure from the Disney ethos, we are left to work out for ourselves whether Valerian and Galen have sex to render Valerian ineligible for the inevitable lottery of virgins.

While he prepares for his next crime, Dollarhyde's plans are thrown off by the romance that flares up between him and his blind co-worker Reba McClane (Joan Allen). After he has taken her to a veterinary clinic to stroke a sedated tiger, McClane kisses Dollarhyde and the two end up in bed. Later, while Reba is asleep, Dollarhyde weeps, distraught that actual human emotions and experiences now risk destroying the perfect and grotesque fantasy world this proto-incel has created for himself—an inversion of the misogynist trope that "uptight" women just need a good fucking.

Her destiny also decided by her sexual status, Princess Elspeth goes of her own accord into the dragon's den, where Galen soon afterwards discovers the baby dragons feeding on her corpse. Galen kills the brood but fails to put an end to the dragon, and he and Valerian are on the verge of fleeing Urland altogether when a last-minute flash of inspiration sends him back to Vermithrax's cave, where he throws Ulrich's ashes into the waters of the subterranean lake of fire. A swirling green flame appears on the surface of the waters, gradually assuming the form of his dead master, and a final confrontation ensues where Ulrich sacrifices himself, exploding in Vermithrax's claws when Galen, as ordered, destroys the amulet. Leaving a trail of smoke behind it, the body of the dragon falls into the waters of a volcanic lake like a stricken airplane or a meteor, trailing behind it world-changing consequences.

The film ends with two institutional forces co-opting the event to consolidate their temporal power: as dawn breaks, a cross-carrying Greil, now a fully-fledged functionary of the new religious order, arrives with a group of acolytes to see the smashed carcass of the animal lying on the bed of the now-dried up lake. He exhorts his followers to thank God for their "divine deliverance" and to "Forsake forevermore the pagan mysteries and the blind superstitions of the past!" Hot on his heels comes Casiodorus, stepping out of his carriage in dainty slippers to gingerly prod a sword into the still-steaming remains of Vermithrax (who at least never made any spurious claims to moral righteousness) while one of his entourage cries, "All hail Casiodorus Rex—Dragonslayer!" Valerian and Galen trudge away across the moors, Galen now aware that the magic he thought he possessed was only ever ceded to him by his master.

Graham slays his own dragon after realizing that the killer must have seen the families' home movies in order to gather the information that allows him to carry out his crimes, and traces the films to the lab where Dollarhyde works. Meanwhile, after seeing one of their co-workers innocently removing some pollen from her hair, which in his solipsistic insanity he perceives as a glowing Blakean tableau of sexual betrayal, Dollarhyde abducts Reba. In the denouement, Graham throws himself through the window of the killer's art-deco home and shoots him to death while in the background Iron Butterfly's psych-rock anthem "Inna Gadda da Vida," with its references to humanity's prelapsarian state of grace, blasts out like the unresolved tensions and horrors of the 1970s erupting through the pastel-colored glazing of a doomed 1980s.

While Leatherface has his blood relatives and Manson his ad-hoc "family," Dollarhyde appears to have no family of any kind, his MO in fact requiring the elimination of such relations to aid in his "becoming." By 1980, spurred by nationwide no-fault laws, US divorce rates had reached an all-time high,[7] and feverish worries about disintegrating families and their presumably debilitating effects on a generation of latchkey kids came to the surface. Rather than filial or fraternal, Dollarhyde's interactions with Lecktor seem both fannish and collegial—and just as nerdish as the obsessively curated retro environment of his home, with its eight-track player and jet-age Fifties furnishings, looking backwards and inwards: an academic or business relationship where the currency is the thrill of treating other people like the set dressing for your own fantasies, which is about as Eighties as it gets.

The stories of both films hum with sex (or its absence) and gender roles, from the innocent virgins sacrificed to the dragon (whose sex, if it even has one, remains a mystery) to the human dragon sacrificing innocents to his own virginity—because emotionally, at least, Dollarhyde is a virgin until he meets Reba McClaine. Valerian and the princess both certainly are, and it's hard not to conclude that Galen must be too. Graham (with his maternal care for infant turtles), Galen, and even to some extent Dollarhyde, all represent vaguely alternate ideas of masculinity—none of them are stereotypically macho or virile-seeming, while together with Ulrich, Valerian (a woman performing masculinity) is by far the most far-thinking and perceptive "man" we meet in *Dragonslayer*. And while Valerian and Galen seem like children of the pre-1969 Sixties—heirs, it is implied, to a world once filled with grandeur but now decaying into a darkness bereft of wonder—Graham, Lecktor, and Dollarhyde instead evoke the dark, post-hippy 1970s, where bad trips have become the norm. Each character is a professional: one a cop, one a shrink, and one a serial killer. Dollarhyde in particular, with his bald head, pushed-back hair, and loose shirts, could easily be an ex-hippie.

When it was released, *Dragonslayer*, directed and co-written by George Lucas's USC schoolmate and frequent Steven Spielberg collaborator Matthew Robbins, was dismissed by some as yet another *Star Wars* rip-off, but though it clearly nods to its multi-billion-dollar-making predecessor, retrospectively it seems like the more honest film of the two. As the murdered mentor who returns in the hour of his protege's need to assist him, Ulrich certainly resembles Obi-Wan Kenobi, and Galen does use his mentor's magic to destroy the film's Death Star. But Ulrich is un-heroically tired and disappointed by life and his role in it, and Galen carries out his quest as much out of vainglory as out of altruism. While his actions end the immediate cycle of death, we are left feeling as though his heroics may have simply paved the way for a new cycle of oppression. And though the story's fantasy is nominally made up of its dragons and backward-harking medievalisms, the whole narrative implicitly dissects the shared fantasies that we continue to carry forward with us today: the kings of the real world are just as much fictions crafted to appeal to potential fans as anything coming out of the role-playing and video game industries, and the rulebooks of history have been carefully written to ensure the gamesmaster continues to prevail. Ulrich and Casiodorus both indulge in mythmaking aimed at capturing the imaginations of the proles, Casiodorus with his pomp and trimmings of divinely ordained right and Ulrich with his costume and his stage effects. *Dragonslayer* hints cynically, or perhaps even altruistically, that many of America's foundational myths may have been concocted in the same way.

While the problem in *Dragonslayer* isn't individuals but old, dying systems and the way the accommodations humans make with them turn into unhealthy new ones, the problem in *Manhunter* is the turbulent human depths that modernity seems to enable. There isn't really any "evil" in *Dragonslayer*, just an aging and peevish dragon trying to guarantee a future for its offspring, while the dragon in *Manhunter* is on a pathological quest for self-realization unmoored from any human empathy, and what better definition of "evil" is there? Both films hint at a country losing itself in its dreams and fantasies, unable to look at itself except through some kind of lens or in some kind of mirror. Galen and Dollarhyde are each, in their way, symbols of something that had always been present in one part of the countercultural mentality: the vain and shallow Galen with his quest—well-intentioned but clearly underscored by a desire to feel special—to put an end to an obviously corrupt system, but generally ill-equipped and unwilling to imagine or build what might take its place; and Dollarhyde, the malignant embodiment of the New Age concepts of "self-realization" and "self-actualization" that are actually just cover for entitled narcissism: to hell with what "becoming" costs those around you.

11. "SOMEBODY'S GONNA DROP THE FUCKIN' BOMB ANYWAY, RIGHT?": *TESTAMENT* AND *PARTING GLANCES*

If you can ignore the somber titles that appear over a black background and the ominous tolling bell that precedes it, the opening scene of 1983's *Testament*—white curtains fluttering in the morning breeze, a sunny California bedroom, the voice on an exercise tape declaiming *"right, left... right, left"*—almost seems of a piece with the opening scene of 1986's *Parting Glances*, where, to the sprightly tinkling of a piano quartet by Brahms, a handsome young man in red Adidas shorts and tank top takes a morning run through a sunny New York City park while his cerebral partner sits on a bench reading a book. Both beginnings share a buoyant, almost weightless feeling of possibility that evokes a Hallmark Movie of the Week, or Reagan's "Morning in America," even though that's very much the opposite of what the films are about.

The United States spent the 1980s living in the shadow of two apocalypses. One of them, the AIDS epidemic, actually happened, albeit initially in silence and aided by the Reagan administration's covert refusal to do anything about it. Fortunately for the continued existence of all life on Earth, the other didn't. Not quite. It did, though, leave the decade irradiated with the terrifying possibility of a slow and agonizing death among the ruins of civilization, which is precisely the concern of 1983's *Testament*. Previously, films depicting nuclear war tended to come at the issue from the perspective of the military, as with 1959's *On the Beach*, 1964's *Doctor Strangelove*, and 1977's *Twilight's Last Gleaming*, or they'd been post-apocalyptic exploitationers like 1962's *Panic in Year Zero!*, 1977's *Damnation Alley*, and 1981's *Mad Max 2*, whose immense success flooded cinemas with low-rent fictions based in post-nuke wastelands. Based on a short story by Carol Amen and brought to the screen by producer, Public Broadcasting Service television reporter, National Education Television documentarian, and director Lynne Littman, *Testament* took a different approach: instead of the cathartic pantomimes that came before it, the film substituted punishingly mundane horror set in suburbs even more placid than those in *Poltergeist*.

Parting Glances was the debut feature of director Bill Sherwood, who started making short films while studying at the public Hunter College after dropping out of the private Juilliard. Much of what had historically fallen under the banner of gay cinema before *Parting Glances* had either been prohibited from referring to its subject matter with anything more than innuendo or else been focused on the more traumatic aspects of homosexual life. *Parting Glances*, which was shot in 1985, when the death of Rock Hudson and Ronald Reagan's first public mention of the disease had put the burgeoning AIDS crisis bang in the public eye, presents homosexuality not as the dramatic *raison d'être* of its story but as a done deal: after they return home from the park, bookish Michael (Richard Ganoung) and bland, sporty hunk Robert (John Bolger), the couple at the heart of the film's story, are already in the sack, the absolute normality of their relationship as much a given as it is with that of Carol (Jane Alexander) and Tom Wetherly (Willian Devane), the protagonists of *Testament*, with the same friction between the pleasure and frustration of familiarity.

Littman says that her model for *Testament* was a film whose effects on her had been so violent that she'd thrown up after seeing it: *The War Game*, a grueling 1965 black-and-white pseudo-documentary that *Punishment Park*'s Peter Watkins made for the BBC about the possible consequences of a nuclear war upon Great Britain (the British establishment considered it so incendiary that it was withdrawn and not shown on TV until 1985).[1] Littman, though, approached the issue differently, adopting a calm tonal palette more reminiscent of the intimacy of a TV movie about domestic tragedy on the scale of divorce or alcoholism—though watching her film requires in any case a strong stomach. Sherwood claimed that what initially spurred him to make *Parting Glances* was partly "dismay at the way gays are always portrayed in movies, which is, you know, as psychotic murderers or child molesters or whatever, so I thought it would be nice to have a movie with just nice normal gay people in it, for a change."[2] Of his decision to keep the AIDS crisis then raging violently through gay communities as something simmering in the background of the film and not its dramatic fulcrum: "I knew that there would be all kinds of plays and television movies dealing with the subject by the time [*Parting Glances*] was released [...] so I just wanted it to have a smaller place in the film, kind of be part of the overall fabric or story of present day gay life in a big city in the US."[3]

Central to the narrative of both films is the departure—temporary or definitive—of a lover. In *Testament*, it's Tom's departure on business from the Wetherlys' home in the leafy suburb of Hamelin for San Francisco shortly before the US is attacked with nuclear weapons, while in *Parting Glances* it's Robert's being transferred to Africa for two years on the orders of the international aid organization he works for—though perhaps the departing lover is actually Nick (Steve Buscemi), Michael's ex who is living with a terminal illness that nobody in the film wants to name out loud and for which there is no cure. This initial section of both films highlights the reassuring, comfortable domesticity of the world the two couples inhabit and the ephemera that fills it: in Diane's case, it's mainly the toys, games, magazines, records, *E.T.* t-shirts, bikes, and He-Man figures of her three kids, teenagers Brad (Ross Harris) and Mary (Roxana Zal) and little Scotty (Lukas Haas). Michael's aesthetic, on the other hand, is more highbrow: Rothko prints, wooden dinosaur skeletons, pot plants, bonsai trees, ethnic ornaments. But despite the differences in tastes, the worlds they inhabit, whether that of the West Coast professional class or the East Coast intellectual class, are solidly middle-class 1980s.

There are tensions in both relationships, though: in *Testament*, dynamic dad Tom, clad in an "All American" t-shirt, takes Brad out for a bike ride through their idyllic neighborhood as he tries to instill his anxious and diffident son with some of his own confidence, urging Brad to push himself past his self-imposed limits, and his blithe self-assurance and the incautious remarks he throws about in front of the impressionable Scotty seem sometimes to annoy the more thoughtful Diane. On the opposite coast, despite their clear affection for one another and many years together, the relationship between Michael and Robert also seems strained—Robert's healthy, handsome blandness, and a life together that's so intertwined they struggle to remember which shirts belong to who, sit uneasily with Michael's more mercurial and emotional character.

Michael is a freelance book editor, currently (and unhappily) working on the "S&M sci-fi porno" novel of his wealthy friend Douglas (Richard Wall). On one of his frequent visits to the record shop where he buys opera and classical LPs, he catches the eye of cute young clerk Peter (Adam Nathan), who pesters him for an invite to Robert's farewell that evening at the loft of their friend Joan (Kathy Kinney). To Robert's mild annoyance, Michael regularly goes over to Nick's apartment to force him to eat healthy food and keep him company, as most of Nick's acquaintances are, we learn, deliberately or unconsciously avoiding him. When Michael arrives, Nick—who is a successful new wave rocker—is listening on headphones to the opera records that Michael has been buying him while waiting for his latest video to show up on one of the multiple old TVs that, *The Man Who Fell to Earth*-like, fill a corner of his apartment. While he's preparing dinner for Nick, Michael cuts his finger. "Have you used that knife lately?" he asks with feigned nonchalance, before hurrying to the bathroom to disinfect the cut while Nick rants about "Bob the bore": "I'll never understand how you fell for that geek," he complains. "I mean, the guy looks like a fuckin' Ken doll." With his consumptive, saturnine good looks and a cynical mien that couldn't be further from Robert's genteel good-naturedness, Nick is Robert's polar opposite, though he's also the most honest, unsentimental, and authentic person in the film, the only one in his community who never seems to be performing—even though performing is his job. He's also the one who seems to have the healthiest relationship with the disease, and bristles at being treated like a victim. Between complaints about the greens Michael forces him to eat, Nick acts as though he's resigned to his situation: "Somebody's gonna drop the fuckin' bomb anyway, right?" he sneers. "So who gives a shit, really? Just glad I won't be around for that."

The bomb gets dropped in *Testament* without any warning or buildup, apart from Diane's offhand mention to Tom of an acquaintance being indicted because he "didn't register for the draft": the cartoon that Diane's kids are watching in the family's sunny lounge simply stops before being replaced by static, which is then replaced by an emergency warning transmission. When the attack itself comes, it's not even a noise—just a silent flash of blinding light. In the aftermath of the bomb, the local community pulls together and, unable to believe that the wider world won't rally, seems determined to struggle through, organizing mutual assistance and continuing with their little world of school plays and piano lessons. But as *Testament* grinds forward, it gradually becomes more and more obvious that there is going to be no struggling through this one. Things are not going to return to normal; they are just going to keep getting worse, and there won't be any school plays when all the children have died and all the adults are busy building bonfires to burn their corpses on.

Unlike *The Day After*, which was released the same year (and which president Ronald Reagan claimed left him "greatly depressed" after viewing it[4]), there are none of the typical signifiers of nuclear war: no model buildings are destroyed, no colorized stock footage of shacks being blown away by 1,000mph winds, no flesh drooping from bones, no radiation sickness makeup—only confusion and denial followed by a dull awareness that spreads through the inhabitants of Hamelin that this might really be it: there might really be no going back. Nobody is blamed for the war, and there's no mention of politics, or enemy countries, or presidents. By definition, it is probably a left-wing film, at least in as much as it aims to affect the opinion of the viewer as regards the effectiveness of a nuclear deterrent, and it is conceivable that to some particularly ideologically-driven idiots at the time, it may have looked like liberal hand-wringing. But really it has no particular ax to grind other than to ask: what is the conceivable purpose of all this misery?

There's no bomb in *Parting Glances* either: no overt mention of HIV or AIDS, no make-up, no hospitals, no dying words—just little hints in the background, like Michael's panicky disinfecting of his cut or the references to "catching you-know-what," that this community is already dealing with an equally lethal kind of invisible death. Despite cases of AIDS in North America going through the roof while *Parting Glances* was being made, with the Centers for Disease Control finding that the 1985 figures showed an increase of nearly 90% in new cases over the previous year and that AIDS patients could expect, on average, to live for about fifteen months after receiving a diagnosis,[5] the White House was still dragging its feet about taking the large-scale action that was clearly long overdue: funding for AIDS research continued to be deplorably inadequate and no federal AIDS prevention plan had yet been approved. Furthermore, much of the general (straight) public was approving of measures to isolate those dying slowly from what the press was calling the "gay plague."[6] The deaths in *Testament* are not immediate either, but as the number of corpses grows too large to be accommodated in the town's graveyard, the gravity of the situation becomes obvious even to those living in denial.

Denial—or dishonesty—causes an argument between Michael and Robert as they return home in a cab after dinner at the elegant apartment of Robert's bourgeois boss Cecil (Patrick Tull) and his wife Betty (Yolande Bavan), where, even while Betty is telling Michael that Cecil has no idea he and Robert are gay, Cecil is recounting one of his many gay trysts to Robert in the kitchen and giving him the address of a place in Nairobi that can be "interesting." Michael calls Robert a hypocrite, and a provoked Robert admits that he allowed the transfer to Africa go through because he was worried life with Michael had been "getting predictable." When the cab driver mutters "Faggots," Michael reacts angrily, earning him a rebuke for being "rude" from the ever-genteel Robert.

The crowd at the farewell party is well-heeled and attractive, the loft airy and luminous, a refined spread of salads on the table. "All these young guys look so perfect, I can't stand it," comments Terry (Andre Morgan), before asking Michael, "Remember how ugly everyone used to look in New York?" "It's the post-Kennedy assassination generation," retorts Michael. Joan has invited a couple of successful and self-consciously edgy German artists to the party in the hope of giving her own art career a boost, increasingly important now that her rent is going up. The film as a whole, and the party scene in particular, is saturated with a feeling that, as the grip of the yuppie mindset on the life of the city has grown tighter and prices continue to rise, things have become increasingly bourgeois, and what was once very real transgression risks now becoming a lifestyle or self-referential performance, like the Germans' "mixed media performance Neo-expressionist postmodern something or other." "Yeah, you can do anything you want nowadays," says Michael, "but sometimes I have this feeling there's nothing left to do." Michael confesses to Joan the guilt he feels over his conflicting emotions about Nick: "sometimes when I'm over there all I can think of is I'm so glad I don't have it." "Who wouldn't be?" replies Joan. "I mean, don't worry, a few years down the road we have lung cancer and heart attacks to look forward to"—if the bomb doesn't get them first. The implication is that, given the dangerous world they inhabit and the hedonism they enjoyed in their younger days, they suspect death is coming for them all sooner rather than later. Yet despite this undertone of resigned gloom, the party scene is at the same time a captivating and vivacious bit of filmmaking, as the camera flits between the various guests, capturing the atmosphere of heady pleasure and confusion.

While Michael is sequestered with Joan and Robert is up on the building's roof talking with Sarah (Kristin Moneagle), his pre-coming-out high school girlfriend and now confidante, Nick appears at the party to the surprise and terror of some of the guests. He flits between the partygoers, commiserating with the sad-looking ex-priest who has left the seminary, teasing the wealthy Douglas about his weight. "I'll have the last laugh," Douglas says to Terry once Nick has gone. "I may have committed the gay cardinal sin of being a bit overweight, but it's that self-same so-called unattractiveness that spared me from the plague." He's articulating the feeling among reactionaries that AIDS was a punishment for a hedonistic, promiscuous, immoral lifestyle—what Pat Buchanan, then Reagan's communications director, called "nature's revenge on gay men."[7]

As the German artist wanders the rooms of the large loft, he's ambushed by Nick, who he had previously been trying to convince to appear in one of his installations: holding a knife to the German's throat, Nick promises he'll sing for him if he gets Joan an art show. It's hard to know how serious the threat is, but the soundtrack's incongruous shift to the kind of unnerving synth that we might more readily associate with imminent violence in a slasher movie suddenly makes more sense; it's a reminder that not far beneath this veneer of happy and good-looking people, farewell parties, good jobs, salad buffets, and "edgy" artists lurks a more precarious reality, of which Nick is the avatar.

Earlier, Nick was cornered by Peter, the guy from the record store, who asked him why Michael plays hard-to-get. "He's a cautious guy," says Nick. "If he's worried about catching you-know-what, it won't be from me." Later, after Peter has apologized for his tactlessness, the two chat on the stairs, and Nick is surprised and perhaps even a little disappointed by Peter's *blasé* acceptance of his homosexuality, echoing the feeling in the rest of the film that what was once thrilling and transgressive risks becoming, in its way, stale and formalized, like Cecil's little jaunts abroad and Douglas's staid gay stable of beefcake at his beach house. Yet *Parting Glances* never becomes didactic, and always maintains a beguiling delicacy of touch. And it's the delicacy of touch with which events are handled in *Testament* that allows the film to make its point all the more forcefully. Its artlessness and lack of pretension make it, if anything, even more upsetting and disorienting: despite its TV drama framing, this is the kind of bleakness we're used to seeing in arthouse film, rendered with the more rarefied aesthetics implied in that genre. The economy with which the characters are sketched lends them a blank credibility, and the absence of any of the iconography of nuclear war (not even a single radioactive symbol) only adds to the film's power. The tone does occasionally get a little preachy, but considering the point the film is trying to make—the stupidity of slowly and agonizingly killing half of the population of the planet—it's a forgivable blip. In any event, *Testament* never feels smug or self-righteous: most of the time, the viewer is simply staring at the screen in dread.

A party features in *Testament* too, only here it's not the happy event that celebrates Robert's departure but the film's grim conclusion, where, in the darkness, Diane, Brad, and Hiroshi (Gerry Murillo) sit around matzo crackers with birthday candles on them while Diane tells Brad to wish that "we remember it all. The good and the awful. The way we finally lived." The film is dotted with poignant little scenes, like the one where Brad takes his late dad's bike from the garage after his own has been stolen, or when mother and son dance together to a (not very good) cover of the Beatles' "All My Loving" played on a battery-powered tape recorder—a pertinent reminder of the finite nature of the technologies we use to remember who we are — or another when Mary, aware of how unlikely it is that she will have the opportunity to find out for herself, asks Carol what it's like to make love, or perhaps the most grueling of all: the final scene showing an old home movie of Tom's birthday, which, in its silent normality, feels like a declaration of love in the face of death that's as touching as Michael's confession to Nick that he's the only person he's ever really loved.

As well as the family Super 8 movies, motifs of recording occur throughout *Testament*—nursery rhymes, exercise cassettes, the answering machine that contains Tom's final message, even the journal that Carol starts writing at the beginning of the story—and they are there too in *Parting Glances*: Nick makes video recordings of himself on VHS where he apologizes to his dad for not telling him about his illness and lays out the conditions of his will ("GMHC [Gay Men's Health Crisis] for care for four people with AIDS and not for medical research, because if the feds can spend a trillion bucks on bombs, then they could spend a little on research, right?"); the book that Michael is finally starting to write for himself, as he moves, perhaps, from a phase of being the editor of his own existence to being the creator of it; and even the opera LPs that Michael brings for Nick—they stimulate his imagination so much that, after leaving the party, he experiences an eerie visitation by the ghost of the Commendatore from Mozart's *Don Giovanni*, who turns out to be Gregg (Daniel Haughey), an old acquaintance who recently died from AIDS. "Heaven's real boring, hang on as long as you can," Gregg tells Nick, before warning him, in a nice little example of the film's ability to deflate its own pretensions, not to let Michael turn him into an opera queen and to stick to baseball: "It's a lot cheaper."

Suicide makes an appearance in both films, perhaps inevitably: at the end of *Parting Glances*, Nick calls Michael from Fire Island saying he "can't take it anymore," spurring Michael to rent an air taxi he can't afford to try and stop him, while Diane, Brad, and Hiroshi climb into the station wagon, that archetypal symbol of middle-class optimism, and prepare to gas themselves to put an end to the nightmare (the conclusion of Amen's original version of the story, which, according to Littman, Catholic literary magazine *The Saint Anthony Messenger* forced her to change). When Michael gets out to the island, he learns it was just a ruse to lure him out to the place where he and Nick had once raided a respectable pool party at Douglas's large beach house. And Diane can't go through with it, slumping onto the steering wheel and turning off the ignition, her blind need to continue existing more powerful than the horrors that she knows await.

Both films feature families of choice or contingency: in *Parting Glances*, that of the tight-knit gay community of which Michael is a part; and in *Testament*, the one created by the need to care for vulnerable members of the community, like Larry (Mico Olmos), the son of the next door neighbors who never came back from work, or Hiroshi, the son of Asian American gas station owner Mike (Mako) who Diane takes in after his father has died. *Testament* and *Parting Glances*, overtly or tacitly, show their respective communities facing in their own way the horrors that the institutions meant to protect them are either ignoring or actively encouraging as they follow their own blinkered, calculated agendas. Where they differ is in their conclusions: in *Parting Glances*, it's implied that, despite everything, optimism and hope still exist for Michael, Robert, and even Nick, and that new memories, sad or happy but in any case vital, are waiting to be forged; in *Testament*, what is vital is the preservation of the memories that are left, because they're the last ones. All that's left now is the slow decay of existence into nothingness.

12. "ARE YOU REALLY CRAZY?":

LETHAL WEAPON AND *FATAL ATTRACTION*

The first American buddy cop movie wasn't *Freebie and the Bean* (1974) or *Nighthawks* (1981) or *48 hrs.* (1982). It was 1970's *Cotton Comes to Harlem*, about two hardboiled Black detectives, Grave Digger Jones (Godfrey Cambridge) and Coffin Ed Johnson (Raymond St. Jacques), who butt heads with dopers, mobsters, militants, honkies, their own police force, and a Back-to-Africa con man (Calvin Lockhart) in a hunt for the $87,000 he fleeced from the Black community. Their captain's (John Anderson) description of the pair is a good one for most of the cops and private dicks of the next twenty years: "too quick with their fists, too flip with their talk, too fast with their guns"—"damn maniacs on a powder keg." The film, based on the 1965 Chester Himes novel of the same name, was co-written and directed by stage and screen actor, playwright, civil rights activist, and Malcolm X eulogizer Ossie Davis, and it was the first by a Black director to become a crossover hit. Meant to entertain above all, Davis's "residual message" was clear: "black people outwit the establishment and stay one step ahead of the wolf's teeth."[1]

After the uprisings in Watts and other major cities across the country throughout the second half of the 1960s, Black police officers were increasingly sought out for what various white commissions and agencies assumed would be their "special effectiveness" in Black communities.[2] 1969's *The Black Cop*, a documentary produced by Kent Garrett for Detroit's public broadcast *Black Journal*, "about Blacks and for Blacks," portrays a much more complicated reality. David Walker, patrolling Harlem like Digger and Ed (but paired with a white partner), wants to "[fulfill] my own life" and "be a service to the community," but "We're being used like tools for the system, a Black cop today." He's "caught in the middle," afraid he may be propping up the racism and inequality he wants to dismantle. Many of the people interviewed on the street describe Black cops as more "brutal" than their white counterparts, because they're trying to prove their loyalty to a police force that serves the interests of "white society and the status quo"; one man takes it even further: "a Black man as policeman is out of the category of being Black any longer, because just the mere thing of him being a policeman shows that he's turned against Blackness."[3] The same friction plays out in *Cotton Comes to Harlem* when Digger and Ed put themselves (literally) between the police station and the angry mob that wants to burn it to the ground. "Now we may have broken some heads," says Ed, attempting to placate, "but we never broke no promises." Earlier, after the captain chews them out, Ed threatens to quit and Digger brushes him off: "You quit, I quit. And then who'll protect the Black folks from the white folks?" To which Ed dryly responds, "Who's gonna protect the Black folks from themselves?"

In 1967's *In the Heat of the Night*, Philadelphia's "number one homicide expert" Virgil Tibbs (Sidney Poitier) is paired with racist Mississippi Police Chief Bill Gillespie (Rod Steiger) to solve the murder of the town's industrialist savior—a murder initially pinned on Tibbs (who's visiting his mother) because he's Black and has money in his wallet. Tibbs is both caught in the middle and a fish out of water in the very town he grew up in, the town he escaped. "Why you wanna help the police like that?" the town's abortionist (for well-paying white women) chides him. "They stealin' your soul. They chew you up and spit you out." But Tibbs, like Digger and Ed, like David Walker, thinks he can make a difference. At the end of the film, Tibbs and Gillespie part on a note of reluctant respect, but they know they can never be friends: the racial rift can't be bridged. The tone has shifted dramatically by the time we get to 1984's *Beverly Hills Cop*. In another fish-out-of-water story, working-class Detroit detective Axel Foley (Eddie Murphy) bucks his inspector's orders and heads to upper-crust paradise Beverly Hills to find out who murdered his friend, a low-level thief who stole from the wrong people (Foley himself is a former juvenile delinquent). Both Tibbs and Foley are young and ambitious, superior cops with instincts honed on the mean streets, but where Tibbs is meticulous and disciplined—until, famously, he returns the slap of a racist white suspect—Foley is rash and insubordinate, a "cowboy cop," and his unlikely mentorship of and eventual friendship with two bumbling white Beverly Hills cops "neutralized racial difference," says Gabrie'l J. Atchison, and "portrayed a racial utopia where racism could be resolved through friendship."[4]

1987's *Lethal Weapon* is generally lumped into this same category, although homicide detective Roger Murtaugh (Danny Glover) is an outlier in the buddy cop mix: middle-aged (he turns fifty as the film begins), clean-living, a respected LAPD sergeant and a Vietnam vet who served in Army Airborne, he's a family man who can't wait to retire and spend time on the boat he putters around with in the driveway. (The boat is pulled by the family station wagon: in Frankenheimer's

Seconds, soon-to-be-reborn Arthur Hamilton has the same setup.) Murtaugh lives in the suburbs, importantly, a luxury not often bestowed on cinematic Black families, especially ones that include a cop. Digger and Ed, Tibbs, and Foley all live in the urban communities they patrol. It's the white officers, explains the NYPD's Arthur C. Hill in *The Black Cop*, who commute from "a foreign environment… like suburbia." But during the 1980s, middle-class Black families did increasingly move to the suburbs[5]—under cover of what Reagan called a "colorblind society,"[6] federal aid to the inner cities was largely scrapped (a deliberate rebuff to liberal mayors), just as crack cocaine wrought fatal addiction and murderous turf wars, and conditions that were already dire became doomed. By the end of the decade, almost twice as many Blacks lived in ghetto poverty.[7]

In *Lethal Weapon*, it's Martin Riggs (Mel Gibson) who's out of luck. In all-too-obvious contrast with Murtaugh, who we meet first, he lives in a broken-down trailer at the beach with his dog, smokes too many cigarettes, drinks beer for breakfast, sleeps with his gun, gets high on violence, and carries around a special bullet he thinks a lot about eating. "He's on edge," the police psychologist (Mary Ellen Trainor) tells Captain Murphy (Steve Kahan). "I'm telling you he may be psychotic." She advises him to pull Riggs out of the field, which of course is exactly the thing that should be done, but he dismisses the evaluation as "a bunch of psych bullshit" and assures her that Riggs is a "tough bastard" who can take it. We're supposed to believe Riggs is "a crazy son of a bitch" and "a real burnout, on the ragged edge" because he "recently" lost his wife in a car crash. And without the "civilizing, humanizing influence" of a woman, to quote Robin Wood again, he has devolved into a savage with a "death wish." The parallels to *Dirty*

Harry's trigger-happy SFPD Inspector Harry Callahan, who has recently lost *his* wife in a car wreck ("a drunk crossed the centerline") and deals with suicide jumpers as dismissively as Riggs, are obvious, but the differences are just as important. "Guys in the Eighties aren't tough," Sergeant McCaskey (Jack Thibeau) jokes with Murtaugh in the station. "They're sensitive people; they show their emotions in front of women and shit like that. I think I'm an Eighties man."

MURTAUGH: How you figure?

MCCASKEY: Last night, I cried in bed. So how's that?

MURTAUGH: Were you with a woman?

MCCASKEY: I was alone. Why do you think I was cryin'?

It's a set-up for a one-liner, but it's also an ironically intimate description of Riggs in the previous scene, where he weeps while cradling his wedding photo, talks to his dead wife, and puts a gun in his mouth—a display the laconic and impassive Callahan, the definitive Seventies man, would never think of making. Riggs is "crazy" not because he misses his wife ("I'll see you much later," he tells her picture, unable to pull the trigger), but because her loss has surfaced the ever-present trauma of his past: he's a vet too, made a Special Forces sniper while still a teenager, one of the best. Unlike the older Murtaugh, though, he can't come to grips with what he saw and did in Vietnam, with what his government turned him into.

The captain, hedging his bets, quickly pairs Riggs with the cool-headed, rock-steady Murtaugh, a situation they both, in the beginning, resent with extreme prejudice. Their first meeting is an inversion of the racist profiling practices of American police: Murtaugh mistakes the shaggy-haired and unkempt Riggs for a criminal, charges him, and gets thrown to the ground by the younger man, who's "heavy into martial arts." (In 1982's *First Blood*, decorated Special Forces vet John Rambo [Sylvester Stallone], shaggy-haired and unkempt, is unwisely chased out of town by a police chief [Brian Dennehy] who doesn't want "guys like you" around.) But Murtaugh, who studies Riggs' file, susses out the problem—"There's something eating away at this guy," the psychologist will soon tell him—right away.

MURTAUGH: It's over, you know.

RIGGS: What is?

MURTAUGH: The war.

RIGGS: Uh, yes, I know.

MURTAUGH: Just thought I'd remind you.

The plot revolves around the death of Amanda Hunsaker (Jackie Swanson), the daughter of Murtaugh's old "Vietnam buddy" Michael Hunsaker (Tom Atkins). Originally filed as a suicide—in director Richard Donner's virtuosic opening scene, Amanda snorts coke and dives off the balcony of a high-rise building—it turns out she was poisoned by a prostitute (Lycia Naff) paid off by former members of Shadow Company, a unit of the CIA-fronted Air America that "secretly ran the entire war out of Laos" and, years later, smuggled heroin from Southeast Asia into the States. Hunsaker wanted out, and they killed his daughter. And right after he spills his guts to Murtaugh, they kill him too. And so Murtaugh's suburban sanctuary is shattered, as he thumbs through Amanda's high school yearbook and realizes that she wasn't much older than his teenage daughter Rianne (Traci Wolfe)—who is promptly kidnapped by Shadow Company for no other reason than to make Murtaugh understand that he can't escape his past either.

Hunsaker "took a bayonet in the lungs" for Murtaugh at the Battle of la Drang in '65, and there's a picture on Hunsaker's desk of the two in some bar in Saigon, looking younger and fresher, clasping hands, buddies. The Vietnam War marked the first time American combat troops were fully integrated, the first time many of the men would interact on a day-to-day basis with different races and ethnicities. "There's no racial barrier of any sort here," Lewis B. Larry, a Black platoon sergeant in the 101st Airborne Division, says in the 1967 NBC documentary "Same Mud, Same Blood."[8] The men under Larry's command agree, and Frank McGee, a white correspondent embedded with the troops, concludes that "Nowhere in America have I seen Negroes and whites as free, open and uninhibited with their associations."[9] In 1970's *The Black GI*, his follow-up to *The Black Cop*, Kent Garrett once again uncovers a more troubling situation. While some Black soldiers, particularly the officers, echo McGee—"Here in the military you kind of get away from the Black versus white bit..."—most describe de facto segregation (comparisons to the American South abound), being passed up or held back for promotion (only 2% were officers), disproportionate discipline and imprisonment (almost 35% of courts-martial cases), disproportionate assignment to combat units (23% in

1967, despite representing only 16% of draftees[10]), and in general being expected "to be some kind of little white Negro" and "take second-class standards..." L. Howard Bennett, the Pentagon's Acting Deputy Assistant Secretary of Civil Rights (and the first Black judge appointed in Minnesota) tells Garrett that "Our participation in protecting and securing this nation puts us in a much stronger position to demand every ounce and iota of democracy to which we are entitled." A few of the GIs interviewed said much the same (Murtaugh might have been one of them: by 1965 he had aged out of the draft; he volunteered for service), but Garrett's response cuts to the deplorable chase: "What you're saying is that Black men should give up their lives for something that they should already have [...] by the very fact of being human beings."[11]

All of this subtext is accidental, but not insignificant, in *Lethal Weapon*: Murtaugh's race is not specified in Shane Black's original script. Neither is Riggs'. Suggested by casting director Marion Dougherty, Donner offered Glover the part, and Glover, a civil rights activist since his student days at San Francisco State University, took it because he "loved the relationship between the two guys. And I loved the fact that the white character comes to the black person's home. Usually, we see it the other way around."[12] If race is decontextualized, it's because everything is decontextualized: Murtaugh and Riggs rush unchecked (never once do they take orders or speak to the captain) through a Los Angeles that's much too far-flung to be a real beat or anything but a symbolic new frontier (from city to suburb, beach to desert), spurning police procedure and pesky legalities along the way (Dirty Harry is by-the-numbers in comparison), and wreaking hellish vengeance on the crowded city streets without a single civilian casualty. In the film's only direct evocation of race, Murtaugh and Riggs talk to a group of unsupervised Black kids: one of them saw who planted a bomb at the house of the "hooker" who killed Amanda. "My mama says policemen shoot Black people," six-year-old Alfred (Donald Gooden, wearing a "Free South Africa" t-shirt) says, and all of the kids shout out, in a repeating chorus: "Is it true? Is that true?" Murtaugh and Riggs smile awkwardly, and the truth is avoided by sending the rascals off to get ice cream. The beating of Rodney King, for which all of the LAPD officers involved would be acquitted, was four years away, but the department already had a long history of assaulting and harassing Black and Latino residents,[13] a targeted violence driven by what 1991's independent Christopher Commission described as a "strikingly" racist culture. We see Riggs and Murtaugh "as individuals," Glover said, responding to a question about squaring his character with his politics, "aside from their work as part of this force of occupation [the LAPD]. It's almost as if they are above this in some way."[14]

In early 1985, the LAPD borrowed two "six-ton armored vehicles" from the US Department of Energy, previously used by the Army in Vietnam as personnel carriers, to be used as battering rams on crack "rock houses" in majority-Black South Central Los Angeles.[15] On February 6, 1985, with Police Chief Daryl Gates in the passenger seat and TV crews not far behind, what witnesses described as a "big tank" smashed through the front wall of a Pacoima home (Riggs sends a cop car through the front wall of Murtaugh's house to distract the sinister Mr. Joshua, played by Gary Busey). Heavily armed LAPD officers and a SWAT team rushed through the hole only to find two women, one of them a resident of the house, three terrified children who had been eating ice cream, and less than one-tenth of a gram of cocaine. So drugs are not exactly a MacGuffin in *Lethal Weapon*. Here, at the height of Reagan's catastrophic multi-billion-dollar war on drugs, heroin is a cipher for crack cocaine, the former (which became "the convenient outward symbol [...] for the white man's fear of the black man," wrote Godfrey Hodgson[16]) funneled from Southeast Asia into the inner cities throughout the late Sixties and Seventies, the latter funneled into the inner cities by traffickers in South America (including the US-backed right-wing Contras in Nicaragua, allegedly aided by the CIA) starting in the early Eighties.[17] In both cases, the supply was plentiful and the street price was cheap. Although the victims were overwhelmingly Black, the only casualty in this alternate Los Angeles is a young, attractive, upper-middle-class white woman (Amanda Hunsaker), precisely the nightmare scenario—a racist phantasm, in reality—that haunted Nixon, Reagan, and large swaths of white America. "Why can I have a beer, but I can't smoke a joint? It's not coke, you know," complains Rianne as her dad and Riggs are knocking down Coors cans on the boat; she's been "grounded" for smoking pot in the house. "Because now, at this moment," Murtaugh explains, "beer is legal, grass ain't." It's a deliberate reference to Reagan's "zero tolerance" policies, under which cannabis was grouped in the same "Schedule" as heroin.[18] Once again, young Blacks suffered most: a generation went to prison, sometimes for life.

If Murtaugh and Riggs are "above" all of this, as Glover remarked, it's because *Lethal Weapon* is a post-*Star Wars* Vietnam revenge allegory about the father-son bond that develops between two vets who have to go back to war to get back home.[19] "We do this my way," Riggs tells Murtaugh when they find out Rianne is kidnapped. They're huddled in the living room, eerily lit by the Christmas tree lights (but only the red ones), two primeval warriors plotting around a fire in a cave. "You shoot? You shoot to kill." Murtaugh has to embrace the killer instinct that he thought he left behind, buried in the mud and the blood of the jungle, and reclaim the virility that he fears age has taken from him. In hushed tones, in that same red firelight, he asks Riggs: "Are you really crazy? Or are you as good as you say you are?" As if Riggs can't be both. A note left on the tree in a later scene, which bloodthirsty Mr. Joshua reads in disgust, describes a moral universe that even George Lucas, who made the police faceless and fascist androids in *THX 1138*, might have found childish:

Dear BAD GUYS
No one here but us
COPS
SORRY!
The GOOD GUYS

Now, it's a given that Murtaugh's kids wrote the note, but Riggs too is childlike, an orphan, a true believer: "You know why I don't do it?" he tells Murtaugh, admitting that "Every single day" he thinks of a reason not to blow his head off with that special bullet. "The *job*. Doin' the *job*." He tells us what the job is a little later, the morning after Murtaugh invites him to his home to break bread with his family: "We gotta get up and catch bad guys." But the bad guys in this particular Vietnam story are not Vietnamese communists. They're the corrupt CIA goons and their mercenary lackeys who "secretly ran the war out of Laos"—who secretly *lost* the war—who betrayed their country and the grunts on the front lines. (In 1985's *Rambo: First Blood Part II*, it's the CIA suit and "goddamn mercenaries" who, for cynical political reasons, betray Rambo's mission to rescue American POWs still being held in Vietnam.) Riggs is juxtaposed not only with Murtaugh, but with his dark side, former Special Ops-turned-merc Mr. Joshua, who a prospective buyer (Ed O'Ross) describes as an offering from "Psychos R Us." At one point, Riggs refers to Joshua as an "albino," yet another physical description not in the original script.

Captured while trying to rescue Rianne, Murtaugh and Riggs are removed to a dreary and labyrinthine industrial warehouse—it's the "Hanoi Hilton" and the tunnels of the Viet Cong Hollywoodized into one set—where they're tortured separately and in great detail. Riggs is strung up and electrocuted by Endo, played by Chinese American Al Leong (Rambo is strung up and zapped by a Russian), because "it's essential to find out all the cops know" about the "rather large" incoming heroin shipment. (The bad guys would have simply assumed the cops knew everything and put off the shipment, or changed the drop location, but logic pointedly does not apply here.) When bloodied and swollen Murtaugh refuses to talk, the commander of Shadow Company and the Emperor to Mr. Joshua's Darth Vader, General Peter McCallister (Mitchell Ryan), has Rianne brought out, bound and stripped to her underwear. He'll torture the "real good-lookin' young woman you got there" to get the answers he wants (when Rambo won't talk, the Russian commander threatens to torture a tattered and bedraggled POW). Who's to stop him, after all? His jaded threat is an epigraph—or epitaph—for the tattered and bedraggled soul of post-Vietnam America: "There's no more heroes left in the world."[20]

Riggs, a sensitive Eighties man announcing a new hero for a nation resurrected, a nation that will never again admit defeat or limit, busts down the door, blows the bit players away, and saves Murtaugh and Rianne. The general escapes, but Murtaugh tracks him down and kills him, proving that he's not, in fact, "too old for this shit." Back at the homestead, Joshua reads the Christmas tree note and Riggs gets the drop on him. But in true warrior fashion, Riggs holsters his gun, grants his evil twin "a shot at the title"—a busted fire hydrant has made a muddy jungle out of Murtaugh's suburban lawn—and bests him in hand-to-hand combat. Joshua won't go quietly, though, not in this wild neo-Western: he grabs the gun of the arresting trooper and draws a bead on Murtaugh and Riggs, the two men collapsed into one supercop body, the wounded older man clutching the exhausted younger. The good guys draw and simultaneously (Murtaugh fires first, by a hair) shoot the bad guy dead. Cut to: Christmas day. Riggs says goodbye to his wife at her rainy gravesite. Cut to: Christmas night at the Murtaugh house. The rain has stopped. Riggs gives his special bullet, wrapped in a red ribbon, to adoring Rianne to give to Roger. He's "not really crazy" after all. His virtuosity at dispensing violence, "the only thing I was ever good at," he sheepishly confessed to Murtaugh, has been revenged upon the agents who sent him to war and taught him to be a virtuoso of violence. But "all that killer stuff" is also a gift— like the bullet—that gave him back the family he'd lost.

In 1987's *Fatal Attraction*, the third highest-grosser of the year (*Lethal Weapon* was number eight) and recipient of six Academy Award nominations, high-powered New York editor Alex Forrest (Glenn Close) is "crazy" not because she's good at killing, but because she's a thirty-six-year-old woman without a husband or a family—and it doesn't seem to bother her, at least not until she meets glib attorney and family man Dan Gallagher (Michael Douglas). The Eighties woman, we soon find out, is a *de*civilizing force (remember the police psychologist who wants to restrain the violent instincts that make Riggs such a good cop?), and she'll do whatever it takes to get what she wants. The day after Dan flirts with her at a book launch gala he's attending with his perfect wife Beth (Anne Archer) and lecherous attorney pal Jimmy (Stuart Pankin), who hits on Alex nearly in front of his wife Hildy (Ellen Foley), the two meet at Alex's publishing house, where Dan dispenses some glib legal advice about a novel involving a love affair (hint). Suddenly, as the meeting concludes, a downpour. Dan's diminutive umbrella crumples (at the launch, he referred to all men as "a little insecure") and so does he, clumsily trying to pull his coat over his head. Alex, collected and commanding in a radiant white trench coat—*her* umbrella blossoms, both erect and womb-like—swoops in for the rescue. Dan asks her to get a drink and they land in an upscale bar, where he lights her cigarette and she, touching his hand, asks if he's "discreet." He is. She angles a little more: "What do you think?" Dan demurs: "Oh, I definitely think it's gonna be up to you." Why would he cheat on his perfect wife in the first place? That was set up earlier. When they get home late from the party, Beth reminds her tipsy, tired, and horny husband that he has to walk the dog. He doesn't want to walk the dog (if she were *really* perfect, a side glance suggests, wouldn't she do it herself?), but such is a man's burden. Raring to go by the time he gets back, undressing and smiling naughtily as he pushes open the bedroom door, he finds—bad luck!—five-year-old daughter Ellen (Ellen Latzen) has snuck into bed with mom. "It's just for tonight, honey," Beth reassures him, or tries to. His male sex right violated, what choice does he have but to engage in a gymnastic carnal affair with a Medusa-haired seductress while Beth and Ellen are visiting Beth's parents in the country?

Following the initial marathon—kitchen counter, salsa dancing, elevator—Dan limps home, returns his wife's call after listening guiltily to her blameless words of perfect-wifeness on the machine, and clumsily lies to her about what he's been up to. He hangs up, the phone rings—it's Alex, telling him she'll "be a good girl" and let him do the work he needs to do if he makes another house call (what luck: Beth has to stay over an extra day to check out the country cottage she wants to move the family to). An afternoon of park-frolicking becomes a home-cooked Italian meal at Alex's to the tune of her favorite opera, *Madame Butterfly*, which leads to more frolicking in the bedroom. When Dan tries to leave, Alex gets upset, feels used, tries to rip his shirt off. "You knew the rules," he tells her. "We are adults, aren't we?" We find out that Alex, like Riggs, is suicidal—but in this case very spontaneously suicidal. She doesn't have a special bullet, but she pulls the trigger, promptly slitting her wrists before Dan can make his forever escape. He can't call 911 and risk getting caught cheating, but he does her the kindness of washing the blood off her wrists and wrapping the wounds with pieces of torn cloth. The next morning, he makes her promise to go see a doctor, touches her tenderly, and bolts home to frantically rumple the bed and serve the dog the food Beth left in the fridge for him before the girls get back. When they do, it's ecstatic and lingering hugs for all, and he spends extra quality time with Ellen (he tells Alex she's six, but she's five) at the dinner table. And Beth's "absolutely perfect" country house that Dan grumpily dismissed days earlier? He'll do her the service of seeing it now. He's going to be a better husband, a better father. Alex was his Vietnam, and he's going to make things right (as long as he can keep his war a secret).

Only Alex won't surrender. When Dan ghosts her at work, she starts to call the apartment, hanging up when Beth answers. While her obsession grows and her mental state deteriorates, things are looking up for Dan: he's about to "become a suburbanite" and make partner, and he celebrates by cavorting like a frat boy with Jimmy while Alex hangs limply and blankly on the wall of her living room in what looks like a gown from a psych ward, clicking the lamp off and on, off and on. *Madame Butterfly* blares, and the opera tickets she got Dan as a "peace offering" lie discarded on the stereo. She calls him in the middle of the night, demanding a meeting. She's pregnant, and she wants to have the baby. A true Eighties man, but not necessarily a sensitive one, Dan had assumed that she was using birth control, and, if not, would enthusiastically opt for an abortion, which he generously offers to pay for. In the deep stuff now, Dan breaks into Alex's apartment "looking for something," he discreetly confides to Jimmy in the aisles of the law library, "anything to get a handle on what I'm dealing with here." Alex tries to call Dan at home again, but the number's been changed, and she slams the phone down in fury when the operator won't give her the new one. We know she's struck a new layer of crazy because, on her bed, along with the manuscripts and glossy decor magazines, there's an open bag of Oreos, an open bag of Doritos, an open container of Häagen-Dazs with a spoon inside—and a glass of white wine to wash it all down with.

How crazy is crazy? In the next scene, Dan comes home to find Alex talking to Beth on the sofa, and he approaches in shaky cam from his (high-angle, looking down) point of view. They shake hands, he spies the scar on her wrist, and they act out an elaborate charade of being strangers. Alex is pregnant, Beth tells him, and she's thinking of renting the apartment since the Gallaghers are "moving to the country." Beth volunteers the name of the town, Bedford, and gives Alex their new number on her way out to "keep in touch." "She didn't mention a husband," Beth remarks pityingly. "I get the feeling she's on her own." But Dan has had enough: no mercy. He jets to Alex's place one more time to have it out, telling her whatever she's "up to" is "gonna stop right now." Alex counterpoints: "No, it's not gonna stop. It's gonna go on and on until you face up to your responsibilities." Dan tells her he "pities" her and that she's "sick." Alex counterpoints: "Why? Because I won't allow you to treat me like some slut you can just bang a couple of times and throw in the garbage?" She threatens to tell Beth, and he slams her up against the wall, his hand clutched around her neck: "If you tell my wife, I'll kill you." If it's not obvious yet that Alex is the Riggs in this story and Dan the Mr. Joshua, then you probably agree with Michael Douglas, who was at the time "really tired of feminists, sick of them [...] Guys are going through a terrible crisis right now because of women's unreasonable demands."[21] Or director Adrian Lyne, who said that single career women "are sort of overcompensating for not being men"; they're "crass" and "unattractive," and he much preferred his own "feminine" wife who "never worked. She's the least ambitious person I've ever met [...] I come home and she's there."[22]

The quotes are from a 1988 *Mother Jones* exposé by Susan Faludi, later expanded into a chapter for her 1991 book, *Backlash: The Undeclared War Against American Women*, that tracks *Fatal Attraction*'s beginnings as a "moral tale about a man who transgresses and pays the penalty,"[23] as described by screenwriter James Dearden, into a male revenge fantasy about a "predatory"[24] (Dearden) "raging beast"[25] (Lyne) who manipulates the man into having an affair, attacks him and his family, and herself pays the ultimate price. Under producer Sherry Lansing, the first woman to head up production for a studio (20th Century-Fox), the original ending—Alex slits her throat to the sounds of *Madame Butterfly* (imitating the eponymous protagonist of the opera), framing Dan (his prints are on the knife), who is later cleared by evidence found by Beth[26]—was switched to what Roger Ebert called an "unforgivable *Friday the 13th* cliche."[27] Why? "Market research," said Faludi. The men in the test audiences of the original cut were screaming "Punch the bitch's lights out!" and "Kill the bitch."[28] They wanted Dan "to have some retribution," Dearden remembered.[29] Paramount President Ned Tanen heard them: "They want us to terminate the bitch with extreme prejudice." And he told Lansing and Lyne to make it so. Nobody liked it, least of all Close, who sympathized with a character she felt was both wronged and mentally ill, but Tanen gave Lansing an extra $1.5 million to shoot a new ending with "no strings attached," other than Alex having to be killed by someone other than herself. She thought it was a "brilliant" compromise. "How could you say no?"[30]

Alex isn't just a single woman "overcompensating" for not being a man. She's a debauched city girl, and her apartment, as Faludi points out, is "a barren loft in New York's meat market district, ringed by oil drums that burned like witches' cauldrons," not unlike the steaming complex where Murtaugh and Riggs are tortured. The building's cage elevator is dungeonesque, the hallways dark and dreary, the walls shedding paint and plaster—just like the ill-reputed Bramford in *Rosemary's Baby*. Inside the inner sanctum, everything is aseptically white: brick walls, sheets, ceiling fan, lamps, pillars, telephone, exercise bike. "They lacked soul," Lyne said of the many Polaroids he'd seen of the apartments of single women in the publishing industry.[31] By contrast, the Gallaghers' country estate is warm and cozy and safe: dark wood, aged red brick, flowers and plants, piano, paintings of mothers and daughters, photographic posters (one of New York City, safely distanced), always a fire in the fireplace. The only thing that's white is the picket fence. Beth, like Rosemary, is a country girl at heart. (She's a teacher who wants to go back to work in the original script; she's a housewife with no career aspirations in the final cut.) She is sexual but "safe," "pure," fertile (Alex had a "bad miscarriage" and didn't think she could get pregnant again), rock-steady, devoted to family above all else: the new house is "just up the road from mom and dad." Alex, as Beth sniffed out, is "on her own," and her father died of a heart attack when she was seven. "It happened right in front of me," she tells Dan. Violently separated from daddy, her descent into psychosis, much like Regan MacNeil's demonic possession in *The Exorcist*, was perhaps inevitable.

Thus, she douses Dan's station wagon (a Volvo: too upscale for Murtaugh) with acid and leaves a cassette tape in the rental's passenger seat featuring an unhinged tirade of creepy confessions and threats, at the end of which she questions his masculinity: "I bet you don't even like girls, do you? Flamin' fuckin' faggot!" (The sensitive Eighties man is also not keen on homosexuality: Riggs finds the idea of women being lovers "disgusting" and, when his jacket catches fire from an explosion, calls Roger a "fag" when he tries to smother it.) For her next trick, Alex sneaks into the house when the Gallaghers are away and boils Ellen's new bunny to death on the stove. It is only *now* that Dan decides to tell Beth about the affair, and that he knows who murdered and cooked the rabbit, and that she, Beth, met the culprit, and that the culprit is pregnant with Dan's child. Beth kicks him out of the house, and Alex promptly kidnaps Ellen for a day at the amusement park for no other reason than to make Beth drive around hysterically until she crashes her car, so that Dan can kneel down at her hospital bed and apologize with moist eyes—so that traumatized Beth can invite him back home.

Dan, to prove that he's a real (heterosexual) man, breaks down Alex's door and assaults her, once again throttling her and nearly fulfilling the promise he made the last time he assaulted her. But he relents, thinking that he doesn't want to become the monster that he already is, and Alex, when she starts breathing again, comes at him with a kitchen knife (*she's no Rosemary*). Dan disarms her, puts the knife on the counter, and slowly backs away. This is where Alex is supposed to kill herself and frame her attacker. (The police would have found her fingerprints along with Dan's on the knife, and in any event would know the difference between a self-inflicted wound and a murder, but logic pointedly does not apply here.) Instead, Alex takes the knife, sneaks into the Gallagher house (Dan has forgotten to lock the doors, naturally), and attacks black-eyed and bandaged Beth as she preps for her bath. Dan fights maniacal Alex, reclaiming his virility once more, and drowns her in the overflowing bathtub. But Alex is too crazy to die. When she pops up and gasps for air like the undead corpse of second-wave feminism, she's shot in the heart by Beth, the incarnation of Reaganite family values.

The fairy tale ethics of *Lethal Weapon*—that there are good "guys" and bad "guys," and it's just that simple—are not always wrong, because it's obvious what should have happened in *Fatal Attraction*. Beth (Murtaugh) shoots Dan (Mr. Joshua) through the heart, she and Alex (Riggs) bury the body, and the two of them, with little Ellen and Alex's child (which got aborted after all), live happily ever after. Just like Murtaugh and Riggs. They're a couple too, in a way. The "communion between men" who fight together in combat "is as profound as any between lovers," wrote Philip Caputo in his 1977 memoir *A Rumor of War*. "Actually, it is more so [...] It is, unlike marriage, a bond that cannot be broken by a word, by boredom, or by divorce, or by anything other than death. Sometimes even that is not strong enough."[32] There's Riggs at Murtaugh's front door, back from the dead, reborn. He doesn't want to impose, and heads back to his truck after handing the gift-wrapped bullet to Rianne. Murtaugh comes out to get him, whispers that he doesn't want to eat his wife's "lousy" turkey dinner "by myself" (how is he by himself?), and brings his brother home. The last man in, Murtaugh spies the single dark Christmas bulb on his awning and screws it in until it lights up: the war is finally over. On the opposite coast, in Bedford, the police come and remove Alex's corpse, and Dan and Beth embrace in the foyer, the camera slowly zooming in on the family photograph on the hall table. But Alex's words to Dan are still true, will always be true, a righteous recrimination from beyond the grave: "You mean you've had your fun, now you just want a quiet life."

CONCLUSION

Theodore Roszak expected that the "generational revolt" would take some time to reach "class-wide dimensions."[1] How long, exactly? When might we expect the culture of disaffiliation to "transform the very sense men have of reality"[2]? 1984, he guessed, or close to it, because "Is there any other ideal toward which the young can grow that looks half so appealing?"[3] Apparently, there was. Reagan's reelection was even more lopsided than Nixon's, and young whites overwhelmingly voted for the kindly and ever-chipper Gipper—followed closely by their grandparents and the boomers themselves. Roszak got the year right, but not the ideology. "So, what was accomplished?" high school history teacher and former radical Mr. Burkewaite (Jim Metzler) asks, repeating his skeptical class's question about the 1960s, in 1987's *River's Edge*. "Fundamental changes were made," he insists, citing civil rights and the "women's movement." "We stopped a war, man," he pleads. "We took to the streets and we made a difference." His students don't buy it, and he glumly voices their conclusion: "All the hippies are executives now, and everybody's sold out." And selling out, in a literal sense, *was* the ideology of Reagan—and every White House since. The only way to ensure "human fulfillment," he said in 1981, using the same quasi-religious language as Roszak, was "the willingness to believe in the magic of the marketplace."[4]

In the Reagan campaign's "Morning in America" TV spot, to the sound of saccharine keyboard strings, we watch a small-town fantasy unfold: a paperboy on his bike delivers the morning edition, a briefcase-toting businessman hops into a station wagon, dad and son carry a rolled-up embroidered rug into their new white-picket-fenced home, a young couple marry in a church, a fireman hoists up the American flag. "They can look forward with confidence to the future," the narrator intones. "Under the leadership of President Reagan, our country is prouder, and stronger, and better."[5] There's no mention of the president's refusal to address or even publicly acknowledge the worsening AIDS epidemic, obviously, or the near-nuclear apocalypse of Able Archer 83, or the CIA's arming and abetting of dictators and death squads in poverty-scourged Central America, or the exponential incarceration of young Black men at home as the systematically racist war on drugs ramped up, or the permanent underclass loosed upon the streets by the gutting of federal housing assistance and the strategic starvation of social services, the "trimming" of the safety net until all that remained was a single gossamer thread clinging to the wind. It was magic, alright: a vanishing act.

The commercial was filmed in northern California's historic Petaluma, often the cinematic stand-in for quintessentially quaint, immaculately white suburbia. *American Graffiti* was filmed there; so was *Peggy Sue Got Married*. Politics and Hollywood, both of them sculptors and purveyors of the image, servants of illusion, had converged and conspired to disacknowledge the disillusionment of the age of limits and shared sacrifice, to sweep "the mess we had made of the world" under the unrolled living room rug, where it still lives and spreads—and mutates. No amount of superheroes, Jedi Knights, righteous outlaws, secret agents, serial killers, wise guys, cynical cops, streetwise philosophers, hipster eccentrics, or talking cartoons will ever stop it. And we, the mere mortals of the real world, several generations of diverse adaptations huddled under one beleaguered roof, can only survive so many fallen skies.

ENDNOTES

PREFACE

1   Killen, Andreas. 1973 *Nervous Breakdown: Watergate, Warhol, and the Birth of Post-Sixties America*. Bloomsbury, 2008, p. 129.

INTRODUCTION

1   Roszak, Theodore. *The Making of a Counter Culture: Reflections on the Technocratic Society and Its Youthful Opposition*. Anchor Books, 1969, p. 42.

2   *Ibid*, p. xiii. Compare this to a quote by SDS leader Mark Rudd from a 1968 open letter to Columbia University president Grayson Kirk: "We will take control of your world... and attempt to mold a world in which we and other people can live as human beings." (Quoted in Grunwald, Lisa, and Stephen J. Adler, editors. *Letters of the Century: America 1900-1999*. Random House, 2008, p. 471.)

3   Fiedler, Leslie A. "The New Mutants." *Partisan Review*, vol. 32, no. 4, Fall 1965, pp. 505-25, p. 509.

4   Arthur C. Clarke in a *Los Angeles Free Press* interview, April 25, 1969: "The goal of the future is full unemployment, so we can play. That's why we have to destroy the present politico-economic system." (Youngblood, Gene and Ted Zatlyn, "Free Press Interview: Arthur C. Clarke, Author of '2001'." *Los Angeles Free Press*, vol. 6, issue 249, 25 Apr 1969, pp. 42-3, 47, p. 43).

5   Quoted in Hunter, Marjorie. "Agnew Says 'Effete Snobs' Incited War Moratorium." *New York Times*, 20 Oct 1969, p. 1.

6   Newfield, Christopher. *Unmaking the Public University: The Forty-Year Assault on the Middle Class*. Harvard University, 2011, p. 52.

7   Cannon, Lou. *Governor Reagan: His Rise To Power*. PublicAffairs, 2003, p. 533.

8   Tyler, Timothy. "Out of Tune and Lost in the Counterculture." *Time*, vol. 97, no. 8, 22 Feb 1971, pp. 15-16, p.15.

9   For more, see Braunstein, Peter and Michael William Doyle, "Introduction: Historicizing the American Counterculture of the 1960s and '70s." Braunstein, Peter and Michael William Doyle, editors. *Imagine Nation: The American Counterculture of the 1960s and '70s*. Routledge, 2002. pp. 5-14.

10 *The Port Huron Statement*. Students for a Democratic Society, 1964 (second printing), p. 7.

11 For more, see Harris, Mark. "The Flowering of the Hippies." *The Atlantic*, Sep 1967, theatlantic.com/magazine/archive/1967/09/the-flowering-of-the-hippies/306619, pp. 63-72; Hogdson, Godfrey. *America in Our Time: From World War II to Nixon*. Doubleday, 1976, pp. 329-330, and Sawyer Bishari, Nuala. "Sex, Drugs, and Rock 'n' Roll '67: Prostitution, Overdoses, and STDs." *SFWeekly*, 16 Aug 2017, www.sfweekly.com/news/feature/sex-drugs-and-rock-n-roll-67-prostitution-overdoses-and-stds.

12 Didion, Joan. *Slouching Towards Bethlehem*. 1968. Farrar, Straus and Giroux, 2008, p. 122.

13 Quoted in Farber, David. *The Age of Great Dreams: America in the 1960s*. Hill and Wang, 1994, p. 205.

14 Farber, Jerry. "The Student As Nigger." *Los Angeles Free Press*, vol. 4, issue 137, 3 Mar 1967, pp. 8, 18-19, p. 8. See also Hoffman, Abbie. *Revolution for the Hell of It: The Book That Earned Abbie Hoffman a Five-Year Prison Term at the Chicago Conspiracy Trial*. 1968. Thunder's Mouth Press, 2005, p. 71: "You want to get a glimpse of what it feels like to be a nigger? Let your hair grow long" and

Braunstein and Doyle, *Imagine Nation*, p. 169: Paul Goodman claimed that being homosexual "made [him] a nigger," and John Lennon and Yoko Ono wrote and recorded "Woman Is the Nigger of the World" for 1972 album *Sometime in New York City*.

15 Karen, David. "The Politics of Class, Race, and Gender: Access to Higher Education in the United States, 1960-1986." *American Journal of Education* vol. 99, no. 2, 1991, pp. 208-237, p. 215. See also Cross, Theodore and Robert Bruce Slater. "Only the Onset of Affirmative Action Explains the Explosive Growth in Black Enrollments in Higher Education." *The Journal of Blacks in Higher Education*, no. 23, Spring 1999, pp. 110-5 and Walters, Ronald and Robert Smith. "The Black Education Strategy in the 1970s." *The Journal of Negro Education*, vol. 48, no. 2, Spring 1979, pp. 156-70.

16 Goodwin, Gerald F. "Black and White in Vietnam." *New York Times*, 18 Jul 2017, nytimes.com/2017/07/18/opinion/racism-vietnam-war.html. There is also evidence that Latinos, who were not counted as a distinct ethnic group by the Department of Defense and instead lumped in with the white population, were overrepresented among American war casualties. See Cuevas, Steven. "The Invisible Force: Latinos at War in Vietnam." KQED, 25 May, 2015, https://www.kqed.org/news/10534280/the-invisible-force-latinos-at-war-in-vietnam.

17 Fiedler, "The New Mutants," p. 516.

18 Baldwin, James. *Nobody Knows My Name, More Notes of a Native Son*. 1961. Vintage, 1993, p. 218.

19 Rosenfeld, Seth. *Subversives: The FBI's War on Student Radicals, and Reagan's Rise to Power*. Farrar, Straus and Giroux, 2012, p. 281

20 Quoted in Greenberg, David. "The Man, the Myths." *Slate*, 9 Jun 2004. slate.com/news-and-politics/2004/06/myths-about-ronald-reagan.html.

21 Bloom, Joshua and Waldo E. Martin, Jr. *Black against Empire: The History and Politics of the Black Panther Party*. University of California, 2016, pp. 237-8.

22 Quoted in Cowie, Jefferson. "The 'Hard Hat Riot' Was a Preview of Today's Political Divisions." *New York Times*, 11 May 2020, nytimes.com/2020/05/11/nyregion/hard-hat-riot.html.

23 Lawrence, Stewart J. "The unquiet ghosts of Kent State." *The Guardian*, 4 May 2011, theguardian.com/commentisfree/cifamerica/2011/may/04/vietnam-us-military.

24 Nixon, Richard M. "Address Accepting the Presidential Nomination at the Republican National Convention in Miami Beach, Florida." *The American Presidency Project*, UC Santa Barbara, 8 Aug 1968, presidency.ucsb.edu/documents/address-accepting-the-presidential-nomination-the-republican-national-convention-miami.

25 Quoted in Farber, *The Age of Great Dreams*, p. 167.

26 Quoted in Cook, David A. *Lost Illusions: American Cinema in the Shadow of Watergate and Vietnam, 1970-1979*. University of California, 2002, p. 70.

27 Pach, Jr. Chester J. "Tet on TV: US Nightly News Reporting and Presidential Policy Making." *1968: The World Transformed*, edited by Carole Fink, Philipp Gassert, Detlef Junker, Cambridge University, pp. 55-82, pp. 67-68.

28 Monaco, Paul. *The Sixties: 1960-1969. History of the American Cinema*, vol. 8, University of California, 2003, p. 188.

29 Quoted in McGee, Mark Thomas. *Faster and Furiouser: The Revised and Fattened Fable of American International Pictures*. McFarland, 1995, p. 242.

30 Quoted in Monaco, *The Sixties*, p. 186.

31 Cook, *Lost Illusions*, pp. 3, 9. Hollywood moguls begged the Nixon administration for a bailout, and they got one in the form of lucrative tax credits and tax shelters that subsidized the industry throughout the decade.

32   Frederick, Robert B. "Top 10 Films Yield 40% of Rentals."
      Variety, 6 Jan 1971, pp. 11-12.

33   Murray, William. "Playboy Interview: Francis Ford Coppola."
      Playboy, vol. 22, no. 7, Jul 1975, pp. 53 *et subseq.*, p. 56.

34   Quoted in Biskind, Peter. *Easy Riders, Raging Bulls: How the
      Sex-Drugs-And Rock 'N Roll Generation Saved Hollywood*. Simon &
      Schuster, 1998, p. 164.

35   In Frank Capra's consensus-era *It's a Wonderful Life* (1946), the
      young and idealistic George Bailey (James Stewart), Michael's
      exact contemporary, struggles over the same decision, only in his
      case the family business and the father are unambiguously *noble*.

36   Roszak, Theodore. *Unfinished Animal: The Aquarian Frontier and the
      Evolution of Consciousness*, Harper Colophon, 1977, p. 3.

37   Quoted in Taylor, Mark C. *Abiding Grace: Time, Modernity, Death*.
      University of Chicago, 2018, p. 203.

38   Lawrence, D.H. *Lady Chatterley's Lover*. 1932. Signet, 1959, 1962,
      p. 5.

39   Roszak, *Unfinished Animal*, pp. 3, 5.

40   Roszak, *The Making of a Counter Culture*, p. 75.

41   Quoted in Pollock, Dale. *Skywalking: The Life and Films of George
      Lucas*, Updated Edition. Hachette, 2009, p. 104.

42   Warren, Earl. "Eulogy for John F. Kennedy." *American Rhetoric*, 24
      Nov 1963, americanrhetoric.com/speeches/earlwarrenjfkeulogy.
      htm.

43   Quoted in Jones, Brian Jay. *George Lucas: A Life*. Little, Brown and
      Company, 2016, p. 185.

44   Kael, Pauline. "Contrasts." *The New Yorker*, 18 Sep 1977,
      newyorker.com/magazine/1977/09/26/contrasts.

45   Wilson, John M. "Coming Home: The Return of E.T." *Chicago
      Tribune*, 19 Jul 1985, chicagotribune.com/news/ct-xpm-1985-07-
      19-8502170247-story.html.

46   Jones, *George Lucas*, p. 358.

47 Quoted in Biskind, *Easy Riders*, p. 344.

48 Quoted in Prince, Stephen. *A New Pot of Gold: Hollywood Under the Electronic Rainbow*, 1980-1989. *History of the American Cinema*, vol. 10, University of California, 2003, p. xv.

49 Vanderbilt, Mike. "Read This: The fight over racism in Star Wars." *The AV Club*, 16 Dec 2015, avclub.com/read-this-the-fight-over-racism-in-star-wars-1798287363.

50 Biskind, *Easy Riders*, p. 323.

51 Kael, Pauline. "The Current Cinema: After Innocence." *The New Yorker*, 1 Oct 1973, newyorker.com/magazine/1973/10/01/after-innocence.

52 Ebert, Roger. "Heaven's Gate." *RogerEbert.com*, 1 Jan (*sic*) 1981, rogerebert.com/reviews/heavens-gate-1981.

53 Quoted in Prince, *A New Pot of Gold*, p. xvii.

54 "Reagan, After Rambo: 'I Know What to Do.'" Associated Press, 30 Jun 1985, apnews.com/article/90843d33d588fab169cb2f0356755938.

55 Prince, *A New Pot of Gold*, pp. 84-9.

56 Cook, *Lost Illusions*, p. 238.

57 Prince, *A New Pot of Gold*, pp. 43-5.

58 Montañez Smukler, Maya. *Liberating Hollywood: Women Directors and the Feminist Reform of 1970s American Cinema*. Rutgers University, 2019, p. 7.

59 Harmetz, Aljean. "Suit to Allege Sex Bias By TV and Film Makers." *New York Times*, 25 Feb 1981, nytimes.com/1981/02/25/movies/suit-to-allege-sex-bias-by-tv-and-film-makers.html.

60 Montañez Smukler, *Liberating Hollywood*, Chapter 4, pp. 232-77

61 Ugwu, Reggie. "'They Set Us Up to Fail': Black Directors of the '90s Speak Out." *New York Times*, 3 Jul 2019, nytimes.com/2019/07/03/movies/black-directors-1990s.html

62   Carter, Jimmy. "Energy and the National Goals - A Crisis of Confidence." *American Rhetoric*, 15 Jul 1979, americanrhetoric. com/speeches/jimmycartercrisisofconfidence.htm.

PART ONE: APOCALYPSE AMERICANA (1968–1973)

1. *"Aren't* You His Mother?"*: Rosemary's Baby* and *Bloody Mama*

1   Quoted in Thompson, Hunter S. *The Great Shark Hunt: Strange Tales from a Strange Time*. 1979. Simon & Schuster, 2001, p. 225

2   "From the Notebooks of Ira Levin," *Rosemary's Baby*, *The Criterion Collection*, Blu-Ray edition insert, 2012, p. 22.

3   In 1977, Roman Polanski drugged and raped thirteen-year-old Samantha Jane Gailey in the Los Angeles home of Jack Nicholson (Nicholson was in Colorado at the time), fleeing the US less than a year later when threatened with imprisonment. Five other women have since accused Polanski of sexual assault.

4   Kennedy, John F. "Transcript: JFK's Speech on His Religion." 12 Sep 1960, *NPR*, www.npr.org/templates/story/story. php?storyId=16920600.

5   Hodgson, Godfrey. *America in Our Time: From World War II to Nixon*, Doubleday, 1976, p. 162.

6   Chinni, Dante. "The One Thing All Americans Agree On: JFK Conspiracy." *NBC News*, 29 Oct 2017, nbcnews.com/ storyline/jfk-assassination-files/one-thing-all-americans-agree-jfk-conspiracy-n815371.

7   Levin, Ira. *Rosemary's Baby*. 1967. Signet, 1997, p. 82.

8   Lewis, Anthony. "Panel Unanimous: Theory of Conspiracy by Left or Right is Rejected." *New York Times*, 28 Sep 1964, nytimes. com/1964/09/28/archives/panel-unanimous-theory-of-conspiracy-by-left-or-right-is-rejected.html.

9   Hofstadter, Richard. "The Paranoid Style in American Politics." *Harper's*, Nov 1964, harpers.org/archive/1964/11/the-paranoid-style-in-american-politics.

10   Quoted in Walker, Jesse. *The United States of Paranoia: A Conspiracy Theory*. HarperCollins, 2013, p. 24.

11   Hofstadter, "The Paranoid Style in American Politics."

12   McCarthy, Joseph. "Senator Joseph McCarthy Attacks the State Department." Modern America: A Documentary History of the Nation Since 1945, edited by Gary Donaldson, M.E. Sharpe, 2007, pp. 35-38, p. 36.

13   *Ibid.*, p. 37. The quote was probably taken from Will Durant's epilogue to *Caesar and Christ* (1944), about the fall of Rome: "A great civilization is not conquered from without until it has destroyed itself within."

14   Hofstadter, "The Paranoid Style in American Politics."

15   Hoberman, J. *The Dream Life: Movies, Media, and the Mythology of the Sixties*. The New Press, 2005, p. 44.

16   "Gas and Clubs Used to Halt Rights 'Walk.'" United Press International, *Omaha World-Herald*, 8 Mar 1965, p. 1.

17   *Ibid.*

18   Levin, *Rosemary's Baby*, p. 114.

19   *Ibid.*, p. 39.

20   SimmsParris, Michele M. "What Does It Mean to See a Black Church Burning? Understanding the Significance of Constitutionalizing Hate Speech." *University of Pennsylvania Journal of Constitutional Law*, vol. 1 no. 1, Spring 1998, pp. 127-153, p. 139.

21   King, Martin Luther. "Our God is Marching On!" 25 Mar 1965, Stanford University, *The Martin Luther King, Jr. Research and Education Institute*, kinginstitute.stanford.edu/our-god-marching.

22   Quoted in Banks, Adam J. *Race, Rhetoric, and Technology: Searching for Higher Ground*. Taylor & Francis, 2006, p. 65.

23 Quoted in Kennedy, Robert F. "Topics: 'Things Fall Apart; the Center Cannot Hold...'." *New York Times*, 10 Feb 1968, p. 32.

24 See Ryan, Rebecca M. "The Sex Right: A Legal History of the Marital Rape Exemption." *Law & Social Inquiry*, vol. 20, no. 4, Autumn, 1995, pp. 941-1001, and Pauly, Madison. "It's 2019, And States Are Still Making Exceptions for Spousal Rape." *Mother Jones*, 21 Nov 2019, motherjones.com/crime-justice/2019/11/deval-patrick-spousal-rape-laws.

25 Farrow, Mia. *What Falls Away: A Memoir*. Bantam, 1998, pp. 112-3 and Sylbert, Richard and Sylvia Townsend with Sharmagne Leland-St.John-Sylbert. *Designing Movies: Portrait of a Hollywood Artist*. Praeger, 2006, pp. 101-2.

26 Pope Paul VI. "Visit of His Holiness Pope Paul VI to the United Nations: Homily of the Holy Father Pope Paul VI." 4 Oct 1965, The Vatican web site, Homilies of Pope Paul VI, www.vatican.va/content/paul-vi/en/homilies/1965/documents/hf_p-vi_hom_19651004_yankee-stadium.html

27 Elson, John T. "Theology: Toward a Hidden God." *Time*, 8 Apr 1966, content.time.com/time/subscriber/article/0,33009,835309-1,00.html.

28 Moffitt, Mike. "When the Devil lived in the Richmond." *SFGate*, 30 Apr 2016, sfgate.com/bayarea/article/When-the-Devil-lived-in-the-Richmond-7382271.php.

29 Bugliosi, Vincent with Curt Gentry. *Helter Skelter: The True Story of the Manson Murders*. 1974. W.W. Norton and Company, 1994, p. 74.

30 Roberts, Myron. "The New Violence: An Age of 'Freaky' Crime?" *Los Angeles*, Oct 1969, lamag.com/citythinkblog/manson-murders-1969-los-angeles-magazine.

31 Quoted in Bugliosi, *Helter Skelter*, p. 560.

32 Quoted in Kraus, Olivia. "My Life After Manson." *New York Times*, 4 Aug 2014, nytimes.com/2014/08/05/opinion/my-life-after-manson.html.

33 Quoted in Felton, David and David Dalton. "Charles Manson: The Incredible Story of the Most Dangerous Man Alive." *Rolling Stone*, 25 Jun 1970, rollingstone.com/culture/culture-news/charles-manson-the-incredible-story-of-the-most-dangerous-man-alive-85235.

34 Quoted in Browder, Laura. *Her Best Shot: Women and Guns in America*. University of North Carolina, 2009, pp. 124-6.

35 *Ibid.*, p. 129.

36 Rable, George C. "The South and the Politics of Antilynching Legislation, 1920-1940." *The Journal of Southern History*, vol. 51, no. 2, May 1985, pp. 201-22, p. 205.

37 Bugliosi, *Helter Skelter*, p. 330.

38 Biskind, *Easy Riders*, p. 32.

39 Quoted in Browder, *Her Best Shot*, p. 127.

40 Woodiwiss, Michael. *Organized Crime and American Power: A History*. University of Toronto, 2001, p. 238

41 Hammel, Lisa. "Dr. Spock as a Father—No Mollycoddler." *New York Times* Books, 8 Nov 1968, nytimes.com/books/98/05/17/specials/spock-father.html.

42 Quoted in Hulbert, Ann. *Raising America: Experts, Parents, and a Century of Advice About Children*. Knopf Doubleday, 2004, p. 258.

43 *Ibid.*, pp. 258-9.

44 Shuster, Alvin M. "G.I. Heroin Addiction Epidemic in Vietnam." *New York Times*, 16 May 1971, nytimes.com/1971/05/16/archives/gi-heroin-addiction-epidemic-in-vietnam-gi-heroin-addiction-is.html, see also Westheider, James E. *Fighting in Vietnam: The Experiences of the US Soldier*. Stackpole, 2011, p. 173.

45 Schmidt, Dana Adams. "Addiction in Vietnam Spurs Nixon and Congress to Take Drastic New Steps." *New York Times*, 16 Jun

1971, nytimes.com/1971/06/16/archives/addiction-in-vietnam-spurs-nixon-and-congress-to-take-drastic-new.html.

46　Quoted in Dean, Eric T. *Shook Over Hell: Post-traumatic Stress, Vietnam, and the Civil War*. Harvard University, 1997, p. 63.

47　Schneider, Eric C. *Smack: Heroin and the American City*. University of Pennsylvania, 2008, pp. 159-181.

2. "You Think They Deserve That Flag?": *Wild in the Streets* and *Punishment Park*

1　Adler, Renata. "Going 'Wild in the Streets'." *New York Times*, 16 Jun 1968, nytimes.com/1968/06/16/archives/going-wild-in-the-streets-going-wild.html.

2　Eliscu, Lita. "What Do You Thilm?" *East Village Other*, vol. 3, no. 31, 12 Jul 1968, p. 11.

3　Mintz, Elliot. "Looking Out." *Los Angeles Free Press*, vol. 5, no. 28, 12 Jul 1968, p. 27

4　*Ibid*, p. 27.

5　Marcuse, Herbert. *One-Dimensional Man: Studies in the Ideology of Advanced Industrial Society*. 1964. Beacon Press, 1966, p. 63.

6　Savio, Mario. "Sit-in Address on the Steps of Sproul Hall." *American Rhetoric*, 2 Dec 1964, americanrhetoric.com/speeches/mariosaviosproulhallsitin.htm.

7　Frank, Thomas. *The Conquest of Cool: Business Culture, Counterculture, and the Rise of Hip Consumerism*. University of Chicago, 1998, p. 8.

8　Marcuse, *One-Dimensional Man*, p. 64.

9　Smith, Chris A. "Angels, Protesters and Patriots: What a Long-Ago Skirmish Says About Love of Country." *California*, University of California Berkeley, Spring 2016, alumni.berkeley.edu/california-magazine/spring-2016-war-stories/angels-protesters-and-patriots-what-long-ago-skirmish.

10　Monteith, Sharon. *American Culture in the 1960s*. Edinburgh University, 2008, p. 97.

11 Haut, Woody. "'Anarchy on Sunset Strip': 50 years on from the 'hippie riots'." *The Guardian*, 11 Nov 2016, theguardian.com/us-news/2016/nov/11/sunset-strip-riot-hippie-los-angeles.

12 Timothy Leary, acid guru *par excellence* who at the time of *Wild in the Streets* was quite a bit older than Max Frost's Troops, would say in 1977 that "The LSD movement was started by the CIA." (Quoted in Lee, Martin A. and Bruce Shlain. *Acid Dreams: The Complete Social History of LSD: the CIA, the Sixties and Beyond*. 1985. Grove Press, 1992, p. xx).

13 Church, Frank *et al*. *Alleged Assassination Plots Involving Foreign Leaders: An Interim Report of the Select Committee to Study Governmental Operations With Respect to Intelligence Activities*, United States Senate, 20 Nov 1975. www.intelligence.senate.gov/sites/default/files/94465.pdf. p. 72.

14 Quoted in Church *et al.*, *Alleged Assassination Plots Involving Foreign Leaders*, p. 142.

15 For more on Weinberg's famous quote, see Daily Planet Staff. "Don't trust anyone over 30, unless it's Jack Weinberg." *Berkeley Daily Planet*, 6 Apr 2000, berkeleydailyplanet.com/issue/2000-04-06/article/759.

16 Gomez, Joseph A. *Peter Watkins*. Twayne (Theatrical Arts Series), 1979, p. 103.

17 Watkins, Peter. *Punishment Park*. *Peter Watkins: Filmmaker/Media Critic* website. pwatkins.mnsi.net/punishment.htm

18 For example, see "Weather Underground Announces Fall Offensive." CBS News, 6 Oct 1970, *YouTube*, uploaded by retrogo, 19 Jan 2009, youtube.com/watch?v=TfdJ3FiSva4, where Weather Underground leader Bernardine Dohrn tells Nixon and Agnew in an audiotaped statement to "guard your planes, guard your colleges, guard your banks, guard your children, guard your doors." Dohrn's sister Jennifer would say at this same press conference, "I think it's right on. I think she's far out. I think all

Weathermen are far out." Bernardine Dohrn would be added to the FBI's 10 Most Wanted List a week later.

19 Baskir, Lawrence and William Strauss. *Chance and Circumstance: The Draft, the War and the Vietnam Generation*. Knopf, 1978, p. 24.

20 Quoted in Baskir and Strauss, *Chance and Circumstance*, p. 25.

21 Nixon, Richard. "Statement on Signing Bill Repealing the Emergency Detention Act of 1950." *The American Presidency Project*, UC Santa Barbara, 25 Sep 1971, presidency.ucsb.edu/documents/statement-signing-bill-repealing-the-emergency-detention-act-1950.

22 "Garden Plot & SWAT: US Police as New Action Army." *CounterSpy*, vol. 2, issue 4, Winter 1976, pp. 16-21, 43-59.

23 Ridenhour, Ron with Arthur Lubow. "Bringing the War Home." *New Times*, vol. 5, no. 11, 28 Nov 1975, pp. 18, 20-4.

24 Quoted in Ridenhour and Lubow, Bringing the War Home," see also Katsiaficas, George N. *The Imagination of the New Left: A Global Analysis of 1968*. South End Press, 1987, p. 259.

25 Katsiaficas, *The Imagination of the New Left*, pp. 259-260.

26 Quoted in Smith, Sam. "Mission Creep: Militarizing America." *The Progressive Review*, no. 342, March 1996, pp. 1-12, unz.com/print/ProgressiveRev-1996mar-00009, p. 10.

27 Baudrillard, Jean. *America*. Translated by Chris Turner. Verso, 1988, p. 55.

28 *Ibid*, p. 28

29 *Ibid*, p. 5.

3. "How Do You Know You're You?": *Seconds* and *Watermelon Man*

1 Hoberman, *The Dream Life*, pp. 54-5.

2 Simon, Alex. "John Frankenheimer: Renaissance Auteur." *Venice Magazine*, Oct 1998, thehollywoodinterview.blogspot.com/2008/02/john-frankenheimer-hollywood-interview.html.

3   Bernstein, Adam. "Melvin Van Peebles, fiercely independent filmmaker, dies at 89." *Washington Post*, 22 Sep 2021, washingtonpost.com/local/obituaries/melvin-van-peebles-dead/2021/09/22/b0af14ca-ca9b-11ea-91f1-28aca4d833a0_story.html.

4   Quoted in Gates, Racquel J. "Subverting Hollywood from the Inside Out: Melvin Van Peebles' *Watermelon Man*." *Film Quarterly*, vol. 68, no. 1, Fall 2014, pp. 9-21, p. 14.

5   Rabin, Nathan. "Watermelon Man." *The AV Club*, 18 Oct 2004, avclub.com/watermelon-man-1798200055.

6   Gates, Subverting Hollywood from the Inside Out," pp. 14-16.

7   Stevens, Dana. "Seconds." *Slate*, 6 Aug 2013, slate.com/culture/2013/08/criterion-collection-edition-of-seconds-directed-by-john-frankenheimer-and-starring-rock-hudson-reviewed.html.

8   Appelbaum, Ralph. "John Frankenheimer Speaks to Ralph Appelbaum (1979)." *John Frankenheimer: Interviews, Essays, and Profiles*. Edited by Stephen B. Armstrong, Scarecrow Press, 2013, p. 77.

9   Quoted in Armstrong, Stephen B. "Introduction." *John Frankenheimer: Interviews, Essays, and Profiles*. Edited by Stephen B. Armstrong, Scarecrow Press, 2013, p. xiv.

10   Black, William R. "How Watermelons Became a Racist Trope." *The Atlantic*, 8 Dec 2014, theatlantic.com/national/archive/2014/12/how-watermelons-became-a-racist-trope/383529/.

11   Under Van Peebles' "aegis," said Raucher in a 2016 interview (Fassel, Preston. "Herman Raucher (2016)." *Cinedump*, 13 Sep 2016, cinedump.com/interviews/2016/9/13/hermanraucher), *Watermelon Man* became "more of a black power film than I'd wanted."

4. "Every Girl Should Have a Daddy": *The Exorcist* and *Manson*

1   For more, see the entirety of O'Neill, Tom with Dan Piepenbring. *Chaos: Charles Manson, the CIA, and the Secret History of the Sixties.* Little, Brown, 2019, but specifically Chapters 5-7, pp. 141-235.

2   "Manson (1973)." *AFI Catalog of Feature Films: The First 100 Years, 1893-1993.* catalog.afi.com/Catalog/moviedetails/54554

3   Bugliosi, *Helter Skelter*, p. 320.

4   "August 3, 1970 Charles Manson holds up Nixon Guilty Paper in Court." CBS News, 4 Aug 1970, *YouTube*, uploaded by MichaelsBackporch, 15 Dec 2020, www.youtube.com/watch?v=7HzeItzuiq0.

5   Fine, Gary Alan. "The Manson Family: The Folklore Traditions of a Small Group. *Journal of the Folklore Institute*, vol. 19, no. 1, Jan-Apr 1982, pp. 47-60, pp. 51-3.

6   Lansing, H. Allegra. "You Could Feed The World On America's Garbage! Dumpster-Diving with the Manson Family." *Medium*, 21 Oct 2020, themansonfamily-mtts.medium.com/you-could-feed-the-world-on-americas-garbage-57ae46bb641e.

7   In addition to his learning the ropes from his fellow prisoners, Manson also read self-help authors such as Dale Carnegie (*How to Win Friends and Influence People*) and L. Ron Hubbard (*Dianetics*, Scientology) while incarcerated: see Mozingo, Joe. "Charles Manson crawled from the Summer of Love to descend into Helter Skelter murders." *Los Angeles Times*, 20 Nov 2017, latimes.com/local/california/la-me-ln-manson-california-20500123-story.html.

8   Reich, Wilhelm. *The Mass Psychology of Fascism.* Edited by Mary Higgins and Chester M. Raphael, M.D., translated by Vincent R. Carfagno, 1970. The Noonday Press/Farrar, Straus and Giroux, 1993, pp. 104-5. Emphasis in original.

9   *Ibid.*, p. 53.

10   Typical of these well-marketed audience interviews and
     reactions is *"The Exorcist | Audience Reactions." YouTube*,
     uploaded by *The Exorcist* Online, 24 Mar 2014, youtube.com/
     watch?v=AkIqFK3KoZ4.
     See also Dempsey, Michael. "The Exorcist." *Film Quarterly*, vol. 27,
     no. 4 (Summer 1974), p. 61.
11   Dempsey, "The Exorcist," p. 62
12   McCormick, Ruth. "'The Devil Made Me Do It!': A Critique of
     The Exorcist." Cinéaste, vol. 6, no. 3 (1974), pp. 18-22, p. 21.
13   Dempsey, "The Exorcist," pp. 61-2.
14   McCormick, "'The Devil Made Me Do It!'", p. 19.
15   *Ibid*, p. 21.
16   For more, see Gough, Aidan R. "Community Property and
     Family Law: The Family Law Act of 1969." *Cal Law Trends and
     Developments*, vol. 1970, issue 1, pp. 273-305.
17   Friedman, Lawrence M. "A Dead Language: Divorce Law and
     Practice before No-Fault." *Virginia Law Review*, vol. 86, no. 7, Oct
     2000, pp. 1497-1536, pp. 1504-5.
18   For more, see Melnick, Erin R. "Reaffirming No-Fault Divorce:
     Supplementing Formal Equality with Substantive Change,"
     Indiana Law Journal: vol. 75, issue 2, pp. 711-729.
19   Bianco, Marcic and Merryn Johns. "Classic Hollywood's Secret:
     Studios Wanted Their Stars to Have Abortions. *Vanity Fair*, 15 Jul
     2016, vanityfair.com/hollywood/2016/07/classic-hollywood-
     abortion.
20   Morgan, Thad. "When Hollywood Studios Married Off Gay
     Stars to Keep Their Sexuality a Secret." *History.com*, 10 Jul 2019,
     history.com/news/hollywood-lmarriages-gay-stars-lgbt.
21   McCormick, "'The Devil Made Me Do It!'", p. 21.

PART TWO: A HANDFUL OF RUST (1974–1980)

5. "The Cost of Electricity": *The Texas Chain Saw Massacre* and *Harlan County, USA*

1   Smith, William D. "Energy Crisis: Shortages Amid Plenty." *New York Times*, 17 Apr 1973, nytimes.com/1973/04/17/archives/energy-crisis-shortages-amid-plenty-energy-crisis-paradox-of.html.

2   Jacobs, Meg. *Panic at the Pump: The Energy Crisis and the Transformation of American Politics in the 1970s*. Farrar, Straus and Giroux, 2016, p. 29.

3   Finney, John W. "Nixon Asks $2.2-Billion in Emergency Aid for Israel. *New York Times*, 20 Oct 1973, nytimes.com/1973/10/20/archives/nixon-asks-22billion-in-emergency-aid-for-israel.html.

4   Nixon, Richard. "Address to the Nation About National Energy Policy." *The American Presidency Project*, UC Santa Barbara, 25 Nov 1973, presidency.ucsb.edu/documents/address-the-nation-about-national-energy-policy.

5   Hunt, Jennifer. "Four decades later, has America finally got over the oil crisis?" *The Conversation*, 30 Oct 2014, theconversation.com/four-decades-later-has-america-finally-got-over-the-oil-crisis-33541.

6   Jacobs, *Panic at the Pump*, p. 125.

7   *Ibid.*, pp. 74-5.

8   *Ibid.*, p. 124.

9   Quoted in Jacobs, *Panic at the Pump*, p. 61.

10 Jacobs, *Panic at the Pump*, p. 25.

11 Black, Dan, Terra McKinnish and Seth Sanders. "The Economic Impact of the Coal Boom and Bust." *The Economic Journal*, vol. 115, no. 503, Apr 2005, pp. 449-476, p. 452.

12 Harris, Fred. "Burning Up People to Make Electricity." *The Atlantic*, Jul 1974, theatlantic.com/magazine/archive/1974/07/burning-up-people-to-make-electricity/304563.

13 *Ibid.*

14 "Mining Program: Occupational Safety and Health Risks." *Centers for Disease Control/National Institute for Occupational Safety and Health*, 8 Nov 2012, cdc.gov/niosh/programs/mining/risks.html.

15 Steven, Mark. *Splatter Capital*. Repeater Books, 2017, p. 74.

16 *Ibid.*, p. 79.

17 Wood, Robin. *Robin Wood on the Horror Film: Collected Essays and Reviews*. Wayne State University, 2018, p. 114.

18 *Ibid.*, p. 114.

6. "We've Come This Far, We Must Go On!" *Alien* and *Sorcerer*

1 For more on the (frequent mis-)appropriation of the cargo cult concept, see Lindstrom, Lamont. *Cargo Cult: Strange Stories of Desire from Melanesia and Beyond*. University of Hawai'i, 1993, especially Chapter 2, "The Birth of Cargo Cult," pp. 13-36 ("The label has gone wild. It cannot be effaced. It has escaped the bounds of anthropological discourse and now turns up in a surprising range of texts.") and Chapter 3, "Cargo-Cult Culture," pp. 37-65.

2 Friedkin, William. *The Friedkin Connection: A Memoir*. HarperCollins, 2013, p. 347.

3 *Ibid.*, p. 329.

4 *Ibid.*, p. 327.

5 Bernstein, Gregory. *Understanding the Business of Media Entertainment: The Legal and Business Essentials All Filmmakers Should Know*. Routledge, Revised Edition, 2019, p. 197.

6 "Gulf & Western Inc. History." *Funding Universe*, date unknown, fundinguniverse.com/company-histories/gulf-western-inc-history.

7   Segaloff, Nat. *Hurricane Billy: The Stormy Life and Times of William Friedkin*. William Morrow & Company, 1990, pp. 163-4.

8   Opazo, Tania. "The Boys Who Got to Remake an Economy." *Slate*, 12 Jan 2016, slate.com/business/2016/01/in-chicago-boys-the-story-of-chilean-economists-who-studied-in-america-and-then-remade-their-country.html.

9   "A Brief History of RAND." RAND Corporation, date unknown, rand.org/about/history/a-brief-history-of-rand.html.

10 Canby, Vincent. "'Sorcerer,' Action Movie Set in Latin America." *New York Times*, 25 Jun 1977, nytimes.com/1977/06/25/archives/sorcerer-action-movie-set-in-latin-america.html.

11 Harmanci, Reyhan. "Since WWII, tiki has been mainland's answer to paradise." *SFGate*, 1 Oct 2004, sfgate.com/bayarea/article/Since-WWII-tiki-has-been-mainland-s-answer-to-2690492.php.

12 See Fuller, John. *The Interrupted Journey: Two Lost Hours Aboard a Flying Saucer*. The Dial Press, 1966,

for the tale of the Hills' experiences and Dickinson, Terence. "The Zeta Reticuli Incident." *Astronomy*, Dec 1974, reprinted with commentary at astronomy.com/bonus/zeta, for the Zeti Reticuli theory.

13 Lingeman, Richard R. "Erich von Daniken's Genesis." *New York Times*, 31 Mar 1974, nytimes.com/1974/03/31/archives/erich-von-danikens-genesis.html.

14 von Däniken, Erich. *Chariots of the Gods?* 1968. Bantam Books, 27th printing, 1973, p. 55-6.

15 Roberts, K.E. "Technology Worship and Human Debasement in Erich von Däniken's 'Chariots of the Gods?'" *We Are the Mutants*, 6 Feb 2017, wearethemutants.com/2017/02/06/technology-worship-and-human-debasement-in-erich-von-danikens-chariots-of-the-gods.

16   d'Errico, Peter. "Jeffery Amherst and Smallpox Blankets." *Peter d'Errico's Law Page*, University of Massachusetts, 2001, people. umass.edu/derrico/amherst/lord_jeff.html.

17   Friedkin, *The Friedkin Connection*, p. 342.

7. "Please Don't Blow Up the Domes": *Silent Running* and *Phase IV*

1   Canby, Vincent. "Screen: 'Silent Running.'" *New York Times*, 1 Apr 1972, www.nytimes.com/1972/04/01/archives/screen.html.

2   "Airform 'Bubble House.'" *Los Angeles Conservancy*, date unknown, laconservancy.org/locations/airform-bubble-house.

3   Burnette, Wendell. "The Dome in the Desert." *ArchDaily*, 14 Apr 2013, www.archdaily.com/359748/the-dome-in-the-desert-by-wendell-burnette.

4   Rosen, Jody. "Welcome to the Integratron." *New York Times*, 20 Aug 2014, nytimes.com/interactive/2014/08/20/style/tmagazine/welcome-to-the-integratron.html.

5   Tibbs, Hardin. "Buckminster Fuller and a slight case of the not-really-invented-here syndrome." *Hardin Tibbs*, 15 May 2010, hardintibbs.com/blog/buckminster-fuller-and-a-slight-case-of-the-not-really-invented-here-syndrome.

6   Hoppe, Jon. "The Marine Corps Goes Geodesic." *US Naval Institute*, 28 Jan 2016, Internet Archive, web.archive. org/web/20180612152108/https://www.navalhistory. org/2016/01/28/the-marine-corps-goes-geodesic.

7   "The Teacher Was the Sea: Pacific High School." *Red Legacy*, 3 Dec 2009, red-legacy.blogspot.com/2009/12/teacher-was-sea-pacific-high-school.html.

8   Sitzer, Carly. "Earth Day May Be 50, But Its Message Is as Timeless As Ever." *Green Matters*, 29 Apr 2020, greenmatters. com/p/earth-day-history.

9 Nixon, Richard. "Reorganization Plan No. 3 of 1970." *US Environmental Protection Agency*, 9 Jul 1970, archive.epa.gov/epa/aboutepa/reorganization-plan-no-3-1970.html.

10 Grasso, Michael. "'People Can Stop It': Three Ecology PSAs, 1971 – 1977." *We Are the Mutants*, 25 Sep 2017, wearethemutants.com/2017/09/25/people-can-stop-it-three-ecology-psas-1971-1977.

11 Kohn, Eric. "'2001' VFX Guru Douglas Trumbull on Why CGI Hasn't Outpaced the Visual Effects of Kubrick's Film." IndieWire, 1 May 2021, www.indiewire.com/2021/05/2001-vfx-douglas-trumbull-cgi-kubrick-1234634471.

12 Adams, Sam. "Universal's brief indie fling produced great, odd results like *Silent Running*." The AV Club, 16 Apr 2013, avclub.com/universal-s-brief-indie-fling-produced-great-odd-resul-1798237531.

13 Carducci, Mark Patrick. "Michael Cimino." *Film Directors on Directing*, edited by John Andrew Gallagher, Praeger, 1989, pp. 38-47, p. 46.

14 *Ibid.*, p. 47.

15 Mourinha, Jorge. "'I Never Knew How to Make a Film': Michael Cimino in 2005." *Filmmaker*, 5 Jul 2016, filmmakermagazine.com/99041-i-never-knew-how-make-a-film-michael-cimino-in-2005.

16 Kent, Leticia. "Ready for Vietnam? A Talk With Michael Cimino." *New York Times*, 10 Dec 1978, nytimes.com/1978/12/10/archives/ready-for-vietnam-a-talk-with-michael-cimino-cimino.html.

17 "Phase IV." *The Projection Booth* podcast, 8 Dec 2015, projectionboothpodcast.com/2015/12/episode-248-phase-iv.html.

18 "Phase iv lost ending." *YouTube*, uploaded by john smith, 24 Mar 2017, youtube.com/watch?v=N7wotKNaj_s.

19   *Domebook 2*. Pacific Domes/Random House, 1971, pacificdomes. com/pdf/domebook-2.pdf, p. 78.

8. "A Little Human Compassion": *Death Wish* and *Escape from New York*

1   Quoted in Maronie, Samuel J. "On the Set with 'Escape From New York'." *Starlog*, no. 45, Apr 1981, pp. 28-30, p. 29.

2   Ebert, Roger. "Death Wish." *RogerEbert.com*, 1 Jan (*sic*) 1974, rogerebert.com/reviews/death-wish-1974.

3   Austin, Dr. James and Lauren-Brooke Eisen with James Cullen and Jonathan Frank. "How Many Americans Are Unnecessarily Incarcerated?" Brennan Center for Justice, NYU School of Law, 2016, brennancenter.org/sites/default/files/publications/ Unnecessarily_Incarcerated_0.pdf, p. 3.

4   Frum, David. *How We Got Here: The 70's: The Decade that Brought You Modern Life (For Better or Worse)*. Basic Books, 2000, p. 12.

5   Blumenthal, Ralph. "Recalling New York at the Brink of Bankruptcy." *New York Times*, 5 Dec 2002, nytimes. com/2002/12/05/nyregion/recalling-new-york-at-the-brink-of-bankruptcy.html.

6   Freudenberg, Nicholas *et al.* "The impact of New York City's 1975 fiscal crisis on the tuberculosis, HIV, and homicide syndemic." *American Journal of Public Health*, vol. 96, no. 3, Mar 2006, pp. 424-434., p. 425.

7   Maeder, Jay. *Big Town, Big Time: A New York City Epic, 1898-1998*. *New York Daily News*, 1999, p. 164.

8   Kahn, Matthew E. and Mac McComas. *Unlocking the Potential of Post-Industrial Cities*. Johns Hopkins University, 2021, p. 14

9   McQuay, Mike. *Escape From New York*. Bantam, 1981, p. 6.

10   *Ibid.*, p. 19.

11 Drum, Kevin. "Lead: America's Real Criminal Element." *Mother Jones*, Jan/Feb 2013, motherjones.com/environment/2016/02/lead-exposure-gasoline-crime-increase-children-health.

12 Quoted in Bouzereau, Laurent. *Ultraviolent Movies: From Sam Peckinpah to Quentin Tarantino*. 1996. Citadel Press, 2000, p. 140.

13 *Ibid.*, pp. 140-1.

14 Shuster, "G.I. Heroin Addiction Epidemic in Vietnam."

15 Quoted in Scott, James F. *Martin Scorsese, Woody Allen, Spike Lee: Ethnicity, Race, and Identity in American Independent Film*. Lexington Books/Rowman & Littlefield, 2019, p. 40.

16 Quoted in Rosenbaum, David E. "Nixon Tapes At Key Time Now Drawing Scant Interest." *New York Times*, 14 Dec 2003, nytimes.com/2003/12/14/us/nixon-tapes-at-key-time-now-drawing-scant-interest.html.

17 Reagan, Ronald. "Remarks at the Annual Meeting of the International Association of Chiefs of Police in New Orleans, Louisiana." *Reagan Library*, 28 Sep 1981, reaganlibrary.gov/archives/speech/remarks-annual-meeting-international-association-chiefs-police-new-orleans.

18 *Ibid.*

PART THREE: WORLD WITHOUT END (1981–1987)

9. "The Slums of the Future": *Poltergeist and Suburbia*

1 Madrigal, Alexis. "The Racist Housing Policy That Made Your Neighborhood." *The Atlantic*, 22 May 2014, theatlantic.com/business/archive/2014/05/the-racist-housing-policy-that-made-your-neighborhood/371439.

2 Wallace, Robert. "House of Flying Objects." *Life*, vol. 44, no. 11, 17 Mar 1958, pp. 49-58.

3   Quoted in "Tract Housing in California, 1945-1973: A Context
     for National Register Evaluation." California Department
     of Transportation, 2011, dot.ca.gov/-/media/dot-media/
     programs/environmental-analysis/documents/ser/tract-housing-
     in-ca-1945-1973-a11y.pdf, p. 20.

4   Gordon, Andrew. *Empire of Dreams: The Science Fiction and Fantasy
     Films of Steven Spielberg.* Rowman & Littlefield, 2008, p. 96.

5   MacInnis, Allan. "Penelope Spheeris on Suburbia, Flea, Roger
     Corman, and a civilization in Decline." *Georgia Straight,* 7 Mar
     2018, straight.com/movies/1041431/penelope-spheeris-
     suburbia-flea-roger-corman-and-society-decline.

10. "What Is It You Think You're Becoming?": *Dragonslayer* and *Manhunter*

1   Sheehan, Bill. "Thomas Harris introduced the world to
     Hannibal Lecter, and pop culture would never be the same."
     Washington Post, 9 May 2019, https://www.washingtonpost.
     com/entertainment/books/thomas-harris-introduced-the-
     world-to-hannibal-lecter-and-pop-culture-would-never-be-the-
     same/2019/05/09/56697f88-6ddf-11e9-a66d-a82d3f3d96d5_
     story.html.

2   Martin, Judith. "'Dragonslayer' Devours Itself." *Washington
     Post,* 26 Jun 1981, washingtonpost.com/archive/
     lifestyle/1981/06/26/dragonslayer-devours-itself/6ef1b2ae-
     e83e-489b-b270-487f38ab64f0.

3   Ciabattari, Jane. "Hobbits and hippies: Tolkien and the
     counterculture." *BBC Culture,* 19 Nov 2014, bbc.com/culture/
     article/20141120-the-hobbits-and-the-hippies.

4   Fox, James Alan and Jack Levin. *Extreme Killing: Understanding Serial
     and Mass Murder.* Sage Publications, 2005, p. 60.

5   *Ibid.,* p. 61.

6   For more on the Atlanta Marriott Marquis, see Sisson,
    Patrick. "Neofuturist architect John Portman bet on cities just
    as people fled them." *Curbed*, 26 Aug 2016, archive.curbed.
    com/2016/8/26/12663306/architecture-john-portman-hyatt-
    atlanta-atrium. In the novel *Red Dragon*, Graham and Thomas
    Harris' omniscient narrator note, "The Atlanta FBI office had
    booked him into an absurd hotel near the city's new Peachtree
    Center. It had glass elevators shaped like milkweed pods to let
    him know he was really in town now." (Harris, Thomas. *Red
    Dragon*. G.P. Putnam's Sons, 1981, p. 27.)
7   Abrams, Abigail. "Divorce Rate in US Drops to Nearly 40-Year
    Low." *Time*, 17 Nov 2016, time.com/4575495/divorce-rate-
    nearly-40-year-low.

11. "Somebody's Gonna Drop the Fuckin' Bomb Anyway, Right?": *Testament* and *Parting Glances*

1   Geerhart, Bill. "Interview with TESTAMENT Director Lynne
    Littman." CONELRAD Adjacent, 31 Aug 2010, conelrad.
    blogspot.com/2010/08/interview-with-testament-director-lynne.
    html.
2   Keating, Rian. "Parting Glances Director Bill Sherwood
    interviewed by Rian Keating." *YouTube*, uploaded by Rian
    Keating, date unknown, youtube.com/watch?v=VFaiShW6ki4.
3   *Ibid*.
4   Reagan, Ronald. "White House Diaries: Monday, October 10,
    1983." *Reagan Foundation*, 10 Oct 1983, reaganfoundation.org/
    ronald-reagan/white-house-diaries/diary-entry-10101983.
5   "A Timeline of HIV and AIDS." *HIV.gov*/US Department of
    Health & Human Services, date unknown, hiv.gov/hiv-basics/
    overview/history/hiv-and-aids-timeline.
6   "Poll Indicates Majority Favor Quarantine for AIDS Victims."
    Associated Press/*New York Times*, 20 Dec 1985, nytimes.

com/1985/12/20/us/poll-indicates-majority-favor-quarantine-for-aids-victims.html.

7   Quoted in White, Allen. "Reagan's AIDS Legacy: Silence Equals Death." *SFGate*, 8 Jun 2004, sfgate.com/opinion/openforum/article/Reagan-s-AIDS-Legacy-Silence-equals-death-2751030.php.

12. "Are You Really Crazy?": *Lethal Weapon* and *Fatal Attraction*

1   Patterson, Lindsay. "In Harlem, a James Bond with Soul?" *Black Films and Film-makers: A Comprehensive Anthology from Stereotype to Superhero*. Edited by Lindsay Patterson. Dodd, Mead, 1975, p. 101.

2   Kuykendall, Jack L. and David E. Burns. "The Black Police Officer: An Historical Perspective." *Journal of Contemporary Criminal Justice*, vol. 1, issue 4, 1980, pp. 4-12, p. 8.

3   "Black Cop (1969)." *YouTube*, uploaded by reelblack, 21 Dec 2016, youtube.com/watch?v=DvC-WS8zbkE.

4   Atchison, Gabrie'l J. "Danny Glover." *Race in American Film: Voices and Visions that Shaped a Nation, vol. 1*, edited by Daniel Bernardi and Michael Green, Greenwood, 2017, p. 356-8, p. 357.

5   Schneider, Mark and Thomas Phelan. "Black Suburbanization in the 1980s." Demography, vol. 30, no. 2, May 1993, pp. 269-79, p. 270.

6   "Reagan Quotes King Speech in Opposing Minority Quotas." Associated Press/*New York Times*, 19 Jan 1986, nytimes.com/1986/01/19/us/reagan-quotes-king-speech-in-opposing-minority-quotas.html.

7   Duke, Lynne. "Black Economic Disparity Deepened During 1980s." *Washington Post*, 9 Aug 1991, washingtonpost.com/archive/politics/1991/08/09/black-economic-disparity-

deepened-during-1980s/0735462b-f083-4bcd-ab69-0c24ee727699. See also Jargowsky, Paul A. "Ghetto Poverty among Blacks in the 1980s." *Journal of Policy Analysis and Management*, vol. 13, no. 2, Spring, 1994, pp. 288-310.

8   Quoted in Goodwin, "Black and White in Vietnam."

9   *Ibid.*

10   All statistics from Goodwin, "Black and White in Vietnam."

11   All quotes from *The Black G.I.*; see "Black Journal #22 Black G.I. 1970." *YouTube*, uploaded by Sean Hockabout, 11 Nov 2021, youtube.com/watch?v=TjYLTkoxc74.

12   Blakely, Gloria. *Danny Glover*. Chelsea House, 2002, p. 52.

13   Fleischer, Matthew. "How white people used police to make L.A. one of the most segregated cities in America." *Los Angeles Times*, 11 Aug 2020, latimes.com/opinion/story/2020-08-11/white-people-used-police-brutality-los-angeles-most-segregated-city-in-america.

14   Blakely, *Danny Glover*, p. 50.

15   Viator, Felicia Angeja. "Weapon of Mass Destruction." *Lapham's Quarterly*, 25 Feb 2020, laphamsquarterly.org/roundtable/weapon-mass-destruction.

16   Hodgson, *America in Our Time*, p. 333.

17   For more, see Webb, Gary. *Dark Alliance: The CIA, the Contras, and the Crack Cocaine Explosion*. Seven Stories, 1998.

18   After Rianne goes back into the house, Murtaugh asks Riggs if they've resolved anything, referring to the murder case, and Riggs remarks in part that "Your daughter smokes grass in the house, and it's illegal…" The original script reads: "Your daughter smokes pot, which is illegal *but shouldn't be*." [Italics mine.]

19   Frequent Lucas collaborator Walter Murch said that "*Star Wars* is George's version of *Apocalypse Now*, rewritten in an otherworldly context. The rebels in *Star Wars* are the Vietnamese, and the

Empire is the United States." Quoted in Cowie, Peter. *The Apocalypse Now Book*. Hachette, 2001, p. 5.

20 Compare with Reagan's First Inaugural Address: "We have every right to dream heroic dreams. Those who say that we're in a time when there are not heroes, they just don't know where to look." (Reagan, Ronald. "Inaugural Address 1981." *Reagan Library*, 20 Jan 1981, reaganlibrary.gov/archives/speech/inaugural-address-1981.)

21 Quoted in Faludi, Susan. *Backlash: The Undeclared War Against American Women*. Crown, 1991, p. 121.

22 *Ibid.*, p. 121.

23 *Ibid.*, p. 118.

24 *Ibid.*, p. 119.

25 *Ibid.*, p. 120.

26 *Ibid.*, p. 122.

27 Ebert, Rogert. "Fatal Attraction." *RogerEbert.com*, 18 Sep 1987, rogerebert.com/reviews/fatal-attraction-1987.

28 Quoted in Faludi, *Backlash*, p. 112.

29 *Ibid.*, p. 122.

30 Galloway, Stephen. "Sherry Lansing Book Excerpt: Screaming Matches and Tears on 'Fatal Attraction' Set." *Hollywood Reporter*, 29 Mar 2017, hollywoodreporter.com/movies/movie-features/sherry-lansing-biography-fatal-attraction-book-excerpt-989565.

31 Quoted in Faludi, *Backlash*, p. 120.

32 Caputo, Philip. *A Rumor of War*. Ballantine, 1977, p. xvii.

CONCLUSION

1 Roszak, *The Making of a Counter Culture*, p. 40.

2 *Ibid.*, p. 267.

3 *Ibid.*, p. 40.

4 Reagan, Ronald. "Remarks at the Annual Meeting of the Boards of Governors of the World Bank Group and International

Monetary Fund." Reagan Library, 29 Sep 1981, https://www.reaganlibrary.gov/archives/speech/remarks-annual-meeting-boards-governors-world-bank-group-and-international-monetary

5 "Presidential ad: "It's Morning Again in America" Ronald Reagan (R) v Walter Mondale (D) [1984—PRIDE]." *YouTube*, uploaded by New York Historical Society, 8 Jun 2020, youtube.com/watch?v=pUMqic2IcWA.

ACKNOWLEDGEMENTS

Kelly

I'd like to thank Jess, Alice, and Kay for letting me sit in the back of the house with the cat and write and edit this book. I love you (although I can't promise it won't happen again). I also need to thank my mom, Sandi, who watched all those horror movies with me as a kid and took me to see *Blade Runner* when I was ten because I told her it was going to be "a lot like *Star Wars*." That was the day I learned to love film.

Mike

First of all, to my parents Joe and Karen: my eternal gratitude for your support and love over my entire life, especially during these very difficult past two years. I couldn't have done this without you.

I'd like to thank the entire team at Repeater Books: Tariq Goddard, Vicky Hartley, Carl Neville, Ellie Potts, Josh Turner, Christiana Spens, Matt Colquhoun, and everyone else who's helped in bringing this book to life. Shouts out to Carl, jonny mugwump, the Acid Communist, and everyone who's been part of Repeater Radio for giving me a place to call home during the pandemic. My sincere thanks to the URIEL crew—Bill Brickman, Brant Casavant, Melanie Hockabout, Rob MacDougall, Leonard Pierce, and Jeff Wikstrom—for creating a virtual 1970s for us to play in; it's been an inspiration, both for this book and everywhere else in my life.

Of course, I'd like to thank my fellow Mutants, Kelly

Roberts and Richard McKenna: meeting you both and starting the magazine nearly seven years ago now has quite literally changed the course of my life. Until the next time we can have a drink together in person again.

And finally, to the one and only love of my life, J: my work on this book is dedicated to you.

Richard
I'd like to thank Minnie and Sunny.

REPEATER BOOKS

is dedicated to the creation of a new reality. The landscape of twenty-first-century arts and letters is faded and inert, riven by fashionable cynicism, egotistical self-reference and a nostalgia for the recent past. Repeater intends to add its voice to those movements that wish to enter history and assert control over its currents, gathering together scattered and isolated voices with those who have already called for an escape from Capitalist Realism. Our desire is to publish in every sphere and genre, combining vigorous dissent and a pragmatic willingness to succeed where messianic abstraction and quiescent co- option have stalled: abstention is not an option: we are alive and we don't agree.